Timperley Boy

'From under the Stairs'

Peter Scott

With illustrations by Peter Richardson

DEDICATION

I dedicate this book to the memory of my Mum
and my pal Harry for all these shared memories

ACKNOWLEDGEMENTS

For their help in obtaining or allowing the use of photographs:

Bill Edge of Reddish Stockport, Philip Harding, Trafford Leisure Services, Mike Brown, Hazel Pryor, Inez Slack nee Downs, Sheffield Newspapers Ltd, Sheffield Libraries, Archives & Information, Manchester Archives & Local Studies, Kent Messenger Newspaper Group, Barry Hollis, Jean Vernon, Ruth Smith (Harry's widow), Bryan Berryman, Lillian Short, Max Payne MBE, my sister Carole Cartledge, Scarborough Evening News, East Coast Radio, GM Radio - The Allen Beswick programme

My apologies to anyone that I have inadvertently forgotten, I have been helped and encouraged by so many for which I will be forever grateful.

I wish also to thank my wife Glenys for her support and proofreading. Also my daughters, Allison and her husband Robert, and Sally and Galen who gave me the computer in the first place.

I am grateful to Peter Richardson for his excellent cartoon drawings.

CHURNET VALLEY BOOKS
6 Stanley Street, Leek, Staffordshire. ST13 5HG 01538 399033
thebookshopleek.co.uk
© Peter Scott and Churnet Valley Books 2003
ISBN 1 904546 05 6

Printed by Bath Press

CONTENTS

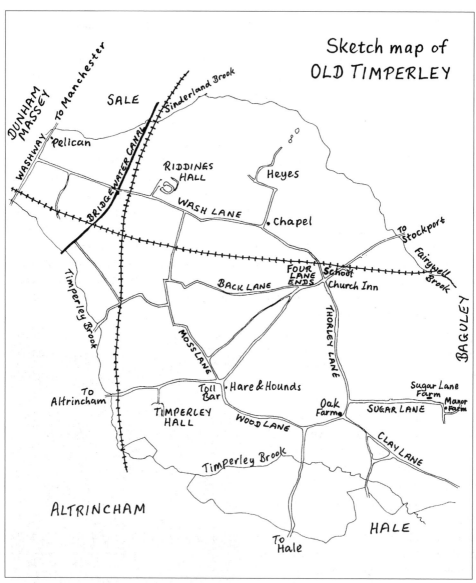

Courtesy of 'Looking back at Timperley', Hazel Pryor

INTRODUCTION

Within just a few seconds your life can change completely. I had just finished cleaning the car ready for our trip to see our daughter and her family when fate hit me where it hurts most, in the heart. My journey, on that balmy July evening of 1995, now became a frantic one in an ambulance. I had had a heart attack, the first of two that night - when your heart requires a jump start there is no better place to be than in a hospital.

It was stress; in my job as a sales and marketing manager the pressure had built up over the months, culminating in a huge row with my boss the previous day. And there was smoking of course, and lack of exercise, and other reasons. I spent nine days in the hospital which gave me a lot of time to think of the past - and the future.

The following year we had a holiday booked for the end of September, but again, instead of lazing on a beach, I found myself stretched out on an operating table undergoing a quadruple heart by-pass. A couple of months later, well on the road to recovery, my son-in-law gave me a computer in the hope that it would help to while away the time for me.

To be honest, the thing frightened me to death. But I persevered and slowly gained confidence, and after a few weeks of Body Works, Encarta and Solitaire, I tried my hand at typing. I would nearly finish a sentence, and about to congratulate myself when I would press the wrong key and my work would disappear into the jungle of my hard drive (whatever that is) never to be seen again.

One day when I was fighting a losing battle with it, and with the added irritation of a radio in the background, I went to turn it off and they started playing a favourite old song, *Memories,* from the musical *Cats.* I thought, why not; why not write the memories from my childhood?

As I wrote my story I realised I had a great deal to thank my parents for. I now realise how much my mother fought against the odds through the War years - I now know she had heart valve disease. Doing a part-time job on top of a family must have been really tough for her. Mum taught me to respect other peoples' feelings, to be truthful and honest. In 1952, just a few years after my story ends, my mother died from her heart condition. Bless you Mum.

Mum and Dad's wedding.

Muriel and myself in our garden at Gerrard Avenue.

1. My family and friends

I suppose my story should begin back in the 1920s, when my parents' families came to live in Manchester. Dad's parents moved from Halifax, Mum's from Sheffield. They happened to buy properties close to each other and they were destined to meet, fall in love, and then marry in September 1927. My sister Muriel was born on 28th June 1929 and I came into the world on 28th July 1933.

Seven years after their marriage they purchased a house on Gerrard Avenue, Timperley, and it was during the removal that I was invested with my first memory. I was sat on the floor in the hall of the new house looking up through the spindles of the staircase, bawling my head off, and Grandma Bagshaw was looking down over the banisters trying to console me. No doubt all the hustle and bustle had upset me.

A few years ago I related this incident to Muriel. She said *"How old do you think you'd have been?"* *"Four or five, I suppose."* I replied. She said, *"Do you understand; we moved to Timperley..... well it was October 1934: you were only fourteen months old."*

It was hard to believe, but Muriel remembered the incident very well. In the excitement of looking round her new home she had left the kitchen door open and I had escaped. Mum had smacked her - *"he could have been trampled on by the removal men, in and out with furniture,"* she said.

Muriel had been only five, but she had been in charge of me. She has a fantastic memory, so I believe her. Memory is such a strange thing: sometimes I cannot remember what I was doing 5 minutes ago, and yet here I have a memory going back 70 years.

Later when I grew old enough to play outside, I became pals with a little girl who lived at number 1. Her name was Sheila Harding and we became inseparable. Her garden led down to the pond, as did four others - ours was the first that did not do this. We loved to watch the moorhens so her Mum would take us down to feed them. They were very funny as they swam about, darting in and out of the reeds. Sheila's Mum told us they were searching for food. She would give us bread to throw for them, although she would end up throwing most of it. She said that the swans were away on a long journey and would soon be back to have babies; then they would be taking most of the bread.

Time has removed many memories of those early years, but I still remember the great closeness I felt to Sheila. Mum told me that we played for hours and she never heard us falling out with each other. One day, not long after we had both had our fifth birthdays, I called for Sheila as usual, but was upset when her Mum said very curtly, *"she's not coming out"*, and shut the door on me. I ran back home, crying. Mum told me that she was very poorly and was not at home; she was in hospital. *"Sheila's Mummy is very worried, that's why she appeared cross with you."*

How do you explain, day after day, to a five year old why he can't play with his best friend? A few weeks later, Mum and Dad took me out for the afternoon around

Courtesy of Philip Harding

this park-like place with a large house. Dad suddenly lifted me on his shoulders and walked towards a big window. My nose came up against the glass. *"Careful George, he'll be in with her if you get any closer,"* my Mum said.

My friend Sheila on her bike

Courtesy of Philip Harding

After my eyes had adjusted to the inside of the room I could see Sheila right in front of me, propped up with pillows, in a large bed. Her head was swathed in bandage with her left eye covered. I waved excitedly and she gently waved back. After a few minutes, Dad told me it was time for me to wave goodbye. As we waved to each other anew I sensed that something was not right with Sheila. We kept looking at each other, as Dad carefully lifted me off his shoulders; neither of us knew that in a week's time she would be dead.

I remember so well when Mum broke the news of Sheila's death to me. I had just got in from school and she took me in to the front room and sat me on her knee, a serious look clouding her face. I thought I was in trouble for something. It may have been the glint of tears in her eyes that told me she was upset. Pressing my head to her chest, *"Peter love"* she said, her voice barely a whisper, *"I have to tell you something, and it's not going to be easy. You know Sheila's been staying in hospital because of her being so poorly,"* I looked up into her face and saw tears streaming down her cheeks.

"I'm sorry, but Sheila has been so very poorly that this afternoon Jesus thought it best for her to go and live with him." Her voice had become very croaky.

Young as I was, I knew what this meant, and it broke my heart. There we were, the two of us crying together in our front room, Mum trying to console me. I cried and cried. Sheila's death had a deep and lasting effect on me.

She was buried on the 27th September 1938 in Hale cemetery. She lies there still, forever young. I think how sad it was for Sheila to have had such a little experience of life. What compounds the tragedy is the knowledge that today, with modern antibiotics, her illness would have been trivial. She died of an ear infection, a mastoid.

I had started school a couple of weeks before her death. I really missed sharing the excitement of it with her. Perhaps the trauma of it threw a spanner in my emotional works because during my first year at school I became a very naughty little boy.

I had better introduce you to some of my friends now, or as some would say, my gang. Geoffrey Long was a year younger than me and lived at number 7. He was shorter than me and had straight, mousy hair. He was an only child, but not a spoilt little brat like some. His dad had a very good job with the telephone company.

Geoff's garden was the last garden that went down to the pond, so this was the route the gang and I would take when we ventured down to the water. His Mum was out at work for most of the day. It frightens the life out of me now when I think of the reckless way we treated this water. Years later we learned that the builders tried to drain it but gave up, saying that an underground stream was feeding it.

Harry Monks was my best pal and sparring partner; he lived at number 17, on the corner of Leicester Avenue. He was of similar build to me but with a heavier face and dark brown hair. What a pair we were; trouble was never far away - not serious trouble - just high spirits. Well, that's what we thought anyhow - not that we thought very often!

Mrs Monks would often refer to Harry as *'Our Lal'* - most commonly it seemed when she was mentioning the fact that *"Our Lal's got a hole in his heart, you know."* I often wondered about this and why it was never mended.

Other partners in crime were Ian Harkness, a rather lanky lad, a bit younger than me, who lived at number 16. Peter Davies lived at the last house on that side of the avenue, number 40. He was in the same class as me at Park Road, stocky and with a head of curly black hair. His dad was a manager at the Manchester and Salford Docks.

Elizabeth Booth who lived next door to Ian was the only girl to join us on our adventures. She was tall and slim, and when she got to about ten or eleven she never bothered with us anymore, other than to pass the time of day.

After a few years, the younger brother of my beloved Sheila would join the gang. Philip was small and a little podgy - and, like me, he suffered with asthma.

So our little gang usually comprised of six members Harry, Geoffrey, Ian, Peter, Philip and yours truly. What a bunch!

Park Road School

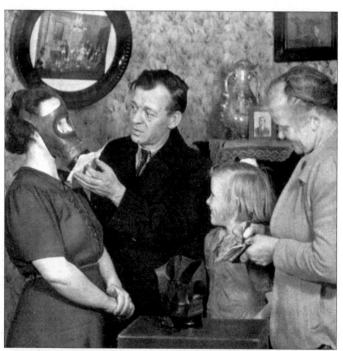

Distributing gas masks.　　　*Courtesy of 'A Childs War', Mike Brown*

2. Off to School and the War

My big sister Muriel had been attending Park Road Junior School since its opening on 7th April 1937. Mum now started the 'drip psychology' treatment. She kept saying to me *"You'll be going to Muriel's new school soon, won't that be nice?"* I wasn't impressed at all; I had better things to do than worry about school.

One day in the summer of 1938 Muriel arrived home from school having just broken up for the summer holidays. She started teasing me in a half singing voice, *"Ha Ha, you'll be going to school when I go back after the holidays, like it or not, Ha Ha"*, and a silly grin on her face. This was no encouragement, and I certainly did not want to go with her.

Mum told her to stop tormenting me. For whatever reason, Muriel seemed to have a nasty side to her. Thankfully my Mum was not daft and got to know her spiteful ways.

Eventually the day dawned for my first day at school. Mum got me up bright and early, gave me a good breakfast, an earful of instructions about my behaviour, and a good wash behind the ears. I was dressed in my new school uniform, white shirt, the tie with green and gold stripes, short grey trousers, black shoes, a green blazer and a school cap to top it all. I was ready for the fray. Mum remembered, more or less at the last minute the night before, to sew the school badges on, a gold tree on a green shield with the letters P.R.S. in a triangle. Very smart.

Turning me round again for what I now hoped would be the final inspection, Mum adjusted my tie, straightened my cap and led me by the hand out of the gate and down the road. As we walked she said, *"Now remember, if you see a lady we know, don't forget to raise your cap and say good morning - or whatever time of the day it is."* We didn't see anyone we knew, so I wasn't able to raise my cap and say *'goodmorningorwhatevertimeofdayitis'*.

Riddings Road came and went, then Park Road and soon we were passing Timperley railway station. As we walked past I thought to myself, what a pity Mum's not taking me on holiday again, which made me even more miserable.

At the bottom of the hill we turned right into Frieston Road. Now we were with other children and their mums, pushing through the Infants & Junior gate. It was a new school, a long building with an upstairs. I could see Muriel's gate at the other end.

"Well, here we are," said Mum, *"It's very nice isn't it, take your cap off, that's a good boy,"* combing my hair with the flat of her hand. Oh no! Out came her hanky, she spit on it though her teeth then wiped a smudge off my face. How I managed to get my face dirty in such a short time, God only knows.

I can't remember much more about the day, other than that Muriel did not seem too pleased about having to escort me back home for lunch, and again after school. Until I got used to going on my own, which wasn't long, Mum gave her this job, which she did begrudgingly, pulling and pushing me because I wouldn't walk quickly enough. In those days parents did not have to worry about children being out and about on their own. Road traffic was minimal and vehicles and drivers were far less aggressive.

I truly believe that Sheila's death affected me in a way that my parents and teachers did not understand, and my subsequent behaviour reflected the turmoil it had caused me. It turned me into a rebel - and I made a proper job of it in that first year. No half measures, I was a rebellious child. I was horrible, unruly and I even turned to crime! I would put my hand up and ask to go to the lavatory, but then I would sneak into the cloakroom and steal money or the like from the other kids' pockets. I'm not proud of it, but it's the truth. I would sneak out of school to spend my ill-gotten gains on sweets that I didn't really want.

Once Auntie Babs came over from Wilmslow. Muriel and I had been home for lunch as usual, so she took us both back to school in her car. As soon as she had turned the car round and left, I also turned round and walked out of the playground and the school for the rest of the day. I went to the sweet shop - Auntie Babs had given me threepence.

When the weather was fine and truancy was the order of the day, I would be out and about getting up to different time-wasting escapades. In the spring or early summer of the following year, I would go into the little park that bordered the school grounds, Newton Park, for the frogs' spawn, which was in abundance. I would lie down and put my hand into the slimy substance, and let it run through my fingers. Soon there were lots of baby frogs to pick up and tease girls with. If I had any money I would go and buy toffees or chocolate. I would go on the canal bank and watch the narrowboats, or as we called them, barges. I would throw stones into the water and watch the circles ripple across the water and be cut in two as a barge passed by. I would sit and wonder where these lovely lumbering barges were going to. I would do this until school was over and then join the other children as they came past, tagging on to go home as if butter wouldn't melt in my mouth.

Muriel was called to the office of Miss Ryder, the headmistress, and given notes to take home to Mum. It seemed that every other week I would be ushered into Miss Ryder's office to find my Mum waiting for me. Miss Ryder would be sat behind her desk with a stern look on her face, in the dark blue suit she always wore. I always climbed the stairs with a feeling of trepidation, like having to go to the dentist.

Later in this first year, my teacher, Miss Henshall, one day chose me to go for her cup of tea at break time. The kitchen was in the middle of the school, some distance from our classroom. Fed up with most of the tea being in the saucer, she taught me to carry it with my thumbs on the cup edge and my fingers under the saucer. She was very kind and understanding and I thank her for being so patient with me. I suppose you could say I became a teacher's pet.

First thing on a Monday morning, after the teachers had called the register, came _"Dinner money! Anyone wanting school dinners this week form a line and have your money ready, no dawdling now."_ A queue formed quickly in front of her desk. Many months later, when we were at war, another queue formed on her instruction. *"Saving stamps, I'm now selling them for who ever wants them, quickly now."* I for one did not have a sixpence every week (not even an illegitimate one!) but we all looked forward to the day when our card finally had the last of the thirty stamps stuck on by our teacher. This announced that we could now go to the Post Office and exchange the card for a little book and have our first National Savings Certificate.

Sometime before the spring of 1939, men and machines arrived at school and started to dig very large holes at the far end of the playing field. It turned out that they were building air-raid shelters, one for each of the six classes. They were fitted out with bench seats on either side, with a double one down the middle, made of slats like park benches, which gave us ridges across the back of our legs. Near to the entrance they installed two chemical toilets, one for girls and one for boys. At the other end there was a round escape hatch, made of sheet steel with a metal ladder. Not long before the start of my second year at school, on 3rd September 1939, Britain declared war on Hitler's Germany. I was coming home one afternoon down Acresfield Road when I saw some men with black things hanging from their shoulders. They were calling at all the houses. I hadn't been home very long when there was a knock on the front door and Mum opened it. *"Good afternoon madam, we are now supplying all households with gas masks; how many people live here?"*

We learned later that children in London had been issued with them as early as January 1938. I spotted a different looking one among the many he carried, it was blue and it had a funny floppy nose made from two thin red pieces of rubber placed together. I found out that these flapped on breathing out. These were called Mickey Mouse masks - to appeal to younger children, so they would not be frightened - with two round windows instead of the large one on the standard masks. I was disappointed - they were for children of less than five; far too young in my opinion to appreciate their comic value!

"Bill. Two adults and two children's, age six and ten for this house. Ta Bill." When he handed them over they were in little cardboard boxes that had a thin rope handle so it could be carried over your shoulder. He then showed Mum how to adjust the straps so they fitted correctly, the right way to put them on, and how to use and look after them. *"Your life may depend on them you know,"* he said, nodding his head. He told us that we were to carry them everywhere that we went; we even had to take them to bed with us, yes even into the bathroom, he emphasized.

I must admit that I was not very keen on the thing. After it had been worn for a while the little oblong celluloid window would steam up. Mum was advised to put a tiny touch of Vaseline on her finger then smear over the inside of the window to stop it steaming up. We found another use for these gas masks in their cases; we used them as goalposts. We also had gas mask drill at school, making sure we could take it out of the box and put it on as quickly as possible. This took place every week like the shelter drill. When the mask steamed up it was like playing blind man's buff; a great game! I am sure the teachers got upset that we made a game out of something that was terrifying to them.

Another way of making sure you got the class giggling was to breathe out hard. This caused the extra air to find another way out, through the sides of the gas mask, which made a farting noise. Did I occasionally see the hint of a smile on some of the teachers' faces?

At the time I was waging a sort of war with Jacky Teague, one of my classmates who lived directly across the road from the Infants' gate. The Teagues could be seen, still sat round the dining table having their breakfast, when all the rest of us were going into school. Was I a bit envious? Despite the fact that he lived just yards away from the school he was always late.

I had a disaster one day. As I ran home from school one hot sunny day it came to me that my Dad would be home. Dad was a furniture salesman at Lewis's in the centre of Manchester, and as he always had to work on Saturdays, he had Wednesday afternoons off. I thought I would help him in the garden when I got home. Suddenly I got stomach ache, I think I must have had a tummy bug. Whoops! It was too late, good job I had underpants with elastic in the legs!

Dad was outside, making a wooden fender for the kitchen fireplace. I just stood near him and watched, I didn't want to tell him about my accident. As I looked at him I saw his nose twitch. *"What's that smell?"* he said looking and sniffing round, then straight at me. *"It's you... you've messed your pants, haven't you? Cor blimey!"* Then a little smile appeared. *"Come on I'll have to get you cleaned up, trust your mother to be out at a time like this."* Whenever I saw that fender it always resurrected memories of that embarrassing incident and that sunny afternoon.

Whilst Dad was cleaning me up in the bathroom and changing my clothes, guess who barged in? Our Muriel. *"Pooh, you've messed yourself; Mum should put you back in nappies!"* she sneered. She was a real expert at sneering. *"Don't take any notice of her, I'll crack her one of these days,"* said Dad to reassure me. But for weeks she tormented me at every opportunity, whispering some remark in my ear so Mum couldn't hear her. She used it to blackmail me into doing chores for her.

A few days after my 'accident' we had a very bad thunderstorm. Claps of thunder followed the lightening. I was terrified. Rather jovially Mum said, *"Oh it's nothing to worry about, it's only God having his coal delivered."* I was never frightened of thunderstorms since. Thanks Mum. And thanks God for using nutty slack!

When I had just turned seven, I was stood in the middle of the road having a rest from kicking a ball about and talking to Harry. Suddenly he said to me, probably learnt from his big brother, *"Who are you going support then, Manchester City or United?"* *"I don't know, I've never thought about it. Anyway... how do you support them?"* We had to admit to each other that we didn't have a clue. *"Who do you support then?"* said I. *"Not telling you till you say which one,"* he answered. I had a penny in my pocket, *"I'll toss up then, heads for United, tails for City"*. It came down heads. I wish some kind benefactor had bought me a few shares in the club all those years ago. Some months later United's ground was badly damaged by bombs and they had to play at City's ground, Maine Road. After the war, when the bomb damage had been repaired, they moved back to Old Trafford. I remember visiting Old Trafford in 1948 to watch United play Huddersfield, when United won 6-0.

"*What's that Dad?*" I asked as soon as I found him in the shed. He was bent over a funny looking object and hitting it with a hammer. "*It's a last,*" he said. "*A last what...?*" I began to say, but before I had finished he picked up the other shoe and put it on this mysterious object. "*There now, it's for mending shoes on; you can watch me.*" He picked me up, sat me on the bench and said "*Don't touch anything!*" (The cue for me to do the opposite.) He ripped the heel off the shoe as it sat on this strange three legged object Then he sandpapered the sole, blew the dust off and coated it with glue from a tube, picked up a black rubber sole, and as if by magic they became two. Now he beat it to death with a hammer.

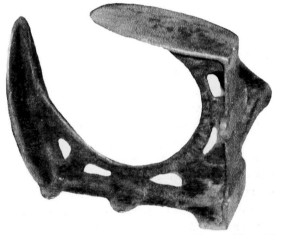

After a lot of sighing, naughty words, and a lot of puffing and panting, he said, "*there now, not bad; mmm, not bad at all.*" Thankfully he lifted me off the bench; my bum was aching and I could hardly walk. I was impressed with his talents as a cobbler, but more with his swearing.

Dad was always up first on Sunday mornings and he would light the fire in the kitchen, then brew a pot of tea and take a cup each back to bed for him and Mum. Our treat during the late summer when apples were in the shops was for Dad to cut one in half, take the core out and bring them up for Muriel and me with a couple of biscuits each. I enjoyed scraping away at the apple and eating the fruits of my labour with my biscuit.

Once a week, Air Raid practice had to take place. A teacher would stand between the eight classrooms and blow a whistle or ring a bell. After a while it was decided that these methods were to be used only by the official wardens during real air raids. We would take part in an organised (so called) dash across the playing field, and down into the shelter. The shelters always had the musty smell of wet earth tinged with the disinfectant from the chemical toilets.

During our second year we were occasionally allowed to take a favourite toy to school. I had just had a birthday and Auntie Babs and Uncle Geoffrey had presented me with a toy excavator. It was far too heavy for me to carry to school, so Mum attached a thin rope so I could pull it. There was a great sound effect from the bucket when it was released! The noise, about the level of Concorde taking off, was appealing to a child, but drove the teacher mad, particularly when the other kids also insisted on playing with it. My teacher's nerves must have been in tatters, for she suddenly shouted, "*Peter Scott, for goodness sake stop making that awful noise, find something else to play with, just as long as it's something quiet for a change!"* She told me not to bring it again.

That day, on my way home, when I reached the top of the station approach, I thought I would make use of my digger, so I rode down the hill sitting on it. The wheels were about two inches thick and very strong. Soon I was on my way down; hurtling is the best description. Oh I wished I had the brains to think ahead as I came whooshing down with my legs stretched out in front of me, far too fast to stop by putting my feet down. The machine went over the kerb and I was catapulted into the road. Astonishingly no bones were broken.

One morning assembly, sometime in the summer of 1940, we were told some important news. *"Now children we have an exciting surprise for you all; next week the King and Queen with the Princesses Elizabeth and Margaret will be coming up from their palace in London to visit Manchester and some of the surrounding towns and villages. But that's not all, because you children will be lining the route. You'll all be given little paper Union Jacks that you can take home after."* Children from other schools were also going.

After weeks of mounting excitement, the day arrived. All the pupils from the six classes of our school were lined up in threes, with a teacher at the front and one behind each class, and we were marched off to take our place on Manchester Road, lining the route the Royal party would take. After standing there for some considerable time we saw a line of large black cars coming towards us, proceeded by an escort of police cars and motor bikes. We waved our flags and the Royals obliged by waving back at us. That was it; a glimpse of the King and Queen sat on the back seat, and their daughters in the smaller seats with their backs to the driver and attendant, and it was over. The most exciting part of the visit was that I had seen Princess Margaret; I decided she was the girl I would marry.

The third years learned to play musical instruments and I was excited, thinking about playing the drums. The day arrived and the teacher marched us into the hall and told us what I had been waiting to hear. She started allocating instruments and explained we would have to share and take turns. *"Peter, here you are."* I could not believe it, she handed me a triangle to play; can you imagine, giving me a triangle? I'm sure that this was my first proper introduction to deep disappointment.

One day Mum had called me in from playing football with Harry, Ian and Geoffrey. *"Right upstairs and get your hands washed, tea will be ready in a minute."* Dad was home from work and as he sat waiting for his dinner, Mum, in the scullery, shouted, *"George, Mr Grummitt died yesterday morning."* *"Good Lord, what happened to him then?"* *"Mrs Harding told me that by all accounts he'd not heard the alarm go off, when he did wake up and saw the time, he jumped out of bed in a panic, and dropped dead with a stroke or a heart attack. They won't know properly until after the post-mortem."*

Mr Grummitt had lived at number 3 with his wife and daughter Enid, a friend of

Muriel. Enid's claim to fame was that her cousin was the famous racing cyclist Reg Harris - the inspiration that drove me to join a cycling club later in my youth. As I was coming home for my lunch, at the bottom of Olive Road, some large black cars were coming towards me and turned the bend of Acresfield Road into Park Road. The first car was the hearse with lots of flowers in it. Then I saw Mrs Grummitt and Enid in another one. I, of course, removed my cap, stood to attention, and bowed my head, like my Mum had taught me. Everyone paid their respects to people who had died, and everyone who was close to the person wore a black arm band for a few weeks after.

It took over three years before I was able to stick my last National Savings Stamp on my card; and by then it was rather dog-eared! I had finally got it full! I rushed home at lunch to show it to my Mum. *"When you come home this afternoon you'll have to go and get a savings certificate won't you,"* she said. I could hardly wait to get up to Mr Morris's Post Office on Arderne Road. With a big grin on my face I gave the lady my card and asked, *"please can I have a stificate"*, pushing the card on the counter as far as I could.

After she had told me I was a lucky little boy to have so much money, she swiftly rolled the certificate over a roller in a tray of water and stuck it on the first page. Now I was doing my bit to win the war. There were a lot of empty pages and I wondered how many I would be able to fill as I said thank you and left the shop.

One afternoon in late spring I had been playing down at the bottom of the garden. The French windows were open, and I could see Mum sat showing Muriel how to sew. Thinking it was time for tea I went up and stood talking to them both. Mum looked at me and asked, *"What have you got in your jacket pockets?"* I said *"Nothing mum."* A determined look came to her face, *"Show me, now please."* I shook my head; at this act of defiance she put her hand in one of the pockets. *"Oh my god, what have you got in there?"* she screamed, withdrawing her hand a lot quicker than she put it in.

The game was up; I had to show her. I withdrew a handful of baby frogs, some dropping to the floor and jumping around as Muriel flew out of the room with a piercing scream. *"Take them back to where you got them from, NOW! Then come back and scrub your hands for your tea."*

When Dad first came home on leave from the army he showed me his gas mask. This one was far better than ours; it had two windows and a corrugated rubber tube that went into a round tin box that stayed in the carrying case on his chest. I wished I could have one. Dad let me hold his new .303 Enfield rifle. I pretended to shoot it from a hiding place behind a chair. To be honest I could hardly hold it. Seeing them at the pictures with the soldiers running about with them gives you no idea that they weigh half a ton.

A year or so later, a corrugated round tin became available for the carrying of our gas masks, but these were very expensive and few could afford them. Some people decorated their gas mask cases by sticking pictures of flowers on them; a few well-off ladies had them incorporated into the bottom of handbags - it takes more than a world war to interfere with fashion.

Whenever I was on my way home I always stopped and looked down at the canal and the railway as I walked over the station bridge - an attraction to an adventurous child. There was a narrow road that led to the towpath and some factories near to Deansgate Lane. Under the bridge the waterway widened out to allow the long boats to turn round. Nearby there were two or three cavernous rooms built of brick. These had a funny, musty smell, so we agreed barge horses must have been put in there at night. When you looked up at the bridge ceiling the reflection of the canal water, together with the light, caused moving reflections on the very wide roof, a little bit eerie sometimes. I would not liked to have stayed the night there. Very ghostly.

The bargees were very proud of their boats and always kept them looking spick and span, with beautifully decorated woodwork. The multi-coloured flowers and patterns painted on the chimney and between the cabin windows were duplicated on the big water jugs, buckets and kettles that they carried. It really was a sight to see the barges being pulled by their well-loved and beautifully kept horses. One member of the family crew would always walk with the horse as it plodded along the towpath, often in deep conversation with it. I suppose this was to prevent them stopping to eat; the barge would have just kept on going, and the poor old horse would have then been dragged behind, possibly

Bridgewater Canal
Courtesy of 'Altrincham: An Illustrated History',
Pat Southern, Trafford Leisure Services

ending up in the water. We referred to the canal as the 'cut'.

Barges carried a variety of cargo; sacks of grain, timber, metals and coal. Coal was usually put into an open barge and pulled behind the mother boat. Most of the cargoes had been unloaded from ocean going ships that had come into Manchester and Salford Docks.

As times changed, horses were replaced with diesel, and the number of barges towed increased to two or maybe three. The men fishing on the canal bank were not very pleased when the barges came along; they had to wind in their lines to clear the way for them to pass, or else risk losing them.

At school I had taken on the role of peacemaker and I would try to sort bullies out. This was not very often, but one occasion was when I was in Miss Lord's class. Miss Lord wore her hair in a tight bun and always appeared very stern, and although she was very strict, she was also very fair and kind. A new boy, called Peter Grundy, who had bright red hair, was teasing and pushing a girl in the playground. I rushed up and told him to stop it. *"Oh yeah, who's goin' to stop me. You?"* he said with a sneer. Looking around I saw a crowd gathering. I wondered, have I met my match. I couldn't let him get away with this. Cries of *"Go on Scotty, give the bully a hiding,"* egged me on.

Up went my fists, and I started my war dance. He did the same and we exchanged blows, then my right hand connected; my hand hurt and there was blood on it. *"I have cut myself"*, I thought, but I looked up; the bully's nose was bleeding like a tap. Shouts of *"good old Scotty!"* echoed in my ears, just as the duty teacher came out and started to wave her arms in the air and shout us in. Peter Grundy was never a problem again.

Opposite the spot where I had the accident with my toy digger, there was a cake shop. Religiously, once a week, I would call in to buy a milk bun for a halfpenny. I took this for granted, until one day, late in 1942, they suddenly told me they could not sell me one, as I had not got a bread unit coupon. I could not understand what the lady was saying; all I knew was that I could not have my bun. When I got home, Mum tried to explain that flour was made from wheat and that it came across the sea in ships from Canada and America, and a lot of ships had been sunk. It was illegal to make the white bread that most people enjoyed, we had to have 'National Bread'. The flour was made with all the wheat grain, including the husk, which gave it the unappetising off white colour. We had to give the shopkeeper Bread Units, known as BUs, for all our bread and cakes - part of the food-rationing programme.

One day, when I was coming home, there were some men working in the middle of Park Road. One was making holes with a road drill, another was pouring black stuff in and another was putting an object into the hole, yellow with two large marble-like things on both sides. I thought it was something to do with the war, and in an indirect way it was. They were 'cats' eyes', a new safety invention that allowed road users to see the middle of the road in the black-out. Magic stuff! The inventor was a Huddersfield man who became a millionaire.

On the corner of Park Road and Frieston Road was a large house which is still there. Whether the apple tree is still in the back garden I don't know, but in the autumn I would chance climbing over the wall. On the odd occasion, at going home time, I met with another couple of boys who liked the apples as well, and as usual, when I was doing something I shouldn't, more often than not I would get caught - and again I was climbing the staircase to Miss Ryder's office.

During the school holidays Mum found me a job I could do to help her. I would go to the Co-op in Timperley Village to collect the rations and a few other items of food. *"Perhaps Harry will go with you; his mum may want some shopping as well."* And Harry did come with me on a few occasions. It entailed a walk of about a mile, but when coming back with a full basket; it seemed more like twenty. For a little lad it was quite a walk, but I enjoyed it really, because the route took us past our favourite shop, 'Constables'. This is where we got our sweet rations. If Harry or I had an odd penny we

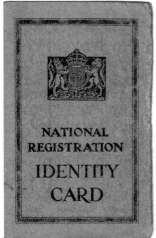

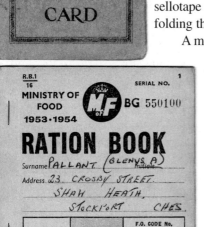

usually went in and bought something like a spearmint chew that we could share.

When I got to the Co-op, I joined the queue on the grocery side of the shop to get what they called dry goods. These were soap, sugar, dried fruit, cocoa, jam and a host of other items. Sugar and dried fruit had to be weighed out into blue paper bags; these were of different shades of blue to distinguish the item inside. When the assistants had some spare time they had to 'weigh up' as they called it. This stock was then put on the shelves in readiness to serve their customers. We did not have such a thing as sellotape in those days; the assistants were expert at folding the bag in a certain way.

A man called Cyril usually served me. He was quite tall and always very pleasant, with a ready smile, but he had what I later knew to be an 'affliction'. Every few minutes his head would jerk to the right and the left corner of his mouth would go up, at the same time as his right elbow moved into his body. When Mum first took me I was fascinated with Cyril and had to have a little giggle - I was staring at him as we were waiting to be served. When we left the shop she put the shopping basket down and pulled my arm so I was facing her and gave me a right good telling off. The tirade ended with. *"How would you like someone laughing at you because you weren't very well? Now don't you ever, EVER embarrass me by doing anything like that again?"* I always remember that last sentence whenever I see someone not as fortunate as myself. Back then, I have to admit that the fascination for watching poor Cyril twitch never left me, but I suppose I also felt sorry for him.

On one such occasion, when he was adding up the shopping list, he did a 'super twitch' and the pencil shot from his hand onto the floor behind him. I heard a couple of ladies have a titter, and I did too, but the thought crossed my mind that 'those ladies should have their mothers with them to tell them off'. I also wondered if my Mum could have stood there and not tittered!

When you'd finished on the dry goods side you had to walk over to the provision side of the shop, and join another queue. There you would hand over the slip giving the total LSD (pounds, shillings and pence) spent with Cyril. On this counter you were

Timperley village in the 1930s above, and the early 1950s below.
Courtesy of 'Looking back at Timperley', Hazel Pryor

served with your family ration of bacon, butter, lard, cheese, margarine and eggs, etc. When these rations had been cut and you saw them on the scales, well, they didn't seem to warrant the amount of paper needed to wrap them in, they were so small.

We now had the familiar ritual of the 'cutting of the coupons' along with the adding up of our purchases. Just think, no adding machines, calculators or electronic tills in these days. When we paid, they would write the amount onto a cheque. I think our number was 26105. The money and the cheque would be put into a metal cup and screwed to a lid suspended from wires. On the pull of a handle it would whiz along to an office up a small flight of stairs. The change was put in for the return journey - money by wire had a different meaning in those days! The cheques, which were a form of receipt, calculated your 'Divi'. Twice a year you got a dividend, a share of the profits. Mum always looked forward to 'divi days', along with thousands of others.

If I had too much for my basket, the shop would give me a paper carrier. They had string handles that cut into your hands. One time the man behind the provision counter packed my shopping in the carrier for me and off I set for home. I had just arrived at the bottom of the railway bridge near the 'Rec' when the bottom of the carrier bag just fell out. I stood and looked at the goods in a heap - and some tins were determined to make their own way home. The sight brought me to my senses and I ran to retrieve them. I thought, *"How am I going to get them home,"* and as I stood there scratching my napper I found the cause of my dilemma, a jar of pickled onions that had been leaking. Over the bridge came a lady carrying her shopping basket and as she drew near she said, *"Oh deary me, what's happened here?"* I looked pleadingly up into her face then down at the pile of groceries. *"Well aren't you the lucky one, you can have this bag as I didn't get a lot this week,"* and she brought a carrier bag from her basket. *"Well I'll have to hurry on now, bye bye,"* she said. Relief flooded through me as I started to gather up my shopping, making sure that I screwed the top on the onion jar tightly this time.

As I restarted my journey home I thought what a good job Harry hadn't been with me, because without doubt we would have called at the 'Rec' to play on the swings, roundabout, seesaw and horse. The horse was a great game, like a seesaw, but hung on long metal rods with a swinging and rocking movement and about six seats in line. We had to be tough in these days, as all the rides were set in concrete and made of iron and wood. Muriel came home one day to tell us that she and Winnie Monks had been on the swings - they must have been fourteen at the time - when a big lad had jumped onto Winnie's swing and standing up behind her had worked the swing up to a great height. Terrified, she kept shouting to him to stop but he just kept on. She said it went all the way over the top, but I never believed this.

Harry and I would sometimes climb over the fence onto the railway line and halfway down the bank we would stop to listen for trains. If all was clear we would run down and place a halfpenny on to the line, then climb back up and wait for the train to come along. After a train had passed we would go and retrieve our now flattened and larger coin. We were unable to spend it of course, so we didn't do it very often. If we had had money to burn I may not be here to write this now! We only ever saw goods trains carrying minerals and rocks, and most of the wagons had ICI in big steel letters on their sides.

During my early school days I was struggling to learn to tell the time, feeling as thick as two bricks. One day I sat in a cardboard box (like you do at that age) that happened to be in the kitchen, intently studying the kitchen clock on the narrow mantle over the red tiled coal fire and oven. Mum saw me doing this, and took the clock down from its safe place and handed it to me to study. It was not much use. Mum, Auntie Babs, and even Muriel, during one of her magnanimous periods, all tried to help me. They used the family alarm clock, and paper and pencil. Once they even used Dad's gold pocket watch before Mum thought better of it.

Despite all this effort, telling the time still eluded me. I sat in my cardboard box one day, now showing wear and tear, still determined to beat this obstacle. Then it suddenly dawned on me, how to do it, in rather a strange way. Auntie Babs had a cocktail watch, small and oblong, with dots in place of numerals and very tiny hands. The watch had been left on the kitchen table and I picked it up and started asking Auntie questions about it. She explained where all the numbers should be, and where the little hands should point. Some days later Mum saw me huddled in the security of my 'time box', closely examining the watch. *"Come on then what time is it?"* she chided as she swept through into the scullery. I replied *"Twenty past six."* She came back into the kitchen and looked straight at the clock on the mantlepiece. *"That was a lucky guess,"* she said, and took a look at the watch. She turned it to another time, *"Right what's it now?"* *"Ten to ten?"* I replied hesitantly. I was the centre of attention; they all had a go at trying me out. OK, so a few were wrong, but I had learnt to tell the time on a watch with no proper hands or numbers!

One morning on my way to school, on turning into Park Road I saw a lot of children and grown-ups outside a house opposite the farm. Ominously, there was a police car there as well. I ran up to find out what was going on. Now, if I was to give you a thousand guesses, you wouldn't get it. There was an aeroplane sticking out of an upstairs bay window. On first sight it looked like a Hurricane but it turned out to be a Barracuda, a plane I had never heard of. It was a single engined aircraft used for training. Though it was an amusing sight (the picture was in all the papers) we learned later that the pilot had been killed, poor man. Eyewitnesses said it appeared to them that he was trying to land in the farm field. The people in the house must have had quite a shock, but no one was hurt. They were having breakfast in the kitchen. The aeroplane was still there when we went to school the next day, but it had gone later in the afternoon when I went home.

Some of us managed to get pieces of the plane as souvenirs. I had a piece of the cockpit window which was made out of thick clear Perspex. I was told it was quite a new invention in those days - the munitions factory workers used it illicitly to make all sorts of things, such as small statues of ladies, animals, chess sets and cigarette lighters. They also made interesting items from bullet cases and shrapnel. They said that they made them during their tea breaks and lunch hours, but I am not so sure.

While on summer holiday during my last year at Park Road, I helped a farmer with his milk deliveries. His farm was opposite the house that the plane crashed into. He did not have an electric milk float, but horsepower, with a leg on each corner and a tail that occasionally lifted to deposit garden manure, as it pulled his two-wheeled cart. I really fancied myself when the farmer let me hold the reins and shout *"walk on girl"*, and *"whoa there."* The milk was carried in two large churns and we had three sizes of ladle for the milk, pints, quarts and gills. All sorts of crockery were left out on people's front steps, but jugs were the favourite. To protect the milk from dirt and flies, some ladies left plates or saucers out, and the posh customers had nets with beads on, to hold them down in the wind.

The various departments of the Co-op also used horse and cart for their deliveries; milk, bread and coal, even house removals. Petrol was in short supply and was needed for the war effort, so it was only sensible to keep the horses working. The horses were shires or similar. There was frequent reference in our house to the 'store's horse' whenever anyone in the family was bursting for a wee. I knew the store's horse pulled the cart that our milk was delivered from, but it was many years before I understood what they meant. Our toilet was upstairs right over the kitchen and the sound travelled through the ceiling. Mum would say, *"the store's horse is at it again."* It seems that the store's horse always emptied its bladder outside our house - a deluge with grand sound effects.

3. Newfield House

During the summer, Muriel and I would go and stay with Uncle George and Auntie Mabel in Sheffield. The visits still hold a fond place in my memory

Mum had two brothers; Jack, the younger, died after being gassed in the trenches during the First World War. Uncle George was my Mum's big brother, and my favourite uncle. Auntie Mabel came from Bridlington. They lived in a house imaginatively called *Newfield,* on Newfield Lane, Dore, near Sheffield. I remember my Mum saying that they would have loved to have children of their own but couldn't.

There weren't many houses on the lane in those days. At the top of the lane towards the Dore Moor Inn were a few cottages and a farm. One of the farmer's daughters, called Nellie, helped Auntie Mabel in the house. Next-door to Uncle's house, and separated by a big hedge with an arched gap in it, was the wooden bungalow of Mr Caplan. Years later I learnt that he owned Uncle's house. It must have been one 'bobby's job', as we said then, to cut this hedge; it must have been about 800 yards long, 8 foot high and 3 foot wide.

At the bottom of Uncle George's garden there was a small block of stables where Mr Caplan kept a few horses. These appeared to have changed every time we went. To this day I still love the pleasant sight of horses looking over the stable door, the equipment in the tack room and the smell of the horses mingled with hay and straw.

The first time I went to visit, they had a pony named Peggy which I was allowed to ride. I was no Harvey Smith; Nellie had to hold me in the saddle as she walked with me. A few years later I remember two young men who were staying with Mr Caplan persuading Muriel to have a ride on a huge carthorse. As it was about to go through the gap in the hedge it hesitated, so one of the boys hit it with a bullrush he was carrying. It made a few backward steps then promptly reared up and threw Muriel off. She was not very pleased! It wasn't just her body that suffered; her dignity took an almighty blow. The temper tantrum that she threw when she got to her feet was something to behold - all because the two young men and I were falling about, laughing. She glared at me and screwing her face up she hissed, *"You just wait!! I'll get even with you!"*

Nellie took us up to the farm and said we could help her father to feed the pigs. All the swill had been boiled in an old wash boiler, and when we arrived it was in the process of being mashed up in a big food mixer. We could help by bringing the buckets to hold under the spout as he filled them. Muriel and I were given a half full one that we carried between us. We lifted it up to the top of the wall, and the farmer, who was in the pig sty, said *"Thanks ter yer both, that's a big 'elp, that were."* as he emptied the bucket into the trough. The swill looked and smelt disgusting, but the pigs enjoyed it. The farmer's wife shouted me over and gave me a small package to take back to Auntie. It turned out to be a packet of home cured bacon.

Whenever we went to stay at Uncle George's, Mum referred to it as going to

'Dore' for a couple of weeks. Sometimes uncle would surprise us by buying us presents. One day he took up his rifle, always kept near the front door, and I heard him say to Auntie, *"Mabel, just going down the lane to the field to try and shoot a couple of rabbits, won't be long."* I asked to go with him but he said. *"No Peter it could be dangerous! Don't want YOU ending up in a pie do I?"* I must have looked very upset, because the next day when he came home from work he bought me a cowboy cap gun and holster, and an Indian chief's head dress. The next day I drove Auntie Mabel mad firing the gun - she came out of the back door saying, *"Peter, for goodness sake, go down the garden away from the house to shoot your gun."*

Uncle George would always arrange some sort of surprise during our stay. One year two rabbits were waiting for our arrival, a white one for Muriel and a black one for me. One day we let them out in the front garden, thinking they would come back like pet dogs. Our mistake! It was a long garden and the grass was high. While we were searching, Auntie Mabel came out. *"Oh crikey! Now we're for it,"* said Muriel. But she had just come out to give us both a piece of juicy water melon. Matters were made worse because Muriel kept saying the usual *"now you're for it, you'll get into trouble now"* routine. I was so relieved when we finally caught them. All I could think about was them ending up in the field where uncle went shooting rabbits. Another year, we looked out of our bedroom window to see two tents had been set up in the garden for us to play in.

Auntie and Uncle had two spaniels, Billy, black and white, and Bobby, brown and white. Every evening Auntie Mabel would let them out of the front door so that they could go to the top of the lane to sit and wait for their master. Uncle George would drive up; open the door and they would jump in for the ride - a much-loved ritual for all concerned. One year Auntie told me that Billy had died of old age. However Bobby still insisted on going up the lane as he had done for all those years. To see him there alone, at his post, was both sad and magnificent.

One day Bobby could not be found anywhere around the house and as this was highly unusual Uncle George started phoning around the neighbourhood. Then they had a phone call, telling him that the old dog had been found in a car. When uncle went to collect Bobby the man explained what he thought had happened. As the man had been loading his shopping, he had left a rear door of the car open and then he had been delayed in the shop by one of his neighbours. They deduced that the dog had smelt the car, which was a Wolseley identical to Uncle's, jumped in the back and gone to sleep. It was not until the driver got home, that the dog was discovered.

We once travelled to Sheffield by train. I remember this, because Mum said that if we opened the carriage window as the train went through Woodhead tunnel the smoke and steam would do my chest good. That was the belief - I ask you?

When our stay had come to an end, Uncle George always drove us home in the evening and the rabbits' eyes shining in the car's headlights, as we motored over those dark and 'ghostly' moors, late at night, had a lasting impression on me.

Every year, at the beginning of November, Uncle would start to buy in stocks of food, extra coal and logs and other items they thought they would need - not forgetting their favourite cigarettes, Players Perfectas. They were often snowed in and unable to get out for weeks on end. They did not seem to mind this just as long as Uncle could get to his hut - a rather large hut - right in the middle of the garden. A little way in front of the hut was a high wooden pylon, with aerials of different shapes and sizes at the top of it. I believe it served as a landmark for miles around. Wireless and communications was Uncle George's hobby - and his livelihood.

Sometimes history happens in front of you and you do not recognise it until later. During our stay in 1938 we were playing in the garden and uncle was working in his hut. Suddenly the door opened and he called over to us *"Muriel, Peter, can you come in here for a minute?"* As we neared the hut he came out with a big smile and said excitedly, *"I've got something to show you - come on in."* We had never been allowed in his shed before - it was like entering the Forbidden City. He was very jolly as he took us over to the wall that was full

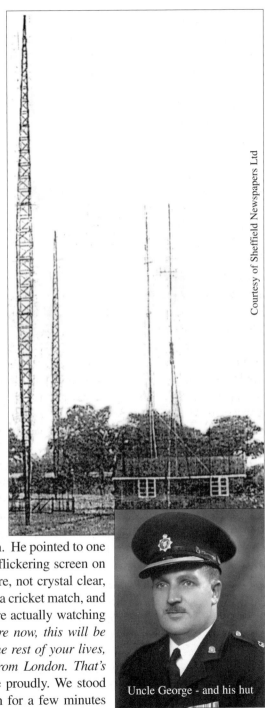

Courtesy of Sheffield Newspapers Ltd

Uncle George - and his hut

of black boxes with knobs and dials on. He pointed to one of the black boxes with a very small flickering screen on it. There was a black and white picture, not crystal clear, but still good enough to see that it was a cricket match, and all the players were moving! We were actually watching a cricket match being played. *"There now, this will be something for you to remember for the rest of your lives, that picture is coming all the way from London. That's called television,"* said Uncle George proudly. We stood spellbound watching the small screen for a few minutes until he told us to go and carry on playing as he had work to do. The next day he showed us a copy of a local Sheffield newspaper that had the headlines, *"GEORGE BAGSHAW GETS TELEVISION OVER THE PENNINES."*

One evening during the latter part of the war, Mum was looking through the family photos, hoping to settle some argument with Auntie Babs. Amongst the pile of photographs I happened to spy one of Uncle George that grabbed my attention. He was stood between two of his favourite Wolseleys cars with another man, and both were in police uniform. *"Mum, who's this with Uncle George?"* I asked. She told me Uncle George had the photograph taken when he had developed a short wave frequency for police car wireless. At the time they were using the same frequency as North Sea fishing boats, and their messages kept interfering with each other. After a lot of hard work he finally succeeded. After the success of the trials, he and the police officer had their photograph taken together with the two cars fitted with the two special wireless sets. I was told he sold the system to Marconi who went to the Home Office and had it accepted throughout the country.

Next day Mum said to me, *"Your favourite inventor uncle has reminded me of a young man your Grandma Bagshaw befriended many years ago when I was a little girl. He had moved into the area to serve a six-year apprenticeship with W. Wichman of Gibraltar Street, a German watchmaker. The young man remained a family friend for years and when he had completed his indenture he started to earn some money by selling various items door to door. Soon he was able to invest money in purchasing more watches, the English lever watch, and he placed adverts in the newspapers for people to have them delivered by post, 5/- down, followed by 5/-a month for ten months. His trade boomed."*

Gradually he extended his range in the mail order business - he was perhaps one of the first. His name was John George Graves and his business developed into a huge company. He became very wealthy, so much so, that he

High-class Waltham Levers.

No. 1334

50/-

The "J. G. GRAVES"
Special **WALTHAM LEVER.**

This well-known watch possesses among its many important advantages the compensating chronometer balance, which enables the watch to automatically adjust itself to all changes of climate and temperature. The Breguet hairspring, the most modern invention for obtaining the highest possible accuracy; Fogg patent reversible pinion; and the fine movement is built entirely on the interchangeable system, so that in the event of breaking or damage, any part can be replaced with promptitude and without in any way impairing the value or efficiency of the watch.

The ideal watch for all heavy occupations. Fitted in extra heavy English Hall-marked Sterling Silver Case, and plainly marked White Enamel Dial.

Warranted for Seven Years.

£2 - 10 - 0

WELL MADE

No. 1334

Accurate and Reliable. Splendid Value and Finish. Good Quality.

No. 1334

View of movement showing compensating balance dust excluding rim cap.

J. G. GRAVES, The Universal Supply Warehouse, **SHEFFIELD.**

was able to bequeath, to the city of Sheffield, Graves Park. In all I believe thirty institutions were to gain from his generosity including the Art Gallery, Library and a new

wing for the Children's Hospital. He shared his success with the people of Sheffield.

It appears that Uncle George was working for J G Graves at the time he made the television breakthrough.

As an afterthought Mum told me, *"Your grandma mended John Graves' britches on many an occasion when he was a young lad."*

In the early 1940s Uncle started his own company called Sheffield Wireless and Telegraph. Much of the equipment in the hut he used for research into wireless waves, television and radar. During the war, as well as being an officer of the Police Special Constabulary, he was an officer in the Voluntary Reserve of the RAF. His main contribution was working on radio and radar.

He had to service complicated radar equipment in which the whole radar cabinet housing had to be dismantled to gain access to the component parts. After a few months he came up with a bizarre idea. One of the ladies who worked in the factory was of a petite build and he approached her with his plan and she agreed to try it out - I can only assume she had a sense of

humour. A pulley contraption was assembled and a parachute harness obtained. The idea was to put her into the harness, hoist her into the air and then lower her into the cabinet to service it. It worked. This simple device saved many hours and enabled the equipment to be returned into service far more quickly.

In the late 1940s Mum told us that she had been speaking on the phone to Brother George - she always referred to him this way - and he had just been over to Sweden to collect a miniature television set for a doll's house for Princess Anne's Christmas present.

Uncle's best friend was Laurie Wilson who also lived in Dore. He owned a cutlery company and made car tools - that company was called Gordon's Tools after his son. They shared the hobby of sea fishing and Laurie Wilson owned a cabin cruiser called *Wappy Two*. Uncle George shared the cost with him and they kept it in the harbour at Bridlington. One day, when I was on holiday in Bridlington, Mum arranged for me to meet up with Uncle George for a trip on *Wappy Two*. On the Friday night he phoned our boarding house to say he could not make it, but I was to go to the harbour, and Laurie Wilson would take me out with him.

When I arrived the 'boat husband' took me on board and showed me round. Soon after Mr Wilson arrived and off we went. We were soon riding the waves towards Flambrough Head. I saw Mr Wilson lean over the controls and pick up a ship to shore radio microphone. He advised the coastguard of his destination and the estimated time of arrival back in harbour. *"Did Uncle George make that?"* I asked. *"Yes he did, and it's a very good one,"* he told me. When we were heading back to the harbour, Mr Wilson called to me, *"want to steer 'er back, young Peter?"* Anticipating my answer, he carried on, *"See yon church spire and that there building over to the left, well now, keep the bows between them two points."* With that he went down into the cabin leaving me with the 'boat husband'. *"Ee's gone fer a drink o' whisky or two,"* said my shipmate with a knowing nod.

Before Uncle George retired, sometime in the mid-1950s, he moved to a flat on the north side of 'Brid', as they referred to it. Many years later, around 1973, I met up with him again; he had sold the flat in Bridlington and was living at The Rising Sun at Bamford near Hathersage. His marriage had broken and Auntie Mabel was living in a flat with her sister Daisy. During a long chat with him he told me many things but one that particularly interested me was his involvement in the First World War when he was *"now't but a lad"*. He was assigned to the Signals Corps. One of the many problems the army had was that the enemy often knew what their next move was to be. He was set to work on the problem. He discovered that the enemy could 'tap' into the single wire system connecting the wireless telephones. After many experiments he found that using two wires, one to send and one to receive, each on a different frequency, solved the problem. He probably saved many thousands of allied lives.

An unsung hero in many ways.

4. Green Gables

Another relative that Mum farmed us out to was Auntie Babs, with Uncle Geoffrey, at Wilmslow. They lived at Green Gables, Pownall Park, and Uncle worked for the family stockbroking firm of Stavacres in Manchester, the largest stockbrokers outside of London.

Auntie Babs was rotund and voluptuous, her hair always in the page boy style. But, did one ever see her with curlers in? Oh no! Although my Mum's younger sister by nine years, you would never have thought they had had the same upbringing; she had married into money, which gave her a lot of 'airs and graces'. But Uncle Geoffrey was a nice man.

Her father-in-law had bought them their lovely house as a wedding present, which they filled with fine furniture and carpets, far beyond anything Dad could afford for my Mum. She had the use of the car while Uncle was at the office, which increased her social status no end. And she just had to have a live-in-maid, who slept in a beautiful blue painted bedroom overlooking the back garden. Despite the elegance of these surroundings, the conditions must have been pretty hard, for the maids were constantly changing.

I preferred Uncle George's because they weren't snobs -and Muriel was Auntie Babs's pet. No doubt it was because they both liked tormenting folk. I suppose we first started these holidays to our aunties and uncles about 1937, spending a fortnight with each at different times of the year. At the time I did not realise that we were being farmed out, but years later I understood it was to give Mum a rest because of her health. She suffered badly with phlebitis, a condition that developed from varicose veins, and was extremely painful. I also discovered later that she had a heart condition. She had to wear pink coloured elasticised stockings that went from her knees to just under the ankles, and the veins had to be painted with a black liquid called belladonna, made from deadly nightshade.

During each stay, on one of the days, Auntie Babs would put us in the car and we would go back to Timperley to see Mum. One time, as soon as the car got onto the main road it started making a funny noise, rather like shaking stones in a tin can. I was very puzzled. *"Auntie, what's that funny noise?"* I asked, feeling worried. *"It's the car picking up stones,"* she replied, with no concern, and continued talking to Muriel, who was in the front seat next to her. It was as if I wasn't there.

Auntie Babs enjoyed cooking; the only trouble was that she could never do anything without a cigarette in her mouth. When she had a long ash she would just turn her head and blow it off. Like many women of her day she would boil sprouts for about an hour, first adding bicarbonate of soda along with the salt. *"It helps to keep their colour,"* I heard her say. The fact that they were soggy and tasteless did not matter. But she did bake very nice cakes. When Auntie made mash potatoes she would put them through a hand press called a 'wormer' - they came out like long worms. Today it would be called 'a potato ricer'. It was very exotic to us.

Green Gables

Auntie Babs in trouble

They had a small breakfast room - which we would have called a kitchen - but when we were there we had breakfast served in the dining room. The toast at breakfast always had to be cut into fingers and crammed into a toast rack. Uncle's daily morning ritual consisted of buttered toast fingers lavishly coated with Rose's Lime Marmalade, and a read of the Daily Mirror. I noticed that he gave most of the articles the merest glance until he got to the 'Just Jane" strip - she was always scantily dressed in frilly underwear with a dachshund dancing round her feet. With their dog Carl being a dachshund I wondered if Auntie was his real life 'Jane'! He always left this paper at home and took the Financial Times with him to read on the train to the office.

Having a maid to do all the housework gave Auntie the time to spend in her bedroom doing her fingernails, hair and face. The one thing on her dressing table that always intrigued me most was a black lipstick in a silver case, which when she put on coloured her lips red. I thought it was magic. Muriel, being a girl, would sit with her most of the time when she did her make-up.

Auntie's bathroom was very impressive; the bath taps were incorporated with a showerhead of very large proportions. A shower was a novelty for me; I enjoyed the 'rain that washed me' as I called it - that was until the night I slipped. In the morning I had a very big bump on my head - nearly as big as the ball of soap on a rope, that was hung near the taps. We were not allowed to use it, on the pain of death, not even Uncle Geoffrey. It was just for show, for God's sake!

I was always getting into trouble there. One time we had gone into the village taking a neighbour's boy with us and Auntie had parked outside John Williams, the grocers, on Grove Street. I wound the rear window down so we could poke our heads out and say hello to people passing by. They just looked at us with disdain and walked on by, so as a way of attracting them we decided to spit at them. When Auntie came back, of course 'goody, goody two shoes' Muriel, just couldn't wait to tell on us. When we arrived home I got a good smacking and was sent to bed.

One morning I woke up with a terrible toothache. It was time for my first visit to the dentist. I was not keen, but Auntie phoned the dentist and made an appointment for that day. The surgery was near the Post Office on Hawthorn Lane, right opposite the cake shop where Auntie Babs bought me my big meringue cakes - there must have been a message there. Auntie told me the tooth fairy might visit me during the night, if I was brave, and leave me a sixpence. Somehow, the thought of having the tooth out did not seem so bad now. The dentist had a good look at my teeth tapping them with an instrument. All was fine until he got to the very back one. *"That hurt,"* I said, tears coming into my eyes. He looked at Auntie and spoke as if I wasn't there. *"Except for the back molar on the right they all seem fine; do you want me to do it now?"* *"Yes, you'd better."*

Later the three of us were sat at the dining room table, and the maid brought Auntie's and Muriel's lunch in for them, and I was about to feel sorry for myself when in she breezed again, with a bowl of tomato soup for me. After every meal Auntie Babs insisted that we helped clear the table - to stop us crashing into one another we had to go "beep-beep" as we went through the doors. But on this occasion I was excused from helping because of my tooth, and in the morning where my tooth had been, there was a shiny new sixpenny piece.

One summer when we arrived we found a large tent in the garden; Sam the gardener came later and seemed to start taking it down. When he pulled the tent off its frame I was surprised - *"look it's a settee hanging on poles."* Muriel snidely remarked, *"Don't you know anything, it's a swinging seat you stupid thing."*

Auntie also had a hammock, the frame made of two black tubes shaped like a banana, between which was tied a yellow canvas hammock that fastened to the end points with a big nut and bolt. I liked to lie on this, rocking up and down.

Early one afternoon Auntie told us that she was taking us both out for a little walk, a turn of events that was very unusual, as she never ventured out without a wheel on each of four corners. She led us out of the gate, turned left and we trooped up the road and turned left again at the corner into Broad Walk. We came to a stop outside a large house with a gypsy caravan parked in the front garden. Directing the question at Muriel she asked, *"Do you know whose house this is and who that caravan belongs to?"* Muriel didn't have a clue, so we were informed. *"Romany, the gypsy writer; he owns them both,"* then she went on to tell us that he came home only yesterday, and no doubt he would be writing another book about his recent travels.

The caravan was a proper gypsy bow top that was pulled by a horse. It looked serene parked on the front lawn at an angle to the house, with its shafts stuck up in the air. It was painted green, like grass, with flowers and symbols painted all over in many bright colours and gold squiggly lines. It looked very beautiful there in the sunlight. Muriel read one of his books after that, it was all about nature and his travels.

Just after the war started, Uncle Geoffrey came home with half a dozen one-inch whitish discs with a safety pin fixed on the back. *"What are they?"* we asked.*" "Wait till it goes dark then you'll see."* We could hold one though, and the whitish side felt like sandpaper and they smelt awful, like bad eggs.

"What are they for Nunky?" pleaded Muriel. She always called him that if she was trying to get round him. *"They're luminous discs and later on tonight you will find that they glow in the dark enabling you to be seen."* We were soon to find out. When he put the lounge lights out, if two people stood close together, it looked like two big ghostly eyes coming towards you.

On the way to the railway station to drop Uncle off to catch the train into Manchester, we now noticed some men painting wide rings round the trees and lamp posts. Uncle Geoffrey told us that it would help us to see them in the blackout, as Mr Churchill had ordered that the street lighting had to be turned off because of the war.

One morning, after we had dropped him at the station, Auntie Babs took us to a small department store called Cleggs, on the corner of Church Street and Hawthorn Lane. After she had done a bit of shopping for herself, we found ourselves in the toy department and she told us that we could choose a toy each. I chose a fort. Auntie and

Uncle were always buying silly joke type things, so Auntie got a camera that squirted water to play a trick on him; she told us this was to get him back for a squirty flower. At bedtime they would play tricks on Muriel and I; things like putting itching powder in our pyjamas, toy spiders and other silly things in our beds and under the pillows. Once they left a bar of soap on the bathroom washbasin and after we had washed our faces it turned our faces black!

For our bedtime drink it was Ovaltine or Horlicks, Milo or Barlova. Imagine my surprise, when fifty odd years later I came across Milo in Sainsbury's. I bought a tin. Auntie loathed mixing Horlicks - in those days it was quite a hard job. You used a glass tube, a metal plunger with holes in and a lot of patience. First the powder was mixed with water to a smooth paste, hot milk was poured on, and then the tube was put in and the hard work began - up and down with the plunger like someone possessed.

Another bedtime ritual was lighting a nightlight on a saucer with some water in it, and woe betide us if we ever touched it.

Uncle Geoffrey took me into the garage one day to get a bottle of ginger beer. The garage had a big hole in the floor covered with heavy planks for making repairs on the car - but I never saw Uncle use it! I noticed a model yacht hanging on a wall. Taking it down, he held it for my inspection and then I took it in my hands, *"Wow, it's a beauty,"* I said. *"It was mine many years ago; my brother and I liked to sail it when we were about your age, I'll ask Auntie if she'll let you go to Lindow Common in the week. How about that?"* I jumped up and down in glee. Then I thought, she won't let me go.

Was I surprised after lunch on Monday when Auntie Babs walked into the garden carrying the yacht? *"Here you are, Uncle Geoffrey told me he'd shown you what to do, I suppose you should be sensible enough at seven to go on your own, off you go then and be careful."* I was allowed to go on my own, to Lindow Common Lake, and sail it! I could hardly believe it. It was only a short walk really from their house and I did feel grown-up. How things have changed, you would not allow a child to do it today - that is if you could even get across the road.

Uncle was very interested in cars, especially racing cars, of which he had a few silver 'Dinky' type models on the lounge table. In the late 1920s and early 1930s racing took place on Southport Beach. He would go to watch and he told us he would have loved to have had a go at roaring around the sands. He was a keen photographer, and he took many photographs of cars that interested him. He would catalogue all the details, make, model, registration number and the place where he had taken the picture. All these photographs now fill a shoebox, over 700 in fact. The locations on the photographs range from Southport to Southend, Llandudno to London and Nice to Monte Carlo. The number of makes is amazing and some of the shapes are fantastic. There is even a photograph of a steam car. I have often wondered why there are no photographs beyond 1938 - someone recently informed me that there was a ban on selling photographic film during the war. If you were caught with a camera in a strategic area the police would arrest you as a spy.

Before the war, Uncle Geoffrey took us all in his car to a firework display at Belle Vue; Mum and Dad, Muriel and Auntie Babs. It was very exciting; everyone seated outside, just like being in a big open-air cinema. We were facing a lake and Uncle said the fireworks would be set off from the other side. The night sky was the ceiling; a few cotton wool clouds skipping between the stars, which shone brighter than diamonds in the clear cold night. I was looking up at the twinkling stars, lost in wonder when they set off the first fireworks. As they soared into the night sky with a loud whoosh, it brought me back to earth very quickly. It was very beautiful, the bursts of colour mirrored in the still water of the lake as it shone near black.

Belle Vue would now be called a theme park. The numerous attractions included a zoo with cages, more like a prison by today's standards. There was motorcycle speedway, greyhound racing, a dance hall, and best of all, the fun fair. As well as the usual attractions of the sideshow they had the big rides. I liked best one of the two big roller coasters, called the Scenic Railway, built in and around a 'mountain'. It had many tunnels where the car would rush down a big dip and burst into the open air, as it turned one of the many bends.

The Bobs was the other one, the normal lattice structure. The dips were steeper. Nearby was the Water Splash with open cars that held about a dozen people. At the top of the climb, the cars turned the bend and would speed down and hit the water trough, the car cutting through the water and shooting it up into the air to hit the big glass screens that protected the onlookers.

The war put a stop to firework displays, so indoor ones took their place at home. Some were black dots on heavy paper and when lit by touching the start spot with a lighted cigarette, a line appeared as it burned to produce a drawing. The Serpent was a disc the size of an old penny, after lighting it a big worm-like mass grew out from the centre. Another slimy one was called Mount Vesuvius, sparks flew out of the top and then molten lava cascaded down its sides. Somehow one or two made a low explosion. My Mum liked the crystals you put in a glass of water which transformed into beautiful flowers of different shapes and colours.

During 1939-40 Auntie Babs followed Mum's example and took in three evacuees from London. To the delight of my sister they were all boys. This was before Uncle was called up for the forces. One day they washed the car on the drive, taking it in turns to use the sponge, which could hardly be seen for the soap suds. I stood and watched, and all was well until they started rinsing the soap off with the hosepipe. At this moment Muriel came to have a nosy and started to interfere. The hose pipe and someone's hand emerged from round the side of the house and started to spray the car - and of course it wasn't only the car that got wet; I think they nearly drowned Muriel! When they started taking it in turns to leather it off, I sat happily in the driver's seat, and went to the seaside in my mind.

Mum and Dad came over one evening when it was Uncle Geoffrey's birthday; I remember it very well for one reason especially - after we had had our dinner we all played pontoon and I won half-a-crown. In 1940 this was a good slice of money; I only got one or two pennies a week pocket money.

Another game we played required the use of a gramophone and a special record. The gramophone was, of course, the wind up kind, the only kind in those days. The game was 'The Grand National' and the record played six horse racing commentaries. All the players placed their bets with a token on a printed mat. Uncle set the record going and one, two, three, they were off! Who won the race depended on which groove the needle went into. It was very exciting with us all cheering our horse on to the winning post. It was always a fight to the finishing line with no quarter given until the last few seconds.

Muriel had started at the High School after the summer holidays of 1940 when she was eleven years old. One evening, after we had had dinner, Uncle Geoffrey helped Muriel to do

Auntie Babs and her evacuees

some homework, she had to add up a column of pounds, shillings and pence, the length of a foolscap sheet of paper. I was amazed when Uncle wrote down the answer when Muriel was only half way down the pence column. He had added the column upside down in his head as he sat in front of her. When it was all checked he had the right answer. No calculators in those days. Auntie said he was a clever 'so and so' when it came to money.

One morning Auntie put us both in the car, saying that we were going to a cafe in a village not far away and that I was to behave myself. It was here that I found out that the salt and pepper were called a cruet. Auntie asked me to go for a cruet off the trolley. *"What's that?"* I asked. *"The salt and pepper, silly boy!"* she whispered.

Uncle Geoffrey had two brothers; David who worked in the family firm along with his wife, and the other who was a botanist out in Nigeria, and called Philip. Unfortunately Phillip lost his life there in tragic circumstances. Uncle Geoffrey would never accept that he committed suicide; he always believed that some Nigerians murdered him.

Uncle Geoffrey now went into the RAF, leaving Auntie Babs living alone in the house, and then the house was 'commandeered' by the War Office. A few miles away was the aeroplane factory of AV Roes at Woodford, who built the famous Lancaster. The War Office wanted it for a test pilot. This meant that she had to come and live with us - but that is another story.

Grandparents Bagshaw

Grandparents Scott

5. Grandparents

THE BAGSHAWS

My mother's family lived in Sheffield where she was brought up and educated. Her grandfather had been a sawmaker and would have worked close to where he lived in one of the many courtyards, reached through narrow passageways between rows of terraced houses, in the centre of the City.

When her brother George was born on October 2nd 1897, her father was an engineer's toolmaker. My Mother was born five and a half years later on 26th March 1903. Grandad's occupation then was described as a shoe tool warehouse manager. When their last child, Isobel (Babs), was born, on 9th February 1912, he was employed as a leather merchant's traveller. I was intrigued when my Mum told me that the company provided him with a pony and trap to do his rounds around the Sheffield area.

In 1919 or thereabouts, Grandad's firm decided that they wanted to expand into the Manchester region and offered him the opportunity of developing this territory. It meant breaking his ties with Sheffield, but he would swap his pony and trap for a Bull-Nosed Morris car. So, with his wife's backing, they upped sticks and crossed the Pennines to live at 25 Greame Street, Moss Side. George was 22 by now and stayed in Sheffield, so just my Mum and Auntie Babs came with them. Whether Grandad Bagshaw died before I was born I don't know, but he had died by the time Auntie Babs got married on September 17th 1935 - he was not on their wedding photos.

The Bagshaw girls, Nellie (my Mum) and her sister Babs, met their future husbands in Manchester - both boys lived but a cock stride away from Greame Street. I hardly knew Grandma Bagshaw - she died soon after we moved to Timperley. Her maiden name was Sarah Isabelle Widdowson.

Grandad's Bull-nosed Morris

THE SCOTTS
At the same period my Dad's family were also moving to Manchester from Halifax. John Isaac Scott was a master tailor and ran a gents' outfitters on Silver Street in Halifax. Later, with a partner, the business was Messrs Ainsworth and Scott, on Commercial Street.

In 1918, when he was 53, they fell out and the firm went into bankruptcy. He moved to Manchester, to 4 Park Avenue (now Smalldale Avenue), Moss Side, and Grandad got himself a job as a shop assistant - it must have been difficult after being your own boss for so many years. The house still faces one of Alexandra Park Gates.

Dad's only sister was called Dorothy Vernon, and his two brothers, Arthur Brear and Frank Preistley. They had another brother, Robert Davenport who died aged 2.

After the family's move to Manchester, my Dad's first job was at Manchester Royal Infirmary, making pills and tablets. One of the tales he told us many years later was that of a mother who brought her daughter into casualty with a poorly leg. The leg was stockingless and clean; the other was encased in the usual thick black stocking worn in those days. But when the doctor came to examine the young lady, he asked for the other stocking to be removed. The mother questioned 'why?' and kicked up a right fuss; but the nurse insisted that it was necessary and she finally removed the stocking to reveal a filthy leg and foot - the mother had only washed the affected leg.

Grandad Scott was an imposing gentleman, probably because he had a large moustache, and Grandma was also a very dignified lady - I never saw her without her 'dangly' crystal earrings. Their daughter, my Auntie Dorothy, was not married and lived at home. Mum always referred to going to Grandma's, as going to Park Avenue.

Grandma had a little monkey called Joey, who would jump off her lap or shoulder and jump all round the room; how he never knocked off the many ornaments I will never know. On his return to her lap he would snuggle up to her for a cuddle.

Their house always smelt different to our house, not a nasty smell, but different. I realised later it was because they had gas lighting. The living room was at the back of the house and rather gloomy and this meant that they had to turn the gas light on towards the late afternoon. One time we were visiting, Grandad said, *"Oh dear the mantle's gone, I'll have to change it."* I looked up and saw a thin tongue of yellow flame coming through the white. Grandad reached up, pulled a chain and the light went out; then he got a little box out of a drawer and laid the contents on the table. He looked at me and said, *"Don't touch"*. I was intrigued to see a small silk purse with red on it and string like handles.

With the aid of some small steps he took off the glass shade and the broken mantle. I had never seen anything like this before, theirs was the only house in the family not to have proper light switches and bulbs. Carefully he picked up the silk purse, as I called it, and tied it on to the fitting. After putting the shade back he took a match and pulled the other chain. It flared up for a second or two and made me jump; when I looked again the silk purse had changed into a white thing again.

Years later it dawned on me that it would have been very difficult finding their way to bed. But when I asked Grandma about it she showed me an oil lamp that they used until the upstairs gas light had been lit.

Whilst the grown-ups talked, Muriel and I had to amuse ourselves, but we had to stay within earshot - Grandad would not allow us to wander about in case we broke any of his ornaments. I remember once, when we all had gone in Auntie Babs' car, I found myself being thrust towards the big brown sink in the kitchen by my Mum. The sides were six inches deep and the taps were set high on the wall and splashed everywhere. *"This is your Auntie's fault,"* Mum told me, sensing I was wondering what was going on. Pushing my head over the sink she cascaded a jug of warm water over my head and rubbed a bar of soap in to it. *"Too frisky my eye,"* she muttered, *"Why she has to interfere, I don't know,"* I didn't know if I was supposed to be listening, so I kept quiet. *"Fancy putting all that sugar in, I don't know, tut, tut."* The jug was now filled with steaming hot water again - I was a bit worried and tried to back away, but Mum realised and added some cold water, and rinsed my golden locks. Towelled and combed I was now able to go back to the living room. It seems Auntie Babs had mixed sugar and water and combed my hair with it to quell its unruly curls; she had added too much sugar and my hair had set like concrete.

Sometimes we played in the larder under the stairs between the living room and kitchen. We played department stores and the larder was the lift. A heavy maroon curtain protected the food but more importantly it was the lift gates - the only problem was that when we were going up and down it was in the dark. We took turns in being the passenger or the lift man but I realised, in the end, why Muriel was so magnanimous in letting me be the lift man most of the time. I had to shout out on every floor, *"Going up (or down), mind the doors please,"* and on top of this I had to try to remember the goods that were sold on each of the six floors - which took me a long time. In the mean time she stood outside and listened to the grown-ups talking!

"Right then Peter, let's go and feed the ducks shall we," said Auntie Dorothy. It was a ritual on our visits. Auntie Dorothy had saved up some old bread and off we would go, hand in hand. Keeping the ducks company would be a few families of moorhens and sometimes there would be visiting geese. and there was an island in the middle of the lake where the birds made their home. Just inside the park gates was a drinking fountain, but my favourite one was another near the big rockery that we passed on the way back. I would always have to stop to have a drink, for the sake of pressing the button to fill one of the four metal cups attached to each of the four taps by a chain. The fountain was quite big; it had steps that led up to a big saucer-shaped bowl. The rockery garden was made with great slabs of stone. It always intrigued me how they got them there, they were bigger than Auntie Dorothy.

In the summertime a band would be playing on the bandstand. People sat around on deckchairs enjoying the music and the sunshine - despite the belief that it always rained in Manchester. We would stand and listen for a few minutes before Auntie said, *"Come on, we have to get back, Grandma will be getting the tea ready."* This was why

My favourite drinking fountain in Alexandra Park.
Courtesy of Manchester Archives & Local Studies

I could never have an icecream from the cart outside the park gates. And, on the way back, we passed by the front-room window with Grandma's prized aspidistra in it; I never liked the plant.

One day during a school summer holiday, in my second year at Park Road, Mum told me we were going to Grandma's straight after lunch. This was very unusual in the middle of the week, so I asked, *"Why Mum?" "Just because, that's why. Now come on in, wash your hands and get to the table."*

When we arrived at Park Avenue, we had no sooner got there, than Mum was telling me to stay with Grandma, as she had to go somewhere. I was not having this; I wanted to go as well - so we were up and off again. Soon we were walking up the steps of a large house, and we sat down in a waiting room with wicker seats. A door opened and a young lady called out, *"Mrs Scott, please come in."* I was left, wondering what on earth was going on. After a marathon wait, the door opened again and Mum walked out holding a blood soaked pad to her mouth. As she could hardly talk, the young lady told me, *"Your mother has had all her teeth out, so look after her on the way home won't you, that's a good boy."* So I took hold of her free hand and walked her back to Grandma's.

One Sunday Dad took me to Grandma's on his own because Mum was in bed feeling poorly. As usual I was soon walking round the park with Auntie Dorothy and I asked her an important question that had been puzzling me for some time. *"Auntie, why do fleas keep biting my Mum?"* A puzzled look came over her face. *"Whatever do you mean Peter?" "Well, Dad said Mum had 'flea bite us'."* A little wry smile came to her lips, then she burst out laughing. How was I to know?

One time Auntie Dorothy said to me *"Would you like to meet a man who eats nails?"* I shuddered at the thought and answered *"Uh, no thanks." "Nails I said, did you think I said snails"* she said with a laugh. Not waiting for my answer, I was ushered out of the park and down Claremont Road and across Princess Road. Soon we were stood outside the cobblers, and in we went, with a ting-a-ling of his doorbell. He greeted us with a nod of his head, in his almost black leather apron, and yes, with lots of nails sticking out of his mouth. It was hard to tell

what he said, until he had used up all the nails, taking them out one at a time, onto the shoe and bashed into the leather with a flat piece of metal. He was very fast; I would bash my fingers flat, I thought!

He took Auntie's shoes down from a shelf, put them in a brown paper bag, and she paid him. He filled his mouth again, mumbled what sounded like good afternoon, and we made our way back home.

Grandad's main hobby was his small backyard garden, full of various containers purchased from the numerous secondhand shops around the area. Then he had a brilliant idea of adding large mirrors to reflect the colourful pots and plants and it also made the yard appear larger. He featured in the Manchester Evening News in 1936, winning one of their awards for gardening; a very proud moment for him. If you positioned yourself in a certain spot between the mirrors your image would seem to travel to infinity. This always fascinated me and I never missed an opportunity to travel out into space. When the war came he was told to remove all the mirrors - the authorities were frightened they would reflect moonlight and be seen by the enemy bombers. He refused saying they were talking nonsense. The whole family tried to persuade him, but to no avail. Mum said he was *'an obstinate old bugger',* and she couldn't understand why they didn't prosecute him.

He used to visit the many secondhand shops in the area and buy all sorts of junk, as Mum called it. No doubt some of the items could be worth a lot of money today on BBC's Antiques Road Show. Years later Auntie Dorothy told me she had given the rag

and bone man the gong that held pride of place on a large ebony carver. It was a magnificent article made of bronze with some lovely artwork on it, and eighteen inches in diameter. I pictured the rag and bone man running off with his prize, as she told us he had done.

My favourite was the knife and fork cleaner. Its crooked handle and various slots for different sized cutlery was, to me then, a joy to behold - just so long as Grandad didn't catch me playing with it. Turning its funny shaped handle was a fascination; it made a whooshing sound that got louder the faster it went, I think this was the carborundum powder.

One Sunday when we all arrived, Grandad was busy in the kitchen, mending a hole in an enamelled saucepan. You had to do things like that in those days, especially during the War. It was not meanness; it was a case of necessity. The Government had confiscated all aluminium cooking utensils, they sent lorries round every district to collect the piles of pans and kettles that youths had collected from around their neighbourhood. The slogan was '2000 pans make a Spitfire'. That is why Grandad and thousands like him had to 'Make

Do and Mend', as another slogan said. Either that or do without. We did not live in a throwaway society as we do today. He was excited about a new product called 'cold solder'. This silvery paste was smeared over both sides of the hole and left to set, mending the hole. *"This is how a hole was mended before,"* he said, showing me another pan. It had two metal disks with leather washers, inside and outside the pan, fastened with a nut and bolt. Very scientific!

I was also intrigued with the taps in the bathroom. I have never seen the like anywhere else. The washbasin was placed over the end of the bath and the taps were like two taps stuck together. The washbasin taps faced forward whilst the bath taps faced sideways pointing down into a hole that lead into the bath.

During the school holidays I would often go to Park Avenue to see Grandma and Grandad. Once Geoffrey decided to come with me. When we got there Grandad had gone out so we had a little chat with Grandma. When the conversation got strained - when she couldn't find out anymore about Geoffrey's mum and dad - we went out to explore the backyard. After we had journeyed into infinity together and laughed at our reflections. Geoffrey said *"There's not much to do is there?"* To cheer him up we went inside and I let him have a go on the knife and fork-cleaning machine, but I must admit that when you've turned the handle a few times without the threat of Grandad, there was not much fun in it.

"Grandma, can we have some bread to go and feed the ducks please?" Thus armed, we set forth to succour the wildlife. I showed him the bandstand, we had a drink from my fountain and then we wandered back home to number four. We sat and tried to make conversation with Grandma again, but there was nothing else to warrant our curiosity. Geoffrey suddenly whispered, *"Me belly thinks me throat's been cut,"* a saying I hadn't heard before. Grandma heard him and she said, *"Would you like a biscuit?"* Egg and chips would have been better! We took a couple of biscuits each and decided to cut our losses and head for the tram stop. At least there would be a chance that we would get home before we starved. On the way to the tram stop I told Geoffrey that behind the tram shed was Maine Road, the home of Manchester City Football Club. That sounded a lot more interesting than going to Grandma's.

Grandad had a few house rules. The first one related to the toilet seat; this had

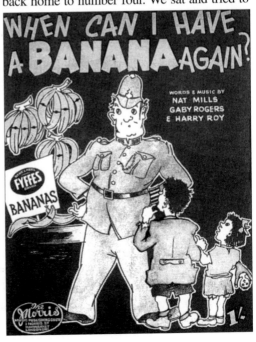

to be left in the up position. Second, he always had the first cup of tea from the pot. Third, no one dared open the newspaper until he had read it. And fourth, if there was any bread and butter left on the plate it had to be eaten before any second helpings of pudding could be had. I am sure he had many more. Dad said he was a very strict 'Victorian' type of man.

There was another side to him though, such as one Christmas when Muriel and I were very young. He went out of the living room and we heard him going up the stairs. About five minutes later Auntie Dorothy went to answer a knock on the front door. She came back into the living room followed by Father Christmas. I knew he was real because he was all dressed up in red clothes with black boots and had a big white beard. There was white fur round his big hood, collar and cuffs. Entering the living room with the festive *'Yo Ho Ho'*, he swung his sack off his shoulder and gave us all a present whilst wishing us a very Merry Christmas. He then told us we would have to take ours home and put them under the Christmas tree until Christmas morning.

Usually we would stay for tea on a Sunday. Then we would look forward to the walk to the tram stop to go home, where Dad would buy Muriel and me an icecream from a cart on the corner of Claremont Road. It was always there, even in winter. Manchester had a lot of Italian ice cream makers in those days, two wheeled carts which held large tubs, each with a large heavy lid. They would ask *"wafer or cornet?"* hardly anything else would pass their lips. There was also the famous 'Stop Me and Buy One' tricycle cart of Wall's icecream. A cornet from them was the size of a night light. They would break it off a long tube that was covered in thin perforated cardboard, and it was left to you to remove the cardboard and stick it in the cornet.

"Tickets please," shouted the conductor as he collected the fares. He wore two straps

Altrincham tram. *Courtesy of 'Altrincham: An Illustrated History', Pat Southern, Trafford Leisure Services*

that crossed his chest and back; one carried his moneybag, the other his ticket punch. The tickets were carried on both sides of a wooden board, printed with the value and held in place by what looked like a row of mousetraps. Before handing the tickets over he had to put them in a slot in his machine and punch a hole on a number of the fare stage.

When Dad had bought the tickets from the conductor I noticed that he always sat holding them. *"Can I hold the tickets Dad?"* I would ask. *"No, I have to keep them safe in case an inspector gets on,"* he replied. When Dad had been called up and was in the Army, and I was on the bus one-day with Mum, she suddenly handed the tickets to me, *"Here Peter, you look after these in case an inspector gets on."* I looked up into her face in surprise; she nodded as she smiled. I felt as if I had been given the King's Crown.

I would wonder at the ravages of consumption, which was the reason, I was told, for the *'No Spitting, Offenders will be PROSECUTED'* signs on each deck of the buses and trams. They rattled and rumbled along, swaying about like a ship at sea, sometimes rather too fast for Mum's liking. Princess Parkway was the end of the tramline. When he reached the terminus, the conductor had to walk up the aisles and push the backs of the seats over, so that the passengers would be facing the other way when the tram was on its return journey. Then he would get off the tram, go to the back, pull the rope attached to the trolley boom, pull it off the electric wire and swing it round from the back, which now became the front. All he had to do now was walk through the tramcar to the rear which now became the front.

We would cross over Altrincham Road and wait for the bus to Timperley village outside a pub called The Royal Oak. When we got to the village, if we had missed the last bus down Park Road, it was a long walk home at night.

Princess Road tram depot. *Courtesy of Manchester Archives & Local Studies*

Altrincham traffic c 1930.   *'Altrincham: An Illustrated History', Pat Southern, Trafford Leisure Services*

6. Near Misses

During my first year at school I became pals with Alan Edwards who lived not far away, on Riddings Road. He let me have a ride on his bike and learning was great fun while he held the saddle. Soon I was riding the small red and white two-wheeler all by myself. Feeling rather proud I thought I would progress onto the road. A wedding must have taken place earlier as confetti littered the footpath and road. Suddenly the little girl who lived next door to Alan decided to venture out of her front garden to collect some. She seemed to appear from nowhere right in front of me, stepping out from behind the cast iron lamppost. I had no chance. Off I came and my left arm hit the post. She wasn't hurt; she ran back into her house. Alan shouted, *"Here's my dad."* Mr Edwards lifted me into his arms. *"I'll soon have you home,"* he whispered, and we were off down Arderne Road.

My Mum was preparing the evening meal, so she was none too pleased. After the initial shock of seeing me in the arms of Mr Edwards, she relieved him of his burden and thanked him very much for his kindness. As soon as she had closed the door, she sat me on the stairs, and phoned for a taxi to take me to hospital.

After being examined by a doctor he handed Mum a piece of paper and told her how to get to the X-ray dept. Sometime later, in increasing pain and feeling very sorry for myself, a nurse called my name to go into the doctor again. Looking at my Mum he said *"He's broken the humerus bone just under the shoulder joint and dislocated the elbow. If you take him into the next room, I'll be in shortly to put the arm in plaster."*

I sat up on a thin bed-type table. A very nice nurse helped me to take off my top clothes, then she showed me a mouth and nose mask covered with gauze. She explained that I could help her to hold it whilst the doctor sprayed something on it that would send me to sleep, that way I would not feel any pain when they mended my arm.

When I came round the arm was folded across my front encased in plaster of Paris. The nice nurse had a quick word with Mum as she handed over yet another piece of paper for something called the dispensary. I heard the nurse telling Mum to bring me back in six weeks. Just as I stepped through the doorway into the waiting room full of people, without any warning, I was horribly sick.

It all took me back to the time I had my tonsils out. I never forgot the experience. I must have been four when one morning Mum called me in from the garden. *"Just look at those knees, I told you to keep yourself clean after you had had a bath, Auntie Babs will be here in a minute."* *"Why?"* I asked. *"She's taking us somewhere."* With that she lifted me up onto the kitchen table with its scrubbed white wooden top and its red knobbly legs. *"Don't move,"* she threatened, and wagged a finger at me as she disappeared into the scullery. Back she swept armed with a face cloth and towel to clean me up thoroughly.

Auntie Babs walked in through the back door and Mum lifted me off the table. *"We've time for a cuppa Babs if you'd like one?"* I was just about to sneak off out, *"Oh no you don't me lad,"* Mum pulled me back into the kitchen. Auntie Babs lit up a cigarette as Mum put the kettle on.

"*Where we going?*" No one took any notice. They had their cup of tea, and soon we were off on a journey I would never forget as long I live. We got out of the car in front of a large building with a very tall chimney and white smoke puffing out of it. I cannot remember anything else until we walked into a big room with a lot of beds. The ether smell was everywhere. A lady seemed to materialise from nowhere, "*Are we going to have our tonsils and adenoids out then?*" She had like a stiff white table cloth folded up on her head. I pressed myself against Mum as if I was trying to get inside her; I felt frightened.

"*Come along then, first a 'baarrth' and then into bed with you.*" "*I've just had a bath,*" I told her, looking pleadingly at Mum, but she just nodded towards the bathroom. "*We all have a baarrth when we come into hospital, so come on now we have a lot of work to do, don't we Mummy?*" They exchanged glances and Mum nodded in agreement. Had I been a little older and wiser I would probably have thought, '*if WE are having our tonsils and adenoids out then why are YOU not having a barrth and getting into bed as well - anyway what are tonsils and adenoids?*"

When I was in bed, Mum and Auntie Babs kissed me good-bye and left me in the charge of the lady with the tablecloth on her head. Soon after they had gone there was a slight commotion near the door where I had come in. A nurse was pulling a big box on wheels into the ward, and when she had finally arrived halfway up the ward, she left it there and walked away. Soon she was back with a white apron over her stiff uniform, and a companion similarly dressed. "*Now I'll see what's in it*", thought nosy little me.

They started taking plates from the bottom part, and then the top was opened. The smell of food wafted across to my nostrils. I sat up, just as the nurse with the table cloth pointed to me, "*No dinner for that one.*" "*Why not?*" I asked, as it dawned on me that I had not had any breakfast either. "*You'll be off to theatre shortly*", she said as she floated away.

After all the plates and cutlery had been cleared away, two ladies came pushing a brown stretcher on a white trolley. "*Sister, where's Peter Scott?*" Unceremoniously they plonked me on the trolley, covered me with a red blanket with a blue stripe at the top and we were on our way out of the big room. I was being pushed down a sloping corridor, with dark brown wood on the bottom half, large glass windows and a glass roof. I could see the sky. Then we were in a white room. The two ladies shouted over my head, "*We'll see you later.*" Without warning a cloth was placed over my face; someone had come from the back of me, and was pressing it over my mouth and nose; and a very strange smell. As I struggled for freedom the hand pressed even harder. Being 'suffocated' wasn't my kind of fun and my legs and arms started to flay about. Other people came to hold me down.

Soon I was in another world, with round pools of water set in tiled floors with marble pillars reaching up to the sky - like Roman baths. Then I was waking up in bed, trying to sit up; and laid in a pool of blood. Out of nowhere came a voice; it was the sister; "*Are we awake then? We'll soon be feeling better won't we after we've changed that dirty pillow, and get you cleaned up. I'll bring us a nice glass of water then we can have a little drink.*"

I started to realise that my throat had been cut - how she expected me to drink water without it leaking out all over the place I could not imagine. I felt very, very sick. She came back with a clean pillow under her arm and a towel, perched on the towel like a budgie was a face cloth and soap, and in the other hand she carried a small bowl of water. She lifted my head, washed and dried my face, then changed the pillows. *"Now I'll just get our nice cold water to sip, that will help to make our throat better, won't it."*

By this time I was getting rattier and rattier, so when she came back with our water I threw it over her, glass and all. Mum was very cross that I should have done such a thing and when she came to see me in the evening I got a good telling off. The nurse must have 'snitched' on me. Mum told me I was to tell her that I was very sorry for what I had done. I was not, but I had to say it. Later I remember having a mug of Bovril, and a big round biscuit.

Some weeks after my broken arm the skin under my plaster started to itch, and I tackled this by pushing a finger down. Bits of plaster started to crumble off but I was going near to mental with the itch, so Mum gave me a knitting needle, which helped a bit. A week or two later I was taken back to the hospital; I had to have another X-ray and they said everything was going alright. The day eventually dawned when I returned to the hospital to have my plaster off. I was a little apprehensive when I saw the large cutters that looked like a crab's claw, but these finally set me free. Oh! what a blessed relief.

But the crease in the elbow joint was raw, and was beginning to fester, no wonder it felt sore. A nurse brought a jar of what looked like egg yolk and putting some on a piece of lint, she placed it over the sore. It was very cool and soothing. Then she bandaged my arm up yet again. She gave Mum some of the lotion, Acriflavine emulsion it was called, and she told Mum to change the dressing every day until the sore had healed.

I was left with a constant reminder for the rest of my life, a slightly deformed elbow joint, but I have never had any pain with it, thank goodness.

We were wending our way home on the bus, when Mum said to me, *"You know, you've always been getting into scrapes one way or another and I don't suppose this will be the last, knowing you,"* as she patted my leg. She went on to tell me of two incidents when I was very young. Both could have had devastating effects. I was two and three quarter years old and she had been chatting to our next-door neighbour, Mrs Long, over the garden fence. All of a sudden, Mrs Long's eyes were drawn up to our bathroom window, a look of horror spreading over her face. *"Mrs Scott, for God's Sake don't look up, just go up to your bathroom as quickly as you can; your Peter's hanging out of the little window."*

Mum said she dashed upstairs *'like someone possessed'*. I was still trying to see her out of the window as she grabbed hold of one of my feet. The elasticated waistband of my trousers had snagged on the window catch and my bare bottom was almost out through the window.

The other time also involved the bathroom; I had clambered into the bath and managed to turn on both taps. Mum told me that it was a good job I had been able to turn on both - and not just the hot. She had been stoking up the fire to get the water very hot for washing clothes.

Doctor Remmers was our family doctor. His surgery was in rooms over Kay's Chemist shop on Riddings Road. His waiting room had chairs all round the walls. You had to remember the person who came in after you when the doctor shouted *"NEXT"*. One of the doctor's hobbies was collecting fountain pens; you could say that he had a fascination for them. He always bought the latest that came onto the market and he took great pride in showing you his new acquisition.

In the late '30s and '40s, ointment did not come nicely packaged in tubes with the instructions printed on them. They were dispensed from large jars by the chemist or mixed as we waited, and then put into various sizes of round waxed cardboard boxes. Medicines were put into corked bottles and pills into little boxes like little ladies' hat boxes.

During the war, when Auntie Babs was living with us, she would often give me a note to go to Kay's Chemist for her. It was usually for Fammel syrup cough mixture, Germolene ointment, Beechams pills or Energen rolls. These rolls were a large box full of special fluffy bread that ladies ate to loose weight; but they didn't work for Auntie Babs. I ran errands for my Mum, but walked errands for Auntie Babs. One day I walked round to Mr Kay's shop with the usual little note, and after a while Mr Kay gave me a brown paper parcel. As he handed it to me I expected it to be heavy, but it was light and soft. When I eventually got home, I asked her what was inside it. She told me they were knee pads to protect her knees when she scrubbed the kitchen floor. I never saw her wearing them, come to think of it, I never saw her cleaning the floor on her hands and knees like Mum did.

I am not sure where we were going but it must have been an important journey; it could have been to the Children's Hospital, but it was a long walk from our house to Manchester Road on that very foggy winter's day. Sometimes the bus would be late or not turn up at all if it was foggy. When the fog was very thick there would be soot floating around in it, which came from the many chimneys and was called 'smog'. We had been stood at the bus stop for what seemed like ages, when Mum said to me *"this pea-souper won't be doing your chest any good you know."* Then she pulled my scarf up over my mouth and nose again as we stood there shivering. The bus appeared slowly out of the fog like a ghostly apparition. As it pulled up I asked, *"Can we go upstairs please?"*

The reason was that I liked Doctor Remmer's house. He lived just up the road from the bus stop in a big house on Washway Road, Brooklands. It had a round turret on one corner which always intrigued me and made me wonder if there was a staircase behind the wall. I never did find out, but I always looked out for his house when we were on the bus going to Manchester.

I was confined to bed on two other occasions, once with chicken pox and about a year later, during my first year at secondary school, with German measles. On both occasions Mum bedded me down in the living room on the pullout bed. I am sure this was so that her and Auntie Babs could keep an eye on me, without having to keep popping upstairs. The bed was called a 'Z' bed, I could never understand why. Dr Remmer visited me a few times but the only treatment I had for the chicken pox was the good old calamine lotion.

One-day Mum had to visit Doctor Remmer's; her legs were painful again. Whilst he was telling her about some new cream I was summoning up my courage to come clean and tell all. Unbeknown to Mum, I had a problem. So when they had finished and Mum was getting up to leave, I confessed, blurting it out in one hurried sentence. *"Doctor Remmers, I was playing with one of those little bullet cartridge cases in my mouth, sucking it onto my tongue - Mum had told me not to do it - and I swallowed it."* As I was regaining my breath, he looked at Mum with a grin on his face, then back at me. *"Don't worry, if you'd been in any danger it would have reported itself."* They both had a good laugh - and Mum explained the joke to me as we walked home.

Not long after I was in trouble again. I had stuck the garden fork into the web between my big toe and the next when I was turning the hen run over. Mum thought she had better take me to Mr Kay or Dr Remmer's. When Mum told Mr Kay the chemist that I had been wearing wellies he told her that these would have cleaned the fork on its way through into my foot. He got a little bottle of water stuff and put some onto my wound. All of a sudden froth appeared and my foot stung. *"Just hydrogen peroxide to clean it"*, I heard him tell Mum, as I writhed in agony.

Many years later Mum told me that I was a little 'so and so' up to the age of about ten or eleven. I was always getting into mischief, I would never think of the consequences or danger of the things that came into my head.

My Dad's Home Guard on parade- the 1st Battalion Cheshire - at Altincham Grammar School.
Courtesy of 'Altrincham: An Illustrated History', Pat Southern, Trafford Leisure Services

Old Park Road, Timperley.
Courtesy of 'Looking back at Timperley', Hazel Pryor

7. Dad's Army

Dad came into the house and looked straight at Mum with a hurt look on his face. *"Aye Nellie, who do you think they've got as the sergeant in charge of us; ruddy Fletcher of all people, that damn butcher, him of all people, that blooming butcher on Riddings Road. God Almighty, what next?"*

"You seem a bit upset George." And at this remark of Mum's, Muriel burst into peals of laughter. They both looked at Dad with his gloomy face and fell about laughing. I joined in but did not understand what they were so hysterical about. It made him even more bad tempered. He searched his pockets and brought out his pipe and tobacco pouch, muttering, *"It's alright for you to be laughing, but it was me who created about last weeks joint. I said I'd never enter his b****y shop again."* His pipe was now into the pouch and his finger was going twenty to the dozen in his effort to fill it as quick as possible and get the thing lit.

Dad struck a match. *"He'll right enjoy putting me through hell and back now won't he?"* *"Why did you join then?"* asked Mum with a giggle. The pipe was taken from his mouth. *"I'd already signed up with the..... oh Hell and damnation,"* he cursed as the match burnt his fingers, *"......the ruddy officer hadn't I - who then takes us into the other room, and there he was, the smug bugger. Just sat there grinning at us all as we sauntered in, whispering something to the other officer sat next to him. I bet it was something about me."* Mum told him he was 'parynoyed', or something like that.

It seemed that Dad had had enough of the Home Guard for tonight. The unsympathetic homecoming was not what he had expected from his nearest and dearest, so he stormed out of the kitchen muttering something about, *"I don't know, you're trying to do your duty and all you get....."* We didn't hear the rest as he slammed the door behind him. When the war started my Dad had just turned 37 in the July of 1939, so, wanting to do his 'bit', he applied to join the Home Guard. He volunteered his body to King and Country and that was the reaction he received when he arrived home. Poor old Dad, he was proper hurt. I went into the scullery for a drink of water and I heard Mum say to Muriel, *"the look on his face, did you ever see the like, just like a little boy, the big soft thing."*

One evening when Mum had gone to a whist drive, leaving Dad to look after me, we listened to the wireless for about an hour, frequently being interrupted by *"Germany Calling, Germany Calling."* This was the start of the propaganda broadcast by Lord Haw Haw (William Joyce) a former follower of the British Nazi leader Oswald Mosley. He was telling us we would lose the war. The twaddle we were hearing must have inspired Dad to suddenly do a bit of parade ground practice, and not having a rifle he used the sweeping brush instead. He did a few attentions, stand at eases, left turns, right turns and about turns, and then things got serious with the brush now taking an active roll. Brush in hand he shouted *"har'tention, shoulder h'arms, pre-sent-a h'arms, shoulder h'arms"*, and marched up and down the living room.

Hearing Mum closing the front door and coming down the hall, he did a halt, and stood to attention, awaiting her entrance into the living room. As she entered he gave her a *"pre-sent h'arms"* in true sergeant-major fashion, to impress her. Oh dear, he did that alright, he was stood right under the light fitting. The pearled glass globe, suspended on three chains from the ceiling rose, was shattered. The pretend rifle went through the globe showering Dad with broken glass and leaving just three remnants of glass swinging on their respective chains.

Even I could tell Mum was not pleased. Dad stood dumbfounded, surrounded by the debris, utterly lost for words as Mum verbally assaulted him. *"Go and get the dust pan and brush and clear up this mess. Now you're going to have to buy another globe, you stupid ******."* This was a change from me getting shouted at, I was thinking. *"And what are you doing up at this time?"* she hurled at me, *"Get up to bed right now."* I did not hang about to get a goodnight kiss I can assure you.

We had to endure a bare bulb for a few weeks until Dad could afford to buy another globe from work. Eventually the incident became a topic of conversation, and, much later, became something to laugh about.

The best story Dad told us happened some months later. By now he had been issued with an old .303 rifle. The platoon were going on a training exercise, night manoeuvres to be exact. Sergeant Fletcher was left in the command after the officer in charge had briefed them all. I do not know his name - it could have been 'Captain Mainwaring'; but one thing for sure, from what Dad said, Sgt. Fletcher was no Sergeant Wilson.

The officer told them to creep along the hedges whilst crossing the fields, and crouch low so as not to be seen. *"Sgt. Fletcher will be out and about to make sure you all do it properly,"* he threatened. Then in an effort to encourage them before they parted, he told them. *"Remember men, one day you might be grateful you did this exercise. Good luck and I'll see you next week."*

Dad said the night was pitch black with heavy cloud cover, and threatening rain. Sgt. Fletcher marched them out into the countryside just beyond the Parish church to the starting point. Dad thought 'now for it'. Sergeant Fletcher bawled. *"Right you lot, you know what's expected of you, right then get on with it."*

They crossed two fields, getting their feet wet in an unexpected ditch, and eventually they arrived at the last field. After climbing the gate they all stood around; this was the field they had been told to cross, and they were told it would take them to a road via a stile. But they had not been told in which direction the stile lay - and it was a very large field and a dark night.

"Can't see a ruddy thing in this light, never mind a blooming stile," said one man, *"can't use a ruddy torch either, not even a match. Ruddy Fletcher."* The field had a slight mound effect and it was impossible to see the other side never mind a gap in the hedge it was so dark. *"Got any suggestions?"* came another voice. At last someone said, *"we'll have to split up, 'arf that way and t'other 'arf t'other way and we'll meet on t'other side."* *"Where's 'e from then; not round 'ere for sure",* said the man close to Dad.

Sgt. Fletcher had warned them before they had set off, *"I'll be watching you, and that stile, and I'll be counting you lot over, so watch it."* Off they went, showing caution, because they did not know when Sgt. Fletcher was going to pounce on them - Dad said he was fond of doing this sort of thing. *"Keeps you lot on your toes, smartens you lot up, by God you need it,"* he would shout.

They had not gone far when all of a sudden they were caught up in gun fire. Without hesitation Dad said they all dropped face down in the mud. A voice, muffled by mud, said, *"Bloody Hell the b*****'s firing a sodding machine gun at us."* Soon silence reigned again.

As they carefully trod the field again, getting over their heart attacks, they kept hearing funny sounds, like heavy breathing and occasional muffled footsteps, but when they stopped all was still and quiet again. They all admitted that it was very scary and it made them all feel very uneasy. The night was casting ghostly shadows and the occasional tiny light clouds that scuttled across the moon only added to the eerie atmosphere, and their fears. They started moving more quickly but the sounds seemed to stay with them.

By now they were all very nervous, and one of the men voiced the opinion that it could probably be Fletcher up to his tricks. All of a sudden *"found it,"* someone said in a heavy whisper, and it floated across to their waiting ears. With the glad news they all ran quickly in the direction of the voice, and it turned into a race as to who could get there first. It was utter chaos; there were eleven men in the party, and when Dad got there two were already getting over the stile, but it did not help that on their chests they had their gas masks, on their backs their rucksacks, and with their rifles slung over their shoulders - and they were all scrambling over each other.

When the melée was eventually sorted out and a semblance of order had returned, the men managed to get over the stile. As the last man steadied himself to climb to safety the sounds came again and got closer and closer. *"What the hell is it?"* he cried in a near hysterical voice, missing the first step in his panic and half knocking his tin hat off. Just at the moment of reaching the top, a sudden push in his back sent him tumbling over the stile into the ditch. When he had regained his senses he heard all the others laughing as he looked up into the face of a big cart horse, tossing its head up and down. It started to neigh, as if to say, *"Serves you lot right for disturbing my peace."*

Their euphoria at all this was short-lived; in the panic they had forgotten about Sgt. Fletcher. *"You lot took your ruddy time didn't you? Had a picnic did you? Looks like you've been enjoying a ruddy mud bath. I saw you all enjoyed the fire crackers."* Then he nearly split his sides with laughter. Dad said they felt like lynching him from the nearest tree. *"Right fall in before I freeze to death, if I do I'll be back to haunt you."* The man next to Dad said, *"I bet you would an all."* And they all laughed, even Sgt. Fletcher.

A few weeks later Dad received a letter telling him to report for a medical somewhere in Manchester, prior to call up, and he joined the army on 28th August 1941. Had he been a few months older he would have been exempt from service. His brother, Frank, a Woolworth's store manager, and Uncle Geoffrey, were already in the forces. Uncle Frank and Dad were assigned to the Army and Uncle Geoffrey the RAF. Dad's other brother, Arthur, was exempt as an engineer, and he stayed at home and worked on munitions.

After his square bashing, Dad was moved from one side of the country to the other where he did his training to be a driver in the Royal Army Service Corps. When he came home on leave he told Mum he was going back to yet another camp, to do training to drive the 'big stuff' as he called it. Sometimes when Dad wrote letters to Mum he would draw me a picture of the type of vehicle he was driving at the time. One was a large water carrier, like a big petrol tanker; another was a tank transporter that had sixteen wheels; he told me it was capable of carrying the largest battle tanks.

In the early years of the war there was an announcement over the air and in the newspapers that Winston Churchill was going to commandeer all metal garden railings, gates and other such items that were not serving a vital purpose. A short time after, we saw gangs of men with lorries and gas burners taking these from public buildings, schools, private houses, factories and parks, in fact anywhere they could be found. Years later I was told by Mum that Grandad Scott was very upset when Alexandra Park gates were taken down as he thought they were a work of art and very beautiful - it was a crime to lose them. Mum said, *"So the country will have to do without guns, tanks and ships then?"* After the war there were a lot of angry people when the railings and gates were found in great masses, rusting on large dumps up and down the country. It turned out Grandad was right.

Later on, I am not sure when, there was a rumour circulating of an imminent invasion by the Germans, but the Navy was given the task of spreading the sea with oil and petrol and setting it alight somehow at the crucial moment. This put paid to the Nazis attempt at landing on our shores.

Harry and me were spurred into action when we heard about an appeal for gold and silver foil; known to us as silver paper. Armed with an old paper carrier bag from the Co-op we set forth on our mission. First we called on people in our avenue that did not go out to work. Very soon we were surprised that we had to go and dump our heavy carrier bag in Harry's garage; we would not have thought it possible in such a short time to have collected so much.

Next we did Leicester Avenue, where one lady who could not hear very well gave us half-a-crown. We tried very hard to explain to her that we were collecting silver paper but she kept saying *"No it's alright, you take it for the war."* Harry said as we walked back down her drive, *"What'll we do with it?"* I think we kept it; well we couldn't put it with the silver paper due to the rules. Well we couldn't could we?

One distinguished old gentleman, with a mop of white hair, kept us on his doorstep for ages. He was asking us a lot of questions, all about what we were doing, and where did we get the authority from. When we asked what authority was he sighed and said *"permission boys, permission"* as he shook his head in disbelief. Then he wanted to know where we had to take it all.

We told him all the answers - it had to be taken to the public library on Park Road. So after we had convinced him that it was all legal he went back in the house and was gone for ages. Harry looked at me and said in a low whisper, *"Wonder what eez doin,"* as he stood on one foot then the other a few times. *"Bet he phones the police or the library,"* I replied, also in a low whisper.

When he eventually reappeared, he came staggering up the hall carrying a large cardboard box. We could tell he was pleased to put them down, and he placed his hand in the small of his back and straightened up with a heavy sigh. He very carefully spent some minutes undoing the knot on the string that fastened the flaps of the lid together. Eventually he opened it up, and with a sort of reluctant pause, he took out a few of the many pads to show us.

They were really lovely; all kinds of foil paper, gold, silver and a kaleidoscope of colours, many embossed with different patterns, very beautiful. Harry and I stood and looked in wonder - the box was about the size of six shoe boxes and it was very heavy. He had only shown us a very small amount of his collection. What others were within we wondered?

We had to leave our carrier bag in his porch whilst we carried his box to Harry's garage between us, and we had to put the box on many a garden wall on our short walk back. I said to Harry as we put the box on the garage floor carefully without dropping it. *"They could have been his prized collection."* We agreed that he did seem very sorry to part with them. We had a good look through them all and wished we could keep some for ourselves. We even discussed going and asking him if he wanted them back. But they joined the rest of the collection for the library.

When we had eventually finished our collecting, along with the man's large contribution, well, to say we had a heavy load was an understatement. Harry's thought of asking Mr. Tattersall to run it round in his car was very tempting. But we wanted to do it ourselves. We could not think of any lady who would trust us with even an old pram in case they did not get the wheels back. Then an idea came to us at the same time as we shouted out *"a wheelbarrow."*

So we spent a full hour walking round and looking into gardens. As some houses had tall wicket gates it was impossible to see into the gardens. We risked sneaking down the paths of some to look through the trellising - then the back door would open and a lady would come out to throw some rubbish in her bin. We dare not risk it again. Reluctantly we started to walk back home down Arderne Road, but suddenly we saw it, standing up against the wall of a house. We stood and looked at each other, and knew what the other was thinking. Who's going to ask for it?

With our arms round each others shoulders we walked briskly through the front gates to the front door. Standing, arms at our sides Harry said *"Go on then, knock on the door!"* My arm started the journey up to the knocker, hesitantly, then suddenly casting caution to the wind I grasped it. *"There's no one in,"* I said, half relieved, and we were just turning to make our get away when it opened. *"Yes, what can I do for you two boys?"*

"P..ple-e-ase c..c.can.. w.w.e.. b.borrow, your w.w.." *"wheelbarrow please,"* interrupted my saviour, Harry. *"What on earth would you want that old thing for?"* she asked. To save me further embarrassment, Harry explained our predicament, and yes, she agreed.

Soon our heavy load was sitting in the barrow, a bit wobbly as Harry pushed it up his garden path and out onto the avenue. Luckily for us the library was only about three hundred yards away. We took turns in pushing it. Squeak, squeak-squeak squeak but we just carried on and parked our gift outside the entrance of the library.

Someone had seen - and heard us - coming, and quickly appeared to tell us. *"Not in here, round the side please, you'll see a hut, Mr Granger should be there to meet you and take your collection."* So after a little rest we squeaked our way round the side, and when we got outside the hut Mr Granger appeared. *"My goodness, that's a good lot there; you have been busy. We'll have to give you a certificate for that lot, you two deserve one each. My, my you have done well."* Pushing our luck Harry said. *"Could we have a drink of water please mister?"* *"I think you can have a glass of lemonade,"* he said, *"and some oil for that wheel."*

Suitably refreshed we stood between the shafts of the wheelbarrow. *"OK"* said Harry, *"you push it first then"*. We rested our certificates in the barrow and started the first leg of our journey home. After giving the kind lady her no longer squeaky barrow back, we said thank you.

"Hey! We'll have to go and show that man on Leicester Avenue our certificates," said I. Harry nodded his agreement and added, *"Then he'll believe us proper!"*

Winnie and our Muriel also organised a concert that was to be performed in Monks' garage, which meant their car had to be put out onto the back garden drive for the time being so that the rehearsals could take place. Later, to make way for the crowds, it would have to be put out onto the road!

Posters were made and painted and pinned up on the telegraph poles, tickets were sold; some people who would not be able to come bought tickets anyway as they wanted to help the war effort and support the girls.

Sydney, Harry's big brother, got into the swing of things and made a few 'props' and many a neighbour promised the loan of chairs, etc. The curtains had been made from all sorts of material by some of the mums and were hung a few days before. This left Sydney to make some final adjustment so *'they'd run right'* as he called it. Harry and I were entrusted with the job of opening and closing them by holding a curtain each and walking towards each other, and trying to keep out of sight. But we didn't, did we, hee, hee!

On the morning of the performance, all kinds of descriptions of chairs were collected and put in place. Ticket sales had gone very well, which meant that we had to give two performances of the programme. This included a short play performed by Muriel, Winnie and Dawn Clifford and another friend. A couple of sketches were performed and many songs were sung. Winnie and Muriel had to sing *In Room 504* for my Auntie Babs or she had threatened that she would not come. The song had romantic memories for her. I recited a little poem about a car. I can only remember the following line: *"I don't know, I can't tell, me press the button, and it went like Hell"*, and would you believe it, Harry and I sung our version of *'I'll Take you Home again Kathleen'*.

A lot of money was raised for the War Effort and every one said that the two girls had done a first class job. The garage was cleared up and the car put back in pride of place again.

Harry's Dad's car played a multitude of parts for the two of us; one day it would be a Spitfire or a Lancaster bomber, another day a battleship or submarine, and last but not least the faithful old bus or charabanc.

Harry's Dad's Armstrong Siddeley

Whenever we played at buses at home it would involve chairs being placed one behind the other. At our house we had a brass ashtray, which was mounted on a stand about 24 inches high with a heavy base. Although the ashtray was only about six inches across it made a smashing steering wheel after we had loosened the screw holding it in place. We did of course have to take turns in being the driver.

8. Air Raids and Evacuees

"Dad, Dad." "Whatever is it now son?" "What's that big paper drum thing in the hall for?" "You'll see, but it's not a drum, so don't get excited about it."
A few days' later I came in from playing to see the drum had been opened and inside there were rolls and rolls of brown paper. Mum and Dad's voices were coming from the back living room and on investigating I found them sticking the rolls in strips on to the windows. I didn't really understand what was going on. Later, I was told that this was to protect us from flying glass in the event of bomb blasts. Whatever a bomb blast was!

Soon, everywhere you went you could see these brown diagonal crosses on windows. Black-out material was another item soon to invade our homes; Mum had to make curtains for all our windows and the front and back doors. If you had to open a door at night the light had to be turned off first because if the Air Raid Patrol warden saw the slightest chink of light he would shout, *"PUT THAT LIGHT OUT!"* For regular offenders many expletives were added, and a summons often followed which carried hefty fines.

All motor vehicles had to have their lights covered with what looked like a mans' top hat with two slots to let some light out. This rule also applied to motor bikes and cycles. The problem was that road accidents rose considerably.

For the first few air raids Mrs Long invited us to share her shelter as we didn't have one - no doubt she welcomed the company as Mr Long had been called up straightaway when war broke out - I heard mum say he'd volunteered! Before going into the army he had erected a steel shelter in their lounge, the height of a table and made with heavy angled steel corners and a top of thick steel, the sides and bottom were heavy wire mesh. These were called Morrison Shelters after the minister, Herbert Morrison. It looked like a great big rabbit hutch, especially when a mattress had been put in.

The period during the latter part of 1939 and early 1940 became known as the phoney war, because nothing happened. It was a period of uncertainty. In his spare time Dad now transformed the coal store beyond the scullery wall into an outside toilet and shed. Maybe the lavatory was to save dad having to take his wellies off whilst he was gardening? Maybe it was to be his own domain, as I often heard mum say, *"George; have you been smoking in the lavatory again? You make the place stink with that filthy pipe thing?"* But the most logical reason, of course, would be for use during air raids.

However, when the job was completed we had no coal store; but not to worry, Dad put down a strong concrete base, just outside the back door and a few days later a small shed was delivered, he painted it green, and now we had a new 'coal hole', as mum called it. The new lavatory required me to cut up more newspaper to hang up on the nail dad had knocked into the wall. Isn't it strange, I heard mum say, that whenever you use old newspaper anywhere, even on the floor just after it had been washed, you always find something to read that you've missed before.

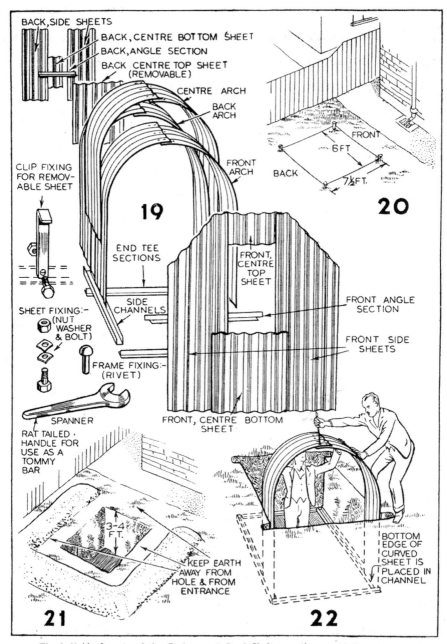

19. The individual parts of the Government Steel Shelter as they are delivered, with details of each part. 20. The actual site chosen should first be marked out in this manner. 21. This diagram shows the hole dug to its final depth. 22. Erecting the steel arches. Two men are required for this part of the task.

Anderson shelter *Courtesy of 'A Child's War', Mike Brown*

The Government were always telling us to save this and that during the war, and one thing was paper. But then they sent out leaflets for nearly everything - Mum called it all bureaucratic drivel. It became known as 'bumf' (bum fodder).

Not content with the coal shed, Dad set to work digging a massive hole. *"Why are you doing that Dad,"* I asked. *"To put the shed in,"* he answered. I couldn't understand this, so I went to call for one of my friends. While I was away Dad took down and re-erected the garden shed in the hole to make our air-raid shelter.

Soon we started to have bombing raids, the wail of the siren warning us that the German bombers were on their way, sending us scurrying for shelter. We soon got to call the siren 'Old Moaning Minnie'.

Outside Peter Davies's house a brick shelter with an eight-inch concrete flat roof had been built. I well remember one evening I'd been to the shops for Mum, and as I turned into our road, 'Moaning Minnie' sounded.

As if by magic an ARP man came up behind me and herded me into this refuge. I was in the dark. Then a few of the local people came in, and thank goodness some of them had torches, although these didn't give out much light - they had by law, to have tissue paper over the front end, secured with an elastic band.

We had our first air raid on the night of July 29th, the day after my birthday. I hadn't been in bed very long when I had to jump out quickly. This was the first time we took advantage of the promised refuge in Mrs Long's shelter.

As soon as Mum heard the air raid siren she would put the kettle on and make a flask of cocoa, half milk and half water, if she had enough milk. Mum always put a piece of greaseproof paper over the neck of the flask before pushing the cork stopper in. Just thinking of it, I can smell it.

During the day of 8th August 1940 we heard the siren start to wail. The Germans had come over to drop a load of paper on us as well. The leaflets were Hitler's 'Last Appeal to Reason', wanting us to withdraw our declaration of war on his country. A parcel that failed to open fell on the head of a local ARP Warden. Luckily he suffered no lasting damage.

During the later part of 1940 Manchester and surrounding districts suffered heavy bombing and incendiary raids. We had 25 in total, with just two that took place during daylight or late evening. The majority lasted for a few hours either side of midnight.

Two days after the raid of the 16th December, Dad was as pleased as a dog with two tails as he announced to us all that he had at last finished our shelter. We all trooped out to explore our haven from the 'Hun'. It was all rather cosy, he had built a set of bunk beds, a small drop down table fitted to one wall. Our two deck chairs were laid upon one of the beds. In one corner stood a paraffin heater and on the table, the matches and candles.

Mum stocked a small box with a few emergency food items that she could spare, *"Let's hope we'll never need this lot,"* she said. She had to raid it on numerous occasions. An enamel bucket was kept near the kitchen sink so she could take fresh water down into the shelter with us.

Our next door neighbours, the Smith's, only had a small garden, and it was even smaller after Mr Smith also dug a big hole and put a shelter in it. His was delivered on a lorry, the first 'build it your self kits' called Anderson shelters, made from corrugated steel sheets (called corrugated iron for some unknown reason). When put together the roof was curved, designed to give added better protection after being covered with sandbags and earth. Wooden steps led down into it and Mr Smith fitted it out similar to ours. With its curved roof it felt cosier than ours, and a lot safer, and it proved to deaden the noise of bombs better than ours did.

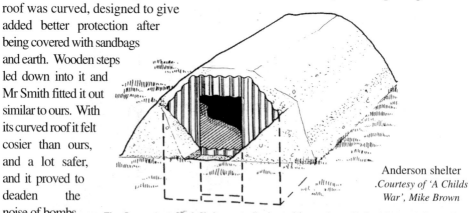

Anderson shelter
.Courtesy of 'A Childs War', Mike Brown

23. The Government Steel Shelter actually in position and provided with an earth capping. The steel parts of which the shelter is constructed will support 3 feet of soil all over, and it is recommended that a minimum of 15 inches of soil be provided.

The day before Christmas Eve was uneventful; Dad had retrieved the Christmas tree from the attic, Mum had decorated it and we were ready for the celebrations to begin. We had finished our tea when Dad came back into the kitchen, *"Right love, I'll be off then Nellie." "Don't let Fletcher upset you now,"* says Mum. Dad was through

Bomb damage in Altrincham
Courtesy of 'Altrincham: An Illustrated History', Pat Southern, Trafford Leisure Services

Below, the blazing oil tank at Broadheath

the back door before she and Muriel could start to laugh. I just shrugged my shoulders knowing they wouldn't tell me why they were laughing. All I knew was that Dad was off to do Home Guard duty.

Not long after Moaning Minnie started her warning. Mum said a naughty word, damped down the fire, put the kettle on the gas stove and did other things at twice the speed of Father Christmas on his sleigh. Soon we were through the back door - tonight we were going to try out our new shelter for the first time.

The night was as clear as daylight. I looked up at the clear moonlit sky, and seconds later a German plane filled my vision, heading for a small fluffy cloud. I will never forget the sight. It was flying very low, *"Look mum"* I shouted, as I pointed up, and we could see the swastika on its tail. It was very exciting - until I saw the guns sticking out of the front end and thought they would soon start firing at us. Mum was ahead carrying the bucket of water; Muriel had the flask. I dashed down after them bumping into Muriel in my eagerness for safety. Even the seriousness of the situation didn't stop her having a go at me.

I was informed years later that the bomber would have been a Heinkel on its bombing run into Manchester or it could have been going in to mark the bombing area for the raid.

The best place for a Heinkel!

This was the first of two consecutive nights of heavy bombing which started on Sunday, December 22nd, at 6.38 pm and Monday, December 23rd 1940, at 7.15 pm, and became known as the Manchester Blitz. The pounding went on until around five o'clock the following mornings; nearly ten hours each night!

On the first night the bombs seemed to be falling in our garden and the surrounding vicinity, they were that close. Mum said, *"Trust your father to be playing ruddy soldiers on a night like this!"* I think she was quite frightened, not just for herself, but also for Muriel and me.

The shelter was vibrating as the bombs exploded, dust and pieces cascading down from the roof timbers. Mum's confidence in our refuge had diminished quickly. Putting the little oil light out, she opened the shelter door, and climbed up a step until her head was poking over the top of the low sandbag entrance. Muriel and I sat on the bunk beds in the near dark, ready to dash round to the Smith's shelter on Mum's command. *"What are you doing now Mum?"* asked Muriel. *"Waiting for a Warden to pass, now hush."* She waited, and waited, until eventually an air-raid warden passed by the front gate.

Except for a few muffled explosions in the distance all was quiet, when Mum made us jump out of our skins with a sudden *"HELLO THERE. Hello. Our shelters not very good and I don't feel very safe with my two children down here; can we go in next door's?"* I think she must have frightened the passing firewatcher half to death.

"Sorry luv, I daren't risk it, not with what's coming down tonight, especially with your kids in there. This is the worst one we've had up to now, and there's lots of flying shrapnel about. Sorry!" So we had to stay put.

A few minutes later we heard and felt an almighty explosion, and the shed shook. *"Oh my God, what ever are we going to do,"* exclaimed Mum, as her arms enfolded the two of us. We found out later that a land mine had demolished a house and part of the adjoining house on Westwood Avenue, opposite Riddings Road, close to where the Barracuda training plane had crashed.

The following morning Mum spoke to Mrs Smith and explained our situation. Mrs Smith told her that she would welcome the company as Mr Smith had also been playing soldiers. We were to spend many a night in Smith's shelter after that, but I think Dad was a little bit hurt. On the second night of the 'Blitzkrieg' he was on Home Guard duty yet again, and Mum was not too pleased at all, but she felt a lot better knowing we were all safer in the Anderson shelter.

When we were out and about, Mum would suddenly cock her ear to the sky and say *"Hush. Oh it's alright it's one of ours"* listening to the continuous steady drone. But if it made a sort of 'er-er' intermittent drone, Mum soon taught us to recognise that it was a 'Jerry' plane.

The men and women 'firewatchers' were renamed Air Raid Precautions Wardens (ARP Wardens) later on, and they played an important part during air raids as they helped to spot the incendiary bombs that caused many fires. The only protection they had was a steel helmet, a whistle and a big rattle, similar to a football rattle. They used the whistle to draw attention to fires and the rattle to warn of life threatening dangers of a gas attack.

When at last we were able to leave the shelter, we looked across the pond in the direction of Manchester. The sky was lit with an eerie red light; just like the one I once heard Dad say was a 'shepherds warning'. I heard Mum say to Muriel, *"Just look at that sky, it would be a beautiful sight, if it wasn't for the horror that has taken place."*

Do you know, I cannot remember what we did with Towser during those air raids; I hope the poor thing wasn't left in the house.

Thousands of incendiaries were dropped that caused many fires, followed by hundreds of high explosive bombs that destroyed factories, shops and homes causing havoc and loss of life. Even a hospital was severely damaged causing bed-ridden patients to be carried to safety during the bombing.

As well as Manchester and Salford and the large surrounding industrial areas including Trafford Park, there were also factories at Broadheath near Altrincham that 'copped it'. Most of these companies were making munitions and Broadheath was only two miles as the 'crow flies' from where we lived.

The nearby Skelton Junction, a spur off the Altrincham to Manchester railway line which passed our 'Rec' going towards Buxton and the mineral quarries, appeared to be an important target, but they never succeeded in getting a direct hit, only near misses. On our way to school one morning, as we neared the top of the station approach, we could see a great pall of smoke rising up into the air, where the previous night's bomb had hit an oil storage tank on the side of the canal near to Broadheath. As the flames and smoke rose into the air, firemen tried to quench them with water from the canal. The water was pumped out with large hoses. We watched the firemen lift them out to clean a big basket on the end; the basket kept getting blocked with mud and rubbish from the canal bed.

One morning as I left for school I found a lump of shrapnel sitting in the middle of our path. It was brown with dashes of red here and there. As I was about to pick it up I wondered if it would still be hot, so I turned it over with my foot. Harry happened to be calling for me as I picked it up. *"Hi'ya Harry, look what I've just found."* I proudly held it out for his eyes to see.

"What's that then?" he said with slight bemusement. *"It's a lump of shrapnel; I just found it on the path." "That little bit; you should see the lump our Sydney found, it'd make fifty of that skinny bit."* I fell in step with him feeling hurt and dejected as we walked to school.

The air raids got less during 1941, only ten, then on 27th July 1942, practically two years after the first, we had the last, and this, they reported, was just a sneak raider who flew above the housetops and dropped a stick of bombs in Beswick on the east of Manchester.

A few years later in the sky above the oil tank, we saw this very unusual aircraft flying around; everyone was quite scared. It had two fuselages with a cockpit in the middle. Each wing had an engine, but they did not appear to have propellers. A small crowd was looking up at it; some even went under the bridge to take shelter and some started to run home. Eventually a policeman riding by on his bike stopped and told us *"Nothing to worry about folks, it's a new plane called a Lightning,"*

Everyone had to have two buckets outside their house; one filled with sand, the other with water, and for every group of houses a stirrup pump was provided. The Air Raid Wardens were in charge of these to fight small fires caused by incendiary bombs.

Bomb damage in Timperley
Courtesy of 'Looking back at Timperley', Hazel Pryor

'Get them out Quick' was the motto. Stirrup pump practice was held at regular intervals, and all the grown-ups had to take part, sometimes pumping, sometimes controlling the nozzle, whilst others brought a steady supply of water. Different types of fire demanded different techniques, so learning the proper method was important. One day, your house may depend on your expertise, they told us. If the grown ups were in a good mood, they would let us boys have a turn, just as long as we had carried some water for them. Occasionally they would light a small fire to make the practice more realistic, and the 'squirter' had to lie down behind a make shift wall of sand bags for protection from the heat and the danger of another explosion.

Strange objects started to appear in various places. Some were oblong others round and some square. Some were built from bricks; some were made of concrete, whilst others had been built using corrugated iron. Even wooden ones had been built. They had large oblong areas painted yellow with a large E W S painted in black on them. Another test of Mum's wisdom was due, as I wandered home trying to work it out. Mum soon stopped my enquiring mind going into overdrive and told me they were tanks for storing water for the firemen. The letters stood for 'Emergency Water Supply'. I don't think I would have worked that one out even if I lived to be a hundred. We boys got our chance at being stirrup pump operatives - when the air raids dropped off in frequency and intensity -watering the gardens in the summer months.

During June 1944 Hitler started a bombardment of a different kind; unmanned flying bombs called V1s. The Londoners soon nicknamed them 'Doodlebugs', and they came over with a spluttering sound. The distance they were to fly was determined by the amount of fuel they carried; when this ran out the engine stopped and they hung there on their little wings for a split second, before they came down. Sometimes the anti-aircraft guns and fighter planes were able to blow them out of the skies. We heard and saw one, much to our amazement, flying over Timperley - someone said that it came down near Liverpool.

Later the Germans launched another more vicious weapon. This was again directed at the unfortunate London populus, the V2 rocket. It was a one-ton bomb, but looked more like the moon rocket in the old Flash Gordon films. This one reached the speed of sound; the only warning anyone received, which was too late anyway, was the slight hissing sound as it came down to earth. It took less than a second to hit the ground and the explosion came with its overwhelming horror, causing destruction over a very wide area.

For their safety during the war, children had to be sent to areas of relative safety throughout the Country - thousands became 'evacuees'. Evacuation was unpleasant but had to be done to save the future generation from the devastation of the Blitz. These were heartbreaking times for parents and children alike. A few belongings were packed into little cases, paper carrier bags, even brown paper parcels, and carrying their favourite teddy, doll or toy, they set off from their homes to their schools, which were being used as assembly points.

With their gas masks over their shoulders and a luggage label with their name, school and destination tied to their clothing, they arrived in great numbers at the railway stations to board the waiting trains.

In the newsreels, women would be seen hanging on to their children's hands for as long as possible. As the train gathered speed they ran with their hands pressed against the window. Mums - and a few dads - stood transfixed, as they watched the back end of the last carriage fade out of sight. They were on a journey into the unknown. As the children looked out of the carriage windows some of the children were seeing cows and sheep for the first time in their lives.

I was only six or seven at the time so I could not possibly have understood the feelings of uncertainty they must have had. We eventually received evacuees in our area but this didn't happen until the evacuation programme was well under way. The first time I met some of them was when Mum answered the door to four girls aged between ten and twelve. After 'hello's had been exchanged and they had said goodbye to the lady escort, mum told me to go out and play. She said the girls were going to have a drink and some cake whilst she got to know them.

Many years later Mum told us what happened. When they had finished their refreshments Mum had called the girls upstairs to have a bath; she said they looked as if they needed one after the ordeal of the last few days; a couple of them did appear quite grubby. As they trooped into the bathroom, three of the girls were making good progress, but the fourth wasn't showing much enthusiasm for the bathing lark; she wouldn't take her knickers off.

Mum tried to persuade her, as did the other girls, but to Mum's annoyance, she refused. Mum tried all the tricks she knew, and resorted to asking her how her mother would react? Eventually she succumbed and got undressed, to reveal that the poor girl was hiding some loose biscuits in her pants. Her mother had told her to hide them as other children may try to steal them from her. Mum consoled her, saying she would throw them away but would find her some replacements. Mum dried her tears and gave her a hug.

They didn't stay long with us, no more than a few days; perhaps our house was used as a stop-over for a short period.

We had a few comings and goings for short stays until a young man, called Bernard, aged about fifteen arrived who was to stay for some time. He had left school at fourteen and was now training to become an accountant with a firm in Altrincham. He was studying for an examination so he was doing a lot of swotting.

One winter's night he was sat at the dining table, wearing his usual Fair Isle pullover. He was working on some important test paper that had to be completed in ink, not pencil (no Biros in those days) to present to his employer next day. Suddenly he erupted *"Oh no, I've made a blot, and I've no more of this special lined paper."* He waved his arms about in blind panic, *"What am I going to do?"* *"Stop your panicking,"* chided Muriel, *"don't worry, I've got some special stuff in my bedroom."* Off she dashed

Kent Evacuees setting off for Cheshire.
Courtesy of 'Evacuees Ready for the Off', Barry Hollis, Kent Messenger Newspaper Group.

upstairs to get it but she was some time in coming back down. In desperation he started to use his ink rubber. Muriel arrived with the magic fluid, two tiny glass bottles with rubber stoppers and small glass rods attached to apply the fluid. The idea was to coat the blot with fluid from the first, add the second fluid, then, using blotting paper, gently press on the area and as if by magic the blot disappeared.

On this occasion however the fluid didn't work. *"That's because you used the rubber and took the surface off the paper; why didn't you wait, you barmy individual,"* scolded Muriel. Again panic set in. Out came his penknife and he started to scratch at it, creating a hole now. He tried sticking some paper underneath the hole and drawing thin lines across it. When he came home the following evening he told Mum that he had been in trouble for the careless paper. Bernard slept on the Z-bed in the downstairs front room. Speaking to Muriel many years later, she told me that one night, Bernard, her and me had had a scuffle on the landing outside our bedrooms; I was trying to help my big sister. Bernard was trying to tickle her then he started to try to pull her pyjama trousers down. Dad, who was on leave, heard the noise and was upstairs like a shot. This was the end of his stay as far as Dad was concerned and he left within a few days. You could say he had blotted his copybook again.

Philip, with his mum, and Norman the evacuee

We were not the only family on the avenue to take an evacuee. Mr and Mrs Harding, Elsie and Dick to my Mum, had a boy of twelve staying with them. His name was Norman Lambert, and he was forever telling us that he was going to be a jeweller when he left school. He joined the scouts; I don't suppose he had much choice - living with a scoutmaster. I was still in the cubs and he tried to teach me semaphore to no avail.

Norman had a bike, a very nice green bike - a racer we would call it. It had 'bent down' handlebars and thinner wheels and tyres than ours, and was lighter in weight. You can imagine it was Norman's pride and joy. Later, when we were attending the secondary school, we played a trick on Norman. Going home one afternoon we noticed three large puddles near the end of Moss Lane. One of the four of us had some sherbet sweets. Sometimes we would muck about with these; one of us would stuff our mouth with a few, and the ensuing froth would force its way through your lips, and down your nose making it look like you were having a fit. Then you would walk into a shop looking gormless. Usually it ended up with the shopkeeper saying, *"Get out you stupid boy"* even before you had tried to ask for anything.

This day I had a brilliant idea to play a trick on Norman. The plan was divulged and a sweet was extracted from the owner, Harry I think. When we saw Norman cycle over the brow of the railway bridge we dropped it into one of the puddles. Very soon it was a pulsating mass of froth about three inches in diameter with four heads bent examining the strange phenomenon - Norman was sure to be inquisitive. As he got nearer we saw the puzzled look on his face and we shouted *"Hey Norman ride through this"* and pointed at the seething mass. He obliged us - then too late asked what it was.

"We don't know," said I. Then on cue Harry says, *"It could be some sort of acid, that bubbles in water couldn't it?"* At this Norman went ballistic, and lifting his front wheel off the ground, spun the wheel through one of the other puddles in desperation. He certainly showed his displeasure as he rode off towards his temporary home. It was quite sometime before we came clean and owned up to the prank we had played on him. We should not have told him; as yet again, he went ballistic. Eventually he forgave us - somehow we thought in the end he appreciated the joke we had played on him.

I never knew what happened to any of the children who passed through our hands so to speak. I have rarely thought about it before, but as far as I know none of them ever wrote to Mum. It now makes me think about the awful trauma these children, and their parents, must have gone through. How had they all coped on returning to London. What did they find? Were their homes still standing? No doubt in many cases it would have taken a very long time to get over it.

9. Hens and other livestock

The New Year was but a few weeks old when I heard Dad rummaging about in his new outside toilet and tool store. Mum helped me struggle my wellies on. *"You'll have to be having some new ones; I could hardly get those on you. Go on then and help your Dad."* *"What's he going to do?"* *"Oh he'll tell you, go on, off you go."*

The store door was slightly ajar and I could see Dad filling his pipe, his spade leant against him. His lips were moving but I could not make out what he was saying. *"Can I come in Dad?"* *"Aye, you can, but I'll have to get started or there be hell to play."* *"Can I get my spade Dad?"* *"Yes but don't be getting in my way there's a good boy."* *"What are we going to do Dad?"* *"Oh you'll see."* He marched out and stood on top of the shelter.

I didn't understand it; he was digging the soil away. *"What's wrong Dad?"* *"Now't - Oh I'm digging the ruddy shed out; seems it's not good enough."* Very soon the shed was pulled to bits and lay on the grass. Then he put all the soil back in the hole. I went to call for Harry. When I got back home I was surprised not to find the shed had been put in the bottom left hand corner of the garden and Dad was now digging small holes, two rows of them. *"What are you doing Dad? "You'll see soon enough."* Some minutes later he said, *"Go and get your wellies off and your shoes on, you can come to Manchester with me."*

We went on the electric train and got off at Old Trafford. We crossed over a main road at Trafford Bar and walked into this shop. Talk about an Aladdin's cave; this was a specialist ironmonger's shop, a cornucopia for just about everything that a man would need to do any job under the sun - *"and very handy"*, Dad said, *"right across from the railway station"*. Dad went with the assistant into the back and some minutes later came out helping to carry a big roll of wire netting, a sack of large staples, some nails and a hoop of thick wire. *"Now, all we've got to do is get this little lot home and we can finish the job."* *"What are we making Dad?"* *"You'll see."*

The roll was so big it had to go in the guard's van. When we eventually arrived home, we were struggling past the back door when Mum shouted; *"Those posts have arrived George."* Dad shouted back, *"Put the kettle on Nellie I'm right parched with this lot."* Dad was soaking the bottom of the posts in a bucket of creosote, just as Mum came with our tea. *"Don't let him get any of that stuff on him George."* When he had painted all the posts he planted them in the holes - I helped him with my spade. *"Right, now I'll have to get the netting on."* It was beginning to go dark. *"Oh b**** it, I've had enough, I'll finish it tomorrow."* So he cleaned his spade, and mine, scraped our boots, and in we went.

By the time I got down to the bottom of the garden next morning, Dad was just finishing making a frame for the gate and was covering it with wire netting. He dug a shallow channel between the posts - I didn't ask why! Soon the netting was stapled to the posts, and now I found out about the channel - Dad filled it in, burying some of the

My dog meat shop in Altrincham.
Courtesy of 'Altrincham, Past and Present', Gillian Fitzpatrick, Trafford Leisure Services

Train in Timperley station.

netting under the ground. I chanced it, *"Why have you done that Dad?" "It's to stop the hens getting out under the wire."* After the gate was fitted, he told me that we had just made *'a pen'*. Yes, we were getting some hens.

I had arrived home from school a week or two later and Mum answered a knock on the front door. I heard her talking to a man who said he had got the chickens in his car; I was rather intrigued. I imagined them all sat in neat rows on the seats, so I just had to see it. Was I disappointed when he opened the boot and took out three sacks. Picking up two sacks he asked Mum if she could manage the other one. I helped her with it and off we all went to put the hens into their new home. When he opened the sacks, blimey, what a lot of noise they made, they were trying to fly all over the place, squawking and clucking.

The small sack revealed a cockerel and two hens and they greeted their new home in the same fashion as the others;but not the cockerel. I think he was put out being shoved in a sack, and he was putting on a show of bravado for the benefit of his 'harem', strutting around as if he owned the place, as Mum remarked. He had two types of hens to rule the roost over. Light Sussex and Rhode Island reds; he was a Rhode Island red. He was a real beauty of a bird. He enjoyed showing off his large purple head dress and his flowing tail of many hues of red. Mum christened him Bertie; she said it suited such a noble bird.

Towser, our Manchester terrier, being inquisitive, just had to run up and down outside of the pen, but after they had settled down he showed no more than a fleeting interest, just so long as none of the inmates escaped, then his attitude changed -he enjoyed a good chase.

A few weeks later, we had the Christening service; we all stood outside the wire with Mum saying, *"That one looks a good Gertie, and look, that one over there, now she'd definitely make a good Mabel."* And so it went on, until they all had names; mostly after members of the family. Who was honoured or insulted I don't know?

When the hens tried to fly the nest, so to speak, Dad had to clip their wings. I helped in this operation; first we got them in the shed and I let them out one at a time as Dad caught hold of them and cut off the tips of their wings. *"That'll put a stop to their flights of fancy,"* he told me with a chuckle.

I remember one hen with affection; she was the light Sussex that Mum called Mabel. She was allowed to grow old gracefully after she had stopped laying eggs; she became a family pet, especially to Harry and me.

Well before my eighth birthday, these birds were playing a significant part in my young life. I collected the eggs, fed and watered them, and changed the straw in their nesting boxes. Every few weeks I would have to turn the hen run over, Mum said '*to keep the ground sweet*'; it was a good job we had a long garden. Every month or so I would have to sprinkle lime over the ground before I started to dig it over. The hens always enjoyed me doing it - it gave them plenty of worms to eat. Some birds were always under my feet but the timid ones would dash in, pick up a worm then run off trying to find a quiet place to eat it in peace. I will never forget the mucking out, ugh! Scraping all their droppings off the drip board from under the perches into a bucket. I got used to it in time, I suppose I had to. If it hadn't been for all the enthusiastic gardeners that were round and about we would have been up to our eyes in hen muck.

Every Saturday morning my job was to take the bus into Altrincham to go and buy the food for our livestock. First it would be for the dog meat, standing in a queue outside a little wooden hut, situated just off Stamford New Road. The meat the lady sold was horsemeat, and by law it had to be dyed purple on at least one side to prevent it being sold for human consumption. Mum said that Towser ate better than we did; his chunk of meat was never fatty and often looked more appetising than ours did, except for the dye of course.

Now for the hens' grub. The 'grain shop' was on Shaw Road, just a short walk across George Street, passing Stanley's Market on the corner that sold fruit and vegetables. The grain shop was a hive of activity on a Saturday morning; a lot of smallholders came into Altrincham for all manner of supplies. I loved to stand and listen to all their gossip, "*The price o' stuff, gud gawd, ke'ps goin' up every bloomin' week.*" They would discuss the price of pigs and fowl, cows and sheep; it was very interesting ear-wigging their chatter, sometimes I was sorry when it was my turn to be served.

To mix with the chopped up boiled potato peelings and scraps, I had to get 7lbs of hen meal, which looked like ground up porridge oats. Then 4lb of corn and 1lb of something that smelled and looked a bit like paprika (not that I had ever heard of paprika in those days) - it was like coloured sawdust. Mum said this was to keep the hens in good condition. The heaviest item was the grit - luckily this wasn't required every week - seashells that had been crushed up. This helped them make the eggshells. On top of this I had to get dog biscuits. I could have done with a packhorse I can tell you. Luckily for me the bus station was very near. Thank goodness the garden lime came from Mr Nelson's shop on Riddings Road!

One week I had to call at Woolworths to buy something for Mum. So getting the joint for the dog first, in case they sold out, I walked down George Street, but had to be careful where I walked because the road was under repair. As I walked out of the store the driver of a steamroller, which had been parked nearby, suddenly blew its steam whistle and started to move off down the road with the normal violent shaking and juddering these monsters made as they started off. It made a lot of people, including me, jump out of our skins; one old lady stood with her hand on her heart. She made a quick recovery, because a few seconds later she was waving her umbrella up at the driver, and

shouting up to him. It was a good job the machine was making such a din or I might have learnt a few words Mum wouldn't have approved of.

Opposite Shaw Road, on George Street, was the office of the Altrincham and Timperley paper. One Saturday Auntie Babs gave me a note to take in along with some money to place an advertisement. I handed the note over to the young lady behind the counter and before I could speak she hurled at me, *"What's a Light Blue Lloyd Loom Bedroom Chair then?"* *"I think it's a sort of thing that's made like a dogs basket,"* I answered. She shrugged her shoulders, *"That's two and threepence."*

The war must have hurried the development of transport As soon as it ended the demise of steam powered vehicles was rapid. Many of the cars, vans and lorries had also been converted from petrol to run on gas. This special gas was carried in huge silver coloured bags that were fixed to a metal framework on their roofs. The diesel engine really developed during this period as well

The bus going to Altrincham one Saturday morning was quite full, and in charge was a very officious lady conductress. We eventually arrived at the bus stop near Navigation Road level crossing and train station; there was a very long queue. As the bus was drawing up she went down, keeping one foot on the last step and hung out, shouting at the queue, *"Only four, I can only take four more standing,"* Oh dear! No one took a blind bit of notice; they just pushed past her, crowding on. Earlier I had stood up to let a lady sit down so I was pushed along to the front of the bus so I couldn't see properly what was going on. Anyway, I heard the bell go and the bus set off amid howls of laughter.

When we got to the bus station I asked a man what it was all about. He told me that the conductress had been very cross, so she pushed past the passengers and stood on the footpath shouting up at them, with a gleam of victory in her eye, *"I'm not letting this bus go until five of you get off."* Someone rang the bell and the bus set off down the road leaving her standing there. He added with a wry smile, *"I wonder if the driver knew what he was doing?"*

In the garden we had big clumps of Michaelmas daisies, a great hiding place for a broody hen. We tried to keep a look out for hens doing this Houdini act, if Mum felt that the eggs were getting less. One day Mum saw a hen squeezing out between a chunk of

George Street, Altrincham, in the war years and below the Market Hall in the 1930s.
Courtesy of 'Altrincham: An Illustrated History', Pat Southern, Trafford Leisure Services

wire that had gone rusty - the hen was off like grease lightening to visit her nest in a neighbour's garden. Mum would sometimes put pot eggs under a broody hen to kid her - she said it was no use wasting eggs if chicks weren't wanted. A neighbour called over to us that they had found a clutch of eggs. It was no use telling them to keep these eggs. Mum said that we would have to let this one sit a batch of eggs, but this meant having to have a little house made with a run for her and her chicks.

So a little hut was made and situated on the grass patch that was our lawn. Soon most of them had hatched and little yellow balls of fluff were following the mother up and down whilst she scratched and clucked *"come here, I've found something interesting for you to eat."* This was the first of many sittings that would swell our stockholding. We would sell the older hens to neighbours, just so long as they could get someone to wring their necks.

When Mum decided to 'sit a hen', I knew we were in for a night of fun; we would sit around the kitchen table to sex the eggs. Mum threaded a darning needle with cotton thread and held it over the egg, and we all had a turn. If it swung in a straight line or went in a circle determined it as male or female, I don't recall which was which. To all you sceptics out there, it worked. This method ensured that only girlie eggs were chosen.

For some reason, Mum fed the birds one evening. She came back into the kitchen in a right state holding her left thumb and with mud all over her dress. Bertie was very agitated, strutting up and down and making a lot of noise, and when Mum had opened the pen door he had flown at her causing her to lose her balance. She had slipped and got a splinter under the nail of her thumb . Unfortunately the wood was rotting slightly and just broke up as Auntie Babs tried to get it out. *"This is no good Nellie, you'd be better going to see what Mr Kay thinks about it, perhaps drawing ointment may remove it?"*

I went round to Riddings Road with Mum but when Mr Kay saw it he just shook his head. *"Drawing ointment won't do anything for that Mrs Scott, I'm very sorry."* She took the Chemist's advice, we caught the bus and Mum was soon being seen by a doctor at Altrincham Hospital. This time it was me that had to wait while Mum had her treatment. I looked around at the other people sat waiting. I saw someone I knew so I went and sat next to him. *"Hello Mr Allcroft."* *"Well, what are you doing here, Peter?"* While I was telling him all about Mum's accident I noticed his hands, they were very badly burnt in places. Mr Allcroft was a fireman and lived up the road from us. He had a daughter called Joyce who was a friend of our Muriel. He had burnt his hands very badly fighting a fire during an air raid. I asked him why he had not worn gloves - he would not have burnt his hands. He gave a little laugh, and explained that the gloves would have melted over his hands and stuck to his skin. This would have made matters a lot worse.

When Mum came out of the treatment room she had a very big bandage that doubled the size of the thumb and she was not well pleased at all. The doctor had to give her an injection against lockjaw and a local anaesthetic to stop the pain whilst he cut most of her nail away. The anaesthetic was wearing off now and her thumb was throbbing.

On the way home Mum was threatening that 'ruddy bird', saying that he was always trouble. Now he would definitely have to go, she meant it as well. The following day a man came and rung the bird's neck and we had him for dinner two days later. The man also brought Bertie's replacement, a Light Sussex, who seemed to like his new home after he had chased his new wives around a bit. Mum said he was showing them that he was their new boss.

The annual fair arrived and set up shop on the usual field in Altrincham on the other side of Timperley Municipal Golf Course. Our transport was the usual in those days, Shanks's pony. Passing our school, we crossed Stockport Road, climbed the wall like paratroopers trying not to be seen, and then, keeping near to the ground so as not to put our lives in danger of flying golf balls or being seen, we picked our way across the hallowed turf. We thought it a dare devil act, crossing the playground of the rich big wigs. We didn't understand then what municipal meant. As soon as we got to the fair we visited a few sideshows. First of all it was the shooting gallery. Paying our money and taking up the air rifles, we were going to show them how to shoot. The clay pipes needn't have been afraid. Perhaps we would show our prowess on the coconut shy? Well we both hit one, but that was all, we both agreed they must be stuck on. Our first ride was on the Queen Mary. This looked like a giant shoebox that rocked up and down on a central axle like a giant seesaw. It had bench seats across and it certainly threw you about as it went very near to vertical.

We waited for one of the bank of six swing boats to become vacant, and we managed to nab it. Then we headed for the Dodgems, where we got told off for doing head on bumps. After the Waltzer we practically fell down the last couple of steps. Holding each other up we made our way to the Coconut Shy, just to show them that we could win one - but we didn't - so we called it a day, buying some candy floss with our last few pennies.

Our kitchen had a small square bay window, just low enough to see out of when sat at the table. Granny Monks, Harry's granny, was a small lady who always wore her hair done up in a bun, right on top of her head. She walked with a bouncing gait and at teatime, every Friday, we would see the top of her head bobbing past the window. She would be bringing the rinds from her bacon ration, all cut up into very small pieces in a twist of grease-proofed paper, to present to Mum. We would hear a little timid knock on the door; the same ritual every week. *"Hello Mrs Scott, I've just fetched some rinds for your hens."* Mum always had her reward ready and waiting, her egg, which had been laid that day. Harry's mum, Mrs Monks, always bought as many eggs as Mum could let her have, so they were never short of an egg at their house. But to Granny Monks, this was her egg, provided by herself. When Mum handed the egg over she would always say, *"Oh no, it doesn't matter, it's only a few rinds,"* as she took the egg out of Mum's hand and bobbed back up the path. Mum always said, *"Bless her, the dear old soul."* The ritual always made us all laugh.

It was not unusual for the neighbours to be found in our kitchen either confiding or seeking advice from my Mum. Mrs Monks was round at our house one day talking to Mum in the kitchen as I was flitting in and out. I kept hearing snippets of conversation like *"She must have been retired over two years now."* Then I heard Mum say, *"Well Cissie, she's not been pulling her weight now for well over a year or so I agree, so you might.... er....."* The talking stopped as I came within earshot. I thought nothing of it - they would be talking about someone up the road, wouldn't they? A few days later Harry and I were out playing and we happened to go back to his house. As we walked in through the gate we could not believe what we saw. Harry's 'uncle' was holding Mabel upside down by her feet, over a grid; blood pouring from her neck. He had cut her throat and she was bleeding to death. She just hung there, showing the occasional signs of life by flapping her wings. This was far too much for Harry and me, how anyone could do such a horrible thing to our Mabel. Spontaneously we charged at him and started to hit him, but it did no good, poor old Mabel died soon after. Harry said that he would not help to eat her. I wonder? When I told Mum she looked at me and said, *"Sorry Peter, but I needed the money."*

At certain times we would have a glut of eggs; so to take account of the hens' rest period in winter, Mum would 'put some down', as she called it. This meant filling an old dolly tub with water and mixing in a tin of waterglass, an egg preserving fluid which sealed the shell so that air could not get in and turn it bad. Throughout the laying season the eggs were added to the tub daily, and they would stay nice and fresh. When we required an egg or two we found it quite convenient for the first few months, because the eggs were near the top of the barrel. But guess who had to get them out when they got towards the bottom of the barrel - you've got it, yours truly. You could bet your bottom dollar my sister Muriel wouldn't. The water was icy cold and the gooey mess clung to your arm like something out of a horror film. Why we never thought of using a child's fishing net I will never know.

Sometime towards the end of the war Mum branched out and invested in three ducks. They got on all right with the hens but later they were separated into a home of their own. Mum thought they would appreciate some water to splash about in, so she managed to acquire a large old bathroom washbasin. I dug the hole to set it into the ground, the plug hole was bunged up, and then we ferried buckets of water from the kitchen. The ducks could smell the water and they quickly marched in to their new swimming pool, one behind the other, quacking loudly. They thoroughly enjoyed it, quacking and flapping for hours, in and out of the basin, looking around as if to say 'aren't we clever'. Their eggs were a lovely greenish blue colour, bigger and that bit stronger than the hens' eggs.

Dad was demobbed on the 20th December 1945, just in time for our first Christmas after the war. To celebrate his safe homecoming we had a family get together. Uncle Geoffrey was home on leave; he had acquired a duck and this went well with two chickens. It must have been difficult for Mum roasting them all. The table looked fit for a king. Nine sat around the table as Grandad and Grandma Scott and Auntie Dorothy came, and Auntie Babs was still living with us anyway.

Towards the end of 1946 Mum and Dad came to the conclusion that it was time to get rid of the livestock and Dad dismantled the pen.

The Bleeding Wolf and the garage next door.
Below: A wonderfully emotive 1940-50s photo in Altrincham.
Courtesy of 'Altrincham, Past and Present', Gillian Fitzpatrick, Trafford Leisure Services

10. My Pals

Harry's mum was Cissie and his dad was Harry. Then came Sydney, Harry's big brother, followed by his older sister, Winnie, who I am glad to say was not as bossy as our Muriel. Not unusually for those days, they had living with them Harry's Granny Monks, who I have mentioned.

Mr Monks was a robust man and he always seemed to be wearing his working overalls, splashed with oil and grease. They were an odd couple, he being so big while his wife was so slim. I don't ever remember seeing Mrs Monks without a cigarette hanging from the corner of her mouth and this gave her a nicotine stain above the right side of her top lip - in contrast to her husband who had nicotine stained fingers. Going into their house was like being in thick smog in the centre of Manchester on a November's day.

Then there also was the dog, Billy, a black and white smaller version of the modern Dulux Dog, I always wondered how on earth he was able to see with all that hair hanging over his eyes. They also had a black cat called Blackie. Harry's mum always referred to Billy's lead as a leash, and a bus as a buzz, due to their origin from Weaste, on the west side of Salford, although as the crow flies it was only ten miles from Gerrard Avenue.

Harry's father was the workshop manager of a garage called The Bleeding Wolf, which was next door to a pub of the same name at Hale. We always thought it was naughty to say the name so we used it as often as we thought we could get away with it. We slipped up sometimes and got a clout.

Mr Monks had a car, an Armstrong-Siddeley, black and yellow and very smart. When we could get away with it, we would sit in it and pretend to go to the seaside. We got caught a few times and got a clip around our ears, because we had been told to keep out of it.

Our Muriel often went round to play with Winnie, and they would do boring things like do their hair and put make up on; they would have to rub it all off before Winnie's mum saw it or else they would be in trouble - it was her make-up they were using. Other times they would just play records. Harry and I, if we hadn't anything important to do, would try to annoy them and sometimes, only sometimes, we would come off worse. Sydney must have started work by then because we didn't see much of him; I only have a few recollections of him, but two incidents come to mind.

One involved my birthday present from Auntie Babs. She had told me weeks before that she had bought me something very special, so on my birthday all I could think was *"when are Auntie Babs and Uncle Geoffrey going to come."* I saw their car turn into the road and immediately left my pals and ran to meet and escort them into our house, but not before Uncle had lifted a box off the rear seat of the car. *"Mum; Auntie's come."* I could hardly contain my excitement.

After they had sat down Uncle said, *"Babs, you'd better give him his present, he's that excited."* But instead of handing me the box she called me to her and said, *"You've got to guess what it might be, so you've got to put this blind fold on."* The rustling of paper came to an end, and then I felt a ring being put on my head. *"What do you think it is?" "A cowboy hat?" "No, have another guess." "Ingun hat with feathers?" "For goodness sake Babs, stop teasing the boy and let him see it."*

When the blindfold had been removed Auntie was holding a mirror in front of my face, as she moved it back I saw a top hat on my head. On inspection I found that it was just like a real one only smaller. After the slight disappointment of it not being a cowboy hat I really liked it. Uncle put a hand in his pocket and gave me a packet of toffee cigarettes; they had one end painted red so that they would look like the real thing. *"There now you can be a proper little toff can't you?"*

Some weeks later I had gone to play with Harry wearing my top hat. Whilst we were playing in his garden Sydney came up behind me and snatched my hat off and ran out of the front gate. Of course we gave chase, but he started to kick it around like a football using the junction of Leicester Avenue as the goal posts. When he eventually got fed up and kicked it back it was a bit battered, but still wearable - no thanks to Sydney.

"Oi! You two," shouted Sydney one day as he beckoned Harry and me towards him. This is my second recollection of Sydney. We followed him into their garden. *"So you two think you're big lads now, do you?"* We just looked at each other and shrugged our shoulders. *"Right then, we'll soon see,"* and he walked off into the garage and came out with a very tall set of steps. *"We're not cleaning windows,"* shouted Harry. Sydney set the steps up on the grass.

"This is what you've to do," he said, and he climbed to the top and cocked a leg over, sitting astride the steps. Within seconds he started to rock the steps forward and backward balancing on the right then the left legs. Back and forth he went defying gravity until after about eight rocks, he could no longer control the movement. We thought he was going to come a cropper but at the last moment he slid off to land on his feet as the steps clattered down behind him.

"There then, how's that for a dare devil trick; come on, our Harry, show what a big lad you are." Harry looked at me; the gauntlet had been thrown down and I watched as Harry climbed to the top and reluctantly cocked his leg over. Goaded on by his big brother Harry started to rock. The second little rock was enough and he jumped to the ground. Somehow the steps managed to regain their upright position as Harry got to his feet.

"*Well that wasn't very good, was it, you big softy. Right, go on up Peter, go on. It's your go now.*" I didn't have much option did I? When I was sat on the top step Harry looked like an ant. "*Go on then Scottie, let's see what you can do.*" I didn't do any better than Harry.

We soon learnt to control gravity longer before reaching the point of no return when you started to drop forward; the trick was to stay sat down and jump off to land on your feet at the last possible moment as the steps fell. Do you know we never considered what may have happened if the point of no return occurred on a backward movement? Within a few weeks we were champions at it and even Sydney said he was proud of us both.

One sunny afternoon my Mum and Mrs Long were having a cup of tea on their terrace. I was playing cowboys and indians with Geoffrey when his mother introduced me to my first cliché Whenever our gang played this game, or cops and robbers, if you got shot, you fell to the ground pretending to be dead, counted to ten, then you could get up and play again. Anyway, I was stood on this high rocky outcrop (the terrace) surveying the prairie (looking for Geoffrey) when he ambushed me good and proper from behind a large bush. As I stood writhing in my death agony, these words of wisdom hit my ears - "*He's dead but he won't lie down,*" followed by some tittering. I thought, "*I'd better do my death dive now,*" so I immediately fell to the ground off the two-foot high terrace wall onto the lawn. Mrs Long and my Mum were quite impressed.

The couple of swans that came home every year had arrived; they flew a couple of circuits over the pond in preparation for their landing. If we were lucky we would all have time to get down to the pond to see them splash down. They would come in low over the detached house on Acresfield Road, and with landing gear down they would skim onto the water and settle. After they had stretched their wings they would fold them into that sort of arch shape and swim around looking majestic.

After parading their magnificence they would put their wings down and paddle over to inspect the patch of bullrushes before starting to re-build their nest ravaged by the winter months. It was the same ritual every year, but we were not always lucky to see them land. When they had settled in we would see them waddle their way up the gardens to be fed. They were quite friendly for a few weeks, but once Mrs Swan had hatched her cygnets then things changed; we had to be very careful, we didn't go too close to the edge of the pond. If we did, one of them would come across the pond skimming the water, spitting and hissing. If you ignored it they would come off the water and chase you with wings flapping - very scary. I think Geoffrey tried to outstay his welcome that bit too long one time - just the once mind you. The swan chased him up his garden with its wing flapping and its beak an inch off his bum. He was so scared that he ended up crying, and not only frightened of the swan, but of his mum as well, as she had been watching him tease the swan. She gave him a good slap and a telling off. We had been told in no uncertain terms to stay away from them as they could break a man's arm with their wings.

Keeping the swans company was a family of moorhens that lived on the pond throughout the year, and they also brought their babies into the world amongst the bullrushes. We loved to watch their quick darting antics as they buzzed around the reed bed, it looked like they were playing hide and seek. They made us laugh with their heads bobbing back and forth. Another bonus of living near the pond was that in the summer time we would see dragonflies flitting around our gardens in the warm air, showing off their multi-coloured bodies and their transparent coloured wings.

The cowboy and indian films must have had an influence on Harry and me, because we were playing at Harry's when he suddenly said to *me, "Let's be blood brothers."* Later Harry came out of the house with Sydney's penknife. *"Come on, let's do it."* We stood there; he put his thumb out and put a little cut in it, the blood started to flow. Oh well, one down one to go. I took the knife and after some hesitation I summed up the courage and cut my thumb, then we held the cuts together for a few minutes so our blood would mingle. *"Now we big blood brothers, just like heap big Indian Chief Sitting Bull,"* said Harry.

There was another bloodletting incident at Harry's. His mum was not feeling very well and we decided that helping her would cheer her up. *"It will help if we chop some sticks for the fire,"* suggested Harry. There was plenty of wood to go at, some about six inches wide and cut into reasonable lengths. We had often seen Sydney chop wood like this, so with the wood stacked and the axe at the ready, we sat cross-legged on the path outside the back door. *"You hold it and I'll chop it,"* I said to Harry. He nodded his head in agreement and we started on the wider pieces first. With uncanny precision I chopped two sticks, then I raised the chopper for the third time and down it came. The next thing I saw, and heard, was Harry grasping his thumb and howling his head off. Blood was seeping between the fingers holding the injury. *"Time I wasn't here,"* I thought - on the way home I fretted *"I've chopped his thumb off"*, and a wave of nausea swept over me.

Minutes later Mrs Monks, now feeling a whole lot worse than before, came round to our house, and not bothering to knock, came into the kitchen and looked Mum straight in the eye. *"We're off to the hospital; you should see what your Peter's done to my Lal's thumb!"* With that she ushered Harry out of the back door and she didn't close it quietly either. The thumb was heavily swathed in a clean white cloth, but blood seeped through staining the top of the 'make do and mend' bandage, made from old sheets - we all resorted to this in those days. Mum looked at me. *"I want the truth now! How did it happen?"*

A couple of hours passed and Mrs Monks and Harry got back. She knocked on the back door and walked straight in. *"Two stitches he's had, and all the blithering time we've been down there, and me feeling bloody awful. Oh I'll 'ave to 'ave a fag."* Mum suggested a cup of tea, during which time she managed to get a few words in. Finally we reached an agreement after Harry and I persuaded his mum that it was an accident. *"I'm not feeling at all well you know; I 'ad to go to bed this afternoon, then that little sod comes and pushes his bleeding thumb under me nose bawling his head off. I could 'ave done without that."* Mum consoled her with a little hug. Poor Mrs Monks, she always seemed to be coming round to complain to Mum, *"Your Peter, he's been hitting our Harry again."*

One evening after we had had our tea, Harry and Ian called for me, and as we walked out Geoffrey came out of his front door. I picked the old tattered tennis ball up from behind the gate and threw it to Ian, saying to Geoffrey *"Your turn in goals."* After a while we tired of the same old game of trying to knock the paint off the gate. *"What shall we do now,"* pleaded Harry. *"Let's play at being Mr Lloyd I suggested, it must be near the time he comes home."* *"Yeah!"* they all said in unison and we all rushed off to get our guns.

"If we're going to ambush him we'd better hide quickly." Just then Philip came out of his gate to join us. *"Well that's one problem solved,"* said I, *"we can now use Phil's garden for one of the ambush points."* We lay in wait for him behind a couple of garden walls. Just in time; around the corner came our scientist, Mr Lloyd, a master spy working in a subversive occupation for the Germans. After he was safely behind his front door, the one of us whose turn it was to be Mr Lloyd would go up to the corner of Acresfield Road and walk down into the trap. As soon as he passed the Harding's gate a policeman would come out behind him, and this was the signal for the other police to show themselves. Then we would capture him, to be dragged to our den for questioning and torture. After the war everything seemed to turn out all right, as they still lived at number five for many years - so our suspicions must have been wrong.

When we were playing cowboys and indians, it soon set Mum wondering how long it would be before I mithered her for the old sheet. *"Can we make a tent in the garden, ple-e-ase Mu-um?"* If she was in a good mood she would soon be out with the clothes maiden and an old blanket. As we grew older and bigger, the maiden was replaced with the washing line which we tied round the tree, and when the covers were thrown over the tent it would be held in place along the sides with bricks; very ingenious.

If it happened to be raining Mum might let us make a tent in the living room. Most times after we had made the tent, playing cowboys and indians would be forgotten as we sat and passed a bottle of pop round in the shade, and a few sweets, and of course planned 'important' things to do.

Occasionally I would go and stay at Harry's for the night. It may have been when Mum wasn't feeling very well. When we eventually got to bed, when Harry's family had had enough of us, we would still be chatting away, trying to frighten each other with ghostly noises. We liked it best when a car came down the road and its lights cast moving shadows of the curtains on the ceiling, changing their shape as they moved over the ceiling. If the wind was blowing, the big rhododendron bushes in the front garden added their shadows to those of the curtains and the light above the track was filled with ghostly heads. We would dive under the bedclothes out of harm's way.

Early on during the war we were told that Harry's father had been arrested by the police for the serious offence of impersonating an officer of the Royal Air Force. The garage where he worked at Hale was very near to Ringway Airport, where a lot of RAF air crew were stationed. This is how he acquired the uniform of a Squadron Leader Pilot. Harry and I heard that he would go into Manchester and live a Walter Mitty existence of a super hero, and of course he would be treated to many drinks. We heard people say that the reason may have been due to his frustration of not being able to join-up.

One day after he had been sentenced to a few years in prison, Harry and I were playing in his garden when a Spitfire flew over the house very low, almost knocking the chimney pots off and frightening us to death. The pilot waggled his wings and soared up into the sky. We wondered was he saying hard luck or serves you right? We would never know.

Mrs Monks was a 'good sort', as people would say, and very down to earth but a bit of a 'rum un'. Her favourite place on a Friday and Saturday night was The Sylvan Hotel. The gang passed the pub on the way to go fishing in Fairywell Brook. One very hot summer's day there was no 'pop' left for Harry, but he kept bothering his mum. *"I've told you, it's Wednesday, the ruddy shop's shut, I haven't got a fizzy drink, now go and play."* *"But mum,"* pleaded Harry. She had just about had enough of his pestering. She got a glass, filled it with cold water, put three spoonfuls of Andrews Liver Salts in and gave it to him, saying *"Here's your fizzy drink, now go and s*** yourself to death and stop your ruddy mithering."*

One day Mum went round to see Mrs Monks and when she came back she told us she had just made a pot of tea, but Mum saw the cat jump up onto the table, stick its head in a cup and have a drink of milk. Mrs Monks knocked the cat flying, but instead of washing the cup, put some more milk in it and asked my Mum if she was stopping for a cuppa. Mum said she came home thirsty.

One of the things our gang enjoyed doing was going fishing. With our fishing nets over our shoulders and a jam jar with a string handle hanging from our mitts, we would trudge down to the brook at the bottom of Sylvan Avenue. At what we called our spot, was the wooden bridge onto Sale Rugby field, but we never had any reason to venture over it. The water of Fairywell Brook was about five foot wide and four to six inches deep, and it contained our prey, tiddlers and newts. Tiddlers were in abundance and we soon had some in our jam jars, but we found it a bit harder to catch the newts. They did not all get away though. When we had had enough we sat on the bridge and dangled our legs trying to reach the water with our toes.

If the mood took us, off would come our shoes and socks and we would have a paddle around, but as soon as we did this, we all knew that we would end up having a splashing match. It always ended with us soaked through, so unless we were feeling brave it was only done in hot weather. Still we must have had some sort of defence mechanism against going home wet, because we would always arrive home quite dry. On occasions our mums would give us a picnic, and then we would sit on the river bank and indulge in swapping sandwiches, and drinking pop purchased from Mr Morris's on our way.

Diagonally to the left of the field there was a public footpath which led to a footbridge over the electric railway and on to the Bridgewater Canal towpath. A small tunnel under the canal led to the other bank. We never caught anything in the canal because the water was so murky - we could not see the fish. *"We will have to get a fishing line,"* I said one day. Harry and Ian suggested that I save up to buy one, seeing it was my idea. Tuppence three farthings they were at Mr Morris's shop.

Three weeks later, I was still a farthing short. Now where was it that I saw that farthing? Whoopee! I remembered, in Mum's jewellery case on her dressing table. I decided to borrow it until I got my spending money on Saturday. I rushed to the post office; what if they'd all sold out? A good few people were waiting to be served, some of them children like me. I hoped they were not all wanting fishing lines. *"Now then young man, what can I get for you, some sweets is it?"* Mr Morris made me jump. *"N-n-no th-th-thank y-y-you, I w-w-want a fishing l-line p-p.-please."* Yes, I had made my purchase, so I rushed back to show the gang and they were suitably impressed. It wasn't far off tea time now so we made plans to go to the canal next day. *"Who's going to dig the worms up?"* No reply, just a shrug of the shoulders. So we messed with the old tennis ball until the first mum shouted *"Tea's ready."* We all agreed to meet up again after tea.

I was just finishing my tea when Mum had gone to answer a knock at the front door; we could all hear her talking to a gentleman. We heard the door close and back she came, sat down and continued her tea. Addressing me in a manner, that I knew was suspicious, she asked, *"And what have you been up to today then?"*

After I had reeled off the day's exploits, and with Muriel and Babs now listening with great interest, Mum continued to ask me things, and then suddenly said, *"Have you bought anything today?"* *"Me? Yes, a fishing line Mum."* *"And where did you get the money?"* The sound of a little knock came at the back door, and Muriel went to see who it was, *"Is Peter coming out?"* *"I don't think so,"* she said closing the door quickly; she couldn't wait to get back. *"Well,"* says Mum; *"I am still waiting for an answer."*

My mind was working overtime, should I tell her that I had borrowed a farthing

The Bridgewater Canal,
and below, Park Road in the 1930s.
Courtesy of 'Altrincham, Past and Present', Gillian Fitzpatrick, Trafford Leisure Services

from her jewellery box; better, I thought. *"From m-m-my spends, I saved up for a few w-w-weeks, b-but I was a farthing short so I b-borrowed one from your b-box on the dressing table; honest I w-w-was going to put it b-b-back, honest Mum."*

"You won't have to now will you," she said, placing the coin on the table in front of me. Before anyone could say anything Muriel piped in with *"Is he going to get a good hiding Mum, is he?"* Mum told her to mind her own business and go and do the washing up. As she opened the door into the scullery, she nastily lifted up Dad's razor strap hanging on the back and let it fall back making a slapping sound. The feel of it hitting my backside came vividly into my now tormented mind. Muriel stood at the sink grinning at me. Auntie Babs pushed her chair back and lit a cigarette, and folded her arms to listen.

Mum told me that my so-called farthing was in fact a half sovereign made of gold and worth a lot of money. *"If it had been mine he'd be getting a good thrash......."* Auntie saw Mum glaring at her, and didn't say another word.

This escapade earned me three smacks with the strap on my trousered bum. OK yes it hurt, but I didn't like upsetting my Mum either. Mum told me she did believe that I would have replaced it with the farthing but, she explained, she would have lost a valuable keepsake of her mother's; had it not been for the honesty of Mr Morris she would never had got it back. *"Just think, if you had spent it anywhere else it would have been lost for ever; why on earth didn't you ask me to lend you a farthing?"*

It turned out that when Mr Morris served me he had known straight away what I had given him and thought it best to keep it and return it safely to Mum. I am very glad he did. My bum was sore for an hour or so, but next day my pride was hurt even more. Mum told me that I had to take the fishing line back.

As I walked past Harry's he was just on his way to call for me. Seeing my glum face he said, *"What's up Pete?"* so I had to tell him my tale of woe. *"Ah 'eck, what are we going to do now?"* I just shrugged my shoulders as we walked in silence to take the precious fishing line back to the post office.

Whilst Mr Long was serving King and Country in far off lands, every month or so he sent a parcel to his wife and son. On most occasions the postman had to leave it at our house because Mrs Long was out at work. Many a time the parcel would arrive in a damaged state. They contained a variety of nuts and some would spill out onto our kitchen table - if they didn't come readily, well they received a little help from Auntie Babs, *"Oh dear look what's happened, never mind we'll enjoy them"* she would say.

Not long after he had been demobbed, Mr Long started clearing a large area of his garden, right against the fence, just past the end of their house. Dad was worried what was going on, and for about a fortnight, it was the same at every meal time. He nodded towards their house and would say, *"Nellie, 'ave yer found anything about what's goin' on yet?"* He had to wait a couple of weeks before it became clear that they were having a brick garage built. Some weeks later, Mr Long came home with a brand new Ford Anglia.

Timperley station
Courtesy of 'Looking back at Timperley', Hazel Pryor

11. The Smokers

Another summer had arrived, and the time had come to make our plans for the school holidays. We called a meeting of the gang after lunch in Geoffrey's greenhouse - always the best place because his mother was at work most of the time, plus the fact that it was further away from the prying eyes of a nosy sister. Lots of important things had to be sorted out, planning adventures, and important issues to discuss - like smoking!

Smoking was very fashionable in these days, and most people were imitating their relatives and cinema screen idols. The questions were, should we, could we, and would we be able to get away with it. The most important question of all was where was the money to come from? Phew! This decision-making was hard work. We put the idea to a vote. Right we would try it. I think Philip wasn't quite sure, but the rest of us agreed - *"well, after all most grown-ups do it, so why shouldn't we?"* One question had to be answered; who would get them? We played stone, paper, scissors to decide. Ian won, as he may have thought, but whichever way you looked at it he had to get them. A packet of five Woodbines would be the cheapest, it was decided.

After the halfpennies, but mostly farthings, had been collected, it was up to Ian to do his stuff. Next day he told us that he had been successful at the newsagents on Riddings Road where he wasn't known and he presented the packet of Woodbines. We hastily called a special meeting. and Ian got a pat on the back, as he had also had the brains to get hold of a few matches from the box on his gas cooker.

One of the gang suggested that we break them in half to try. *"No,"* came emphatically from Harry in a near panic, *"that will make two dog-ends, just light one and pass it round."* We had a vote on this issue and Harry's recommendation won the day. This being so, he had the honour of lighting it, which he did with great aplomb, although he failed to light the match on the seat of his pants like the cowboys did and wasted two valuables matches trying. *"Use the brick"* we all shouted at him as we pointed to one that was sitting right next to him. Harry's initial draw of smoke had no apparent ill effects, and he passed it to me; holding it as 'posh' as I could I placed the cigarette between my lips, and sucked in my cheeks as much as I could, to get a proper turn.

Oh dear me, I wished I hadn't. With such a big mouthful of smoke it was inevitable that some would find its way into my lungs. As the shock waves hit me the fag dropped from my fingers and like Dante's Inferno a cloud of smoke erupted from my facial orifices. I could have sworn it was escaping from my ears as well. What with the choking and spluttering sounds, you can imagine I felt a right Charlie. They all fell about laughing; even Philip had a laugh at my expense. My little experience only spurred them on to do better than their esteemed leader. Which they did of course and I was proud of them.

We all agreed that Harry got the hang of it very quickly. It could have been because all his family smoked - we suspected that he pinched a few on the quiet. Only Auntie Babs smoked in our house, and she didn't give me any opportunity to pinch any.

One day we saw Ian's mum, Mrs Harkness, leaving my house and going next door to Geoffrey's. We sensed all was not well. It turned out Ian had forgotten the rules about hiding the cigarettes in the greenhouse and left them in his pocket. After he'd gone to bed, his mum decided to wash his trousers and 'Oh dear,' we were well and truly dropped in it. Needless to say, Ian lost his position of procurer - I'm sure he wasn't sorry. Trouble was our pocket money was stopped for a couple of weeks as part of our punishment.

At our next meeting it was voted that I should take over the job of acquiring the fags, as we now referred to them, of course when money was next available. As it happened inside the railway station between the two ticket windows there was a small stall which sold newspapers and cigarettes. The cigarettes were kept in an open rough wooden cabinet stacked in columns partitioned with strips of wood. I had got to know the young man who looked after the stall, and I would quite often stop and chat with him on my way home. A few weeks passed and there was still not enough money in the kitty. I was talking to the young man at the station one afternoon when an evil plan suddenly formed in my mind. Whilst he was talking to a customer, I pinched two packs of Woodbines. The stallholder must have seen me out of the corner of his eye as I ran out. Half way down the approach I turned and he was stood at the station entrance waving his arms and shouting after me.

All I wanted to do now was to keep on running to reach the safety of home. I couldn't run any more as I was having an asthma attack so I started walking and thinking. I would have to sneak past him in future - if there was to be future outside of gaol! The fear of what I had just accomplished crept into my mind. When I got home I had feelings of remorse and fear. Panic set in, why did I do such a crazy thing, what can I do, what should I do with them? I stood in Mum's bedroom in front of the wardrobe mirror looking at myself. The thought of the policeman's truncheon which hung in the wardrobe brought fears to me of being locked up. Rational thought eluded me. I'll have to smoke them all, I said to myself. I wished Harry was there - he would help me.

Would you believe it, I tried to smoke three at a time. Muriel would be home soon and Mum soon after. It hadn't entered my head to hide them; it was only when I was part way through the first three that logic manifested itself. I would flush these down the toilet and hide the rest. I managed to do this just in time, as Muriel and Mum came home together. A few hours later it occurred to me that if Mum had gone into the bedroom I would have been for it, as she would have smelt the smoke.

One evening after we had finished our tea, Auntie Babs brought a cigar out of her pocket and lit it up. I had only seen Dad and other men smoke cigars, so I watched fascinated. I said to her *"Ladies don't smoke those, they're for men."* When she had smoked it down to the last inch, she took a side look at Mum, and said to me, with a smile on her face, *"here you are then, seeing that you're a man, do you want to try it?"*

My so-called manhood at nine and threequarters, had been challenged, in front of Muriel as well, so I took the cigar and proceeded to show them. Puff after puff I took in rather quick succession. Oh dear, who's started turning the kitchen round and round?

Putting the 'thing' down, I left the spinning room and literally crawled up stairs, feeling very sick and dizzy. Wanting to be near the lavatory I lay on Mum's bed with my head on the bolster between the two pillows. It felt as if someone was spinning the bed round and round.

Later that night, after I had recovered, I went down stairs to face my tormentors; the laughter that greeted me didn't make me feel any better. They told me that they had seen the colour of my face change to a horrible green very quickly. I had been taught a lesson that I would never forget.

The packaging of cigarettes had to be cut to the minimum during the war; cardboard packets were not allowed, only printed-paper packets. There were no tops to the packets, especially on the smaller popular cigarettes like Woodbines, Player's Weights and Park Drive. There were other varieties towards the end of the war, a Turkish brand called 'Pasha' and another cheap brand called 'Turf'. The larger fags, the ones that we could never afford, were Players Navy Cut, Craven 'A', Senior Service, Gold Leaf, Piccadilly and Four Square.

The variety was greatly increased when the American Forces started throwing them around as gifts. Lucky Strike, Camel, Marlbrough and Pall Mall. The way the Yanks opened their packs was unique, tearing about a half inch square off the top right hand corner to reveal four cigarettes. The packet was tapped on the other hand when a cigarette jumped up about an inch and was placed between the lips whilst the packet was lowered, leaving the cigarette in the mouth ready for lighting. We gang members thought this was very swish but when we tried it with our packs the cigarettes fell on the ground.

All through her life Auntie Babs smoked Du Maurier, a red box with a flip lid. Dad always smoked a pipe and St. Bruno Flake. One day I saw him with what looked like a fat stick of liquorice in his left hand, his penknife in his right and cutting bits off it. *"What's that for Dad? "It's a type of tobacco I'm trying out"* I don't think he liked it very much as I didn't see it anymore!

When I was about thirteen, Harry and I were stood waiting to be served in Mr Morris's newsagents. The man in front of us said *"Tin of the usual please Mr Morris."* We wondered what this 'usual' was, so we paid full attention. We made our purchase, and low and behold the man was outside opening his little tin, so we stood and opened a caramel each and kept a close watch. He appeared to take a deep breath, like a big sigh, then he put thumb and index finger into the tin and, whatever he pulled out, he put on the closed fist of his left hand and to our amazement took a big sniff. *"Ah that's better."* He walked off sniffing loudly.

We asked Sydney about the brown powder and he told it was snuff - made from tobacco. Days later, when we were in Altrincham, Harry and I called at a tobacconists and bought a tin of this snuff. When we got home we couldn't wait to try it. While Harry waited in anticipation I opened the tin, then we both tried to copy the man outside Mr Morris's shop. One, two, three, go, we said in unison. Harry and I never did anything by half, oh no! We were rendered dumb - dumb being the operative word. Tears streamed down our faces; our noses and the backs of our mouths were on fire; even our ears were popping. We nearly sneezed ourselves to death - we thought that we might end up in hospital. Would our noses ever be the same again we wondered as Harry lifted the bin lid and I threw the stuff in.

Unfortunately my childhood smoking pranks were not the end of my smoking. It was a progression to thirty-five a day for most of my adult life. Following a heart attack in April 1993 when I spent three days in coronary care, I stopped. After my quad by-pass operation the surgeon told my wife Glenys that I had emphysema as well. A couple of months later I had three blockages in the main artery of my left leg. I was lucky not to lose it.

When we were young and didn't know better, we always said that anyone who acted daft or appeared to have a screw loose would end up in Macclesfield (Parkside). Sadly Harry's Mum was to end her life in such a place.

I was also very upset when I recently found out that my old pal Harry had died of lung cancer in 1985, just a month after his 51st birthday. Bless you Harry, and thank you for the times we shared together. His sister Winnie also died of the same complaint in her early forties.

My old pal Harry

South Drive, Park Road, TIMPERLEY.

Attractively Designed and Substantially Built

HOUSES for SALE

£850 and £675

FRANK WHITELEY, B.A. (Hons. Architecture)

Builder and Contractor.

One of the many developments in Timperley from the 1930s

12. Life at No 9 with Auntie Babs and Muriel

The large bedroom at the back of our house was occupied by Mum and Dad, overlooking Dad's pride and joy, the garden and the pond. I presume Grandma Bagshaw and Muriel shared the larger front bedroom, and when Grandma died, Muriel had it all to herself.

One Saturday as I dashed in to go to the loo, blimey I thought, there certainly was a great amount of activity going on in Muriel's bedroom. Unable to contain my curiosity I opened the door and was met with Muriel's *"what do you want then? Go and mind your own business."* *"We'll have less of that young lady, just because you've got to make a sacrifice, you'll have to do more than this before you're through and don't you forget it."* *"What's going on Mum?"* I asked. Mum's reply stunned me, *"Auntie Babs is coming to live with us until the war's over."*

If I had understood what depression was, well I would have been depressed. I lumbered down the stairs with my head resting on my shoes thinking I will have to find Harry and tell him my sad news. Then I thought, well it's not all bad news as I realised that what had made Muriel so bad tempered was that she was going to have to share her bedroom. On that fateful day in October 1941, by good luck or good management, I happened to be out when she arrived. When I eventually arrived home she was in residence - and I noticed she hadn't lost any weight.

Our Towser was also having his territory invaded; by Ginger the cat and Karl the dachshund, so I had an ally in the family, that was one consolation.

I was very pleased to still have the small bedroom to myself, although a few boxes did find their way under my bed. When I first sneaked a peek into their room I couldn't believe my eyes, the stuff she had brought with her was stacked high against the fireplace wall completely hiding it. The double bed had been turned up against the opposite wall to make more space, and it left but a thirty-inch corridor from the door to the dressing table in the bay window, which now displayed Babs's make-up and jewellery, alongside Muriel's bits and pieces. And whenever the wardrobe door was opened there was a horrid sickly smell of mothballs.

Whatever possessed me I shall never know. I know I shouldn't have been in the bedroom of her majesty Muriel, but I had had to look through the window at something important. When I left the window, something took my eye, Auntie Babs's bright red button earrings, the clip on type. I picked one up and started to open and close the clip. I must have tried it on all the fingers of my left hand. What I did next will remain a mystery until the day I die. Would you believe I undid my trousers and revealed my little willie and clipped it on the end? When the clip shut tight it brought tears to my eyes within seconds, they where streaming down my cheeks. I could not open it to get it off; I tried and tried with all my might but there was no shifting it.

With tears streaming down my face, I decided to go down stairs and throw myself at the mercy of my Mum. The remarks Mum and Auntie made! I had to wait till they stopped laughing to get the thing off. I never lived it down; I was teased about it for years.

In the spring of 1942 Mum got herself a part-time job as a Home Help, it could have been her part for the war effort. When I was older I often wondered why she went out to work, with her bad health, and Babs stayed at home looking after Muriel and me. Babs had never done a hard day's work in her life and it would have done her the world of good getting her hands dirty. But to be truthful she did keep the house tidy and got our meals.

Mum's boss was a nice lady by the name of Miss Streeter; her office was on Market Street opposite Altrincham Town Hall, just up the road from the hen food shop. Sometimes, when Mum had to go to see her she would take me with her - possibly to get me out of Auntie Babs's way? Mum would give her report and Miss Streeter would give Mum her new assignments.

Auntie Babs arrival was the beginning of two years of torment for me; she and Muriel teamed up and they would take every opportunity to think of ways to stir up trouble for me. I am glad to say that I did not let them get me down.

Auntie's dog Karl was having problems so he had to be taken to the vet quite often; he had something wrong with his back legs. The vet's was in a courtyard off The Downs in Altrincham. In the end he could not walk properly at all; when he started to drag his back legs behind him I felt very sorry for the poor old chap indeed. I think Babs contemplated having a little two-wheel trolley made for him because in all other aspects he was quite lively. However, in the end he died naturally, and sometime later Ginger the cat died also. Both were buried side by side in the garden between our two plane trees.

A few days later I was playing in the garden on my own and I had climbed my favourite tree to survey my kingdom from safety when I looked down and noticed the disturbed earth of their resting places. A thought came into my mind. Scrambling down the tree as fast as I could I set my plan in motion. Very soon I had all the things I wanted and I set about my task with enthusiasm. When it was done, I must admit I was a bit weepy, as I went to look for Auntie Babs. I went to the bottom of the stairs and called up to her. Well, after my third call she stormed out of the bedroom in a right old temper. *"What do you want; I'm trying to have a bit of peace and quiet? What is it?"*

I tried to tell her, between my little sobs and a bit of stuttering. She exploded *"for goodness sake, I haven't got all day,"* as she glared down over the banister rail. When eventually she realised what I had done you should have seen her face. She lifted me up and cuddled me to her. *"What a lovely thing for you to do, come on and show me"*. When she saw the grave with the big letters K and G on it in stones, tears streamed down her face.

But this was soon forgotten; she did not miss an opportunity to give me a clout, even the next day. A few weeks later I was playing with my pals in the avenue when she called me to her. *"Oh no, what have I done now?"* I said. She told me that at the end of the week she would be taking me to Belle Vue, in fact on Friday. Well you can imagine my surprise and excitement. Next day I was playing with Peter Davies and his new neighbour, a boy called David Ainsworth. He and his mother and sister had just moved into the avenue, and I just had to share my good news with them.

Returning home from my adventures two days later, Babs greeted me with, *"I've had a visitor this afternoon"*. Then she gave me a slap across the face, followed by a tirade. *"What do you mean by telling people I'm taking you to Belle Vue? I've had to put up with some boy's mother, this Ainsworth woman, coming here telling me she's just moved up here from London. Then she has the audacity of asking me, if she gives me some money, would I take her son and his sister with us when I take you on Friday. So I told her, there had been a change of plan, we weren't going now, something's come up. Now perhaps that will teach you too keep your mouth shut, won't it?"* So we didn't go to Belle Vue on Friday or any other day.

One late autumn night I had been in bed a while. Suddenly I heard the gate latch go, then footsteps on the drive. Seconds later I heard voices coming from the kitchen; who ever could it be, I wondered? I had better check that Mum's alright, I wonder if Dad's come home on leave? I was putting my dressing gown on as I made my way quietly down the stairs - remembering to stride over the third from the bottom creaky one. As I tip-toed down the hall I heard voices, and somehow there was a familiarity about it.

Very gingerly I opened the kitchen door and peeped in. *"Oh my God, you frightened the living daylights out of me,"* said my Mum with a hand over her heart. *"What on earth are you doing creeping in like that?"* *"He wants a good hiding, if you ask me."* Auntie Babs spouted up. *"Well, no one was asking you,"* admonished my Mum. I tried to explain to Mum - but she said she was alright, thank you - and I was looking at Ronnie Holland. Mum said that it was gone eleven o'clock, and I was to get back up to bed again. In the morning I asked her why Ronnie had called so late; she laughed as she told me that he had been having a drink with some friends and he wanted a mint so his mother wouldn't smell this breath.

This started the occasional Friday night fry-up and chat. Mum would get the frying pan out whilst Auntie Babs prepared the onions. Mum would open a tin of corned beef and chop it up into small cubes, and in went the 'bully beef ' mixed up and fried for a few minutes. The result, goulash; served with some bread it was lovely. I only attended the ritual once or twice, and then only thanks to air raids. Mum said that they enjoyed his visits; he was a lot of fun during these dark days of the war she told me.

One of my jobs was taking the books back to the library on Park Road. Auntie Babs let me borrow her big rubber book holder which had a handle like a brief case. On each side there was a few inches of rubber and a loop. These loops were stretched over the books and it now looked as if you were carrying a small suitcase. When I was old enough I joined the library and remember feeling grown up as I handed in my *Just William* and chose another. My other reading matter was, of course, comics. I took the *Beano* and Harry took the *Dandy* and after we had read them we swapped - well they were tuppence each. When I outgrew these, the *Hotspur* became my comic; my favourite was a footballer, The Cannonball Kid.

How it started I don't know, but suddenly, now two years later, when I got home from school, Auntie Babs had found another job for me. I had to chop up, very finely, mind you, all the potato peelings and vegetable scraps before they were cooked for the hens' food. She presented me with something that looked like a meat cleaver with a handle across the top, and a blade about five inches wide - I had never seen it before - and the job was to be carried out on a bench Dad had fixed onto the back of the coal shed door before he went in the army.

It took me well over a year to cotton on to the fact that Auntie Babs herself had never mashed up the potatoes like this before boiling them. When it did eventually dawn on me, and I realised it had never been necessary, I can tell you 'skin and hair flew'. Auntie Babs was strict, but I realised that she was also a bully. I know I was high spirited, but she enjoyed taking any opportunity to pick on me. Over two years I had suffered heavily at her hands, but I had had enough. When I saw the light on this chopping nonsense I told Mum about it and from next day the peelings were boiled as before.

A few days later Auntie Babs lashed out and hit me across the face again over it, but this time I stood my ground. Summoning up all my courage my arm came back and I hit her across the face just as she had hit me. I have never forgotten the shocked look on her face. I thought, oh blimey, now I am really in trouble. But she never hit me again - and do you know we seemed to be quite good friends after this.

What's sauce for the goose is sauce for the gander - towards the end of 1944 Auntie Babs somehow found out that Geoffrey was seeing another woman down in Hendon where he was stationed. This must have devastated her; Geoffrey was the love of her life, but she started going to Warrington and Altrincham, the towns where the Yanks spent most of their time off duty from their nearby Air Base at Burtonwood. She brought a few of them home to meet us all, and they always gave me some chewing gum and chocolate, and Mum had a couple of parcels of goodies from their PX store. These contained tea and coffee, tinned meats and fruit, and chocolates and sweets. Children would follow the American service men around saying, *"Got any gum, chum?"* This usually resulted in a few sticks being given out. I have to say that the few I met were always very polite, what you would call gentlemen. What the neighbours thought I don't know; at that age I don't think I had thought about it. The well-versed saying then was the Yanks were *"over-sexed, over-paid and over here"*.

I think the Yanks started the graffiti 'Kilroy was here' and another wall drawing 'Chad' - "Wot, no Petrol" or whatever else was in short supply. I remember another poster at the time showed 'The Squaderbug', a sort of beetle that had swastikas all over it and Mr Hitler's hair, and was a warning about wasting the nation's resources - we were encouraged to kill him. We always referred to Hitler as 'Mr Hitler', I think in a sarcastic way.

A sight that made a lot of people's hearts miss a beat during the war was a young man in a navy blue uniform with wide leather black belt and a leather pouch fastened to the front, a little pillbox hat with a red stripe round it, and with a familiar red bike. The Telegraph boys with their little 4 x 3 inch yellow envelopes. No one who had a loved one serving, ever wanted him knocking on their door because it could be bad news.

Mum's heart missed a beat in the early part of May, 1944. She answered the door one evening to find a telegram boy stood on the step, the dreaded yellow envelope in his hand - and yes, it was for Mum. It read something like this:

```
Have w/e pass can't come home-stop-Come to W-S-M Fri-
stop-will phone  Tue night 10o/c-stop.
```

It turned out that Dad and his friend from Cheadle, Fred Townley, had a weekend's leave but were not allowed home. It would be the last leave for quite sometime. So one day in May Mum met up with Fred's wife at the station in Manchester, and they travelled down together to Weston-super-Mare. My younger sister Carole Anne was born as a result of Mum's trip to Weston super Mare.

Why Dad was not allowed home Mum didn't know, but towards the end of June she had another letter from Dad postmarked 'FROM SOMEWHERE IN EUROPE'. A few days after Mum's trip, Dad's lot were moved across country to Hunstanton, and Dad had been on the second landing at Normandy. In letters he wrote later, he told us how he had to drive his truck onto a big net on the ship's deck and keep his engine running at all times. At the landing the ship's crane picked the truck up with him in it, and they were swung out over the side into about three foot of water. He then had to drive up onto the beach and get onto the road as quickly as possible.

We were fortunate to have a telephone which sat on the hall windowsill, a heavy black Bakelite instrument; our number was SAL(e) 2806. If you ever had to make a long distance call it was done via the operator and when your 2 minutes were up she would suddenly come on the line, *'Hello caller, your time's up, do you wish to pay for any further time'*, if you didn't they would give you just enough time to say your goodbyes, then cut you off.

Harry's mum had one of the older types still, on a board screwed to the wall, with the earpiece that had to be lifted off a cradle that sprung up and made the connection. You had to turn a handle before you got a line to dial out a local call. The mouthpiece was attached to the instrument on the wall, so Harry had to stand on tip toe, or get a box to stand on!

Local calls you dialled yourself, the first 3 letters of the exchange followed by the number. The operator had to obtain all other numbers, sometimes ringing you back. An overseas call was a different matter altogether. They had to be pre-booked and not a lot of countries were available. You dialled '0' to get the operator, then you had to give them the name and the number you wished to 'try' to contact - you would be told approximately how long you would have to wait - *"Caller your call will take about two hours to obtain, please stay within proximity of your instrument. If we connect you and you do not take the call you will be charged just the same."* These calls were limited to just three minutes.

It took two of the gang to pull open the heavy door of a red telephone box. Once we were inside we were confronted with a big black box 1 foot wide by 2-foot attached to a large black board. To the right was a box shelf which held the telephone books. After lifting the receiver the two pennies were inserted into the slot adjacent to the button

'A'. When the call was answered you could hear them but they couldn't hear you until the 'A' button was pressed and you would hear your pennies drop into the box. Button 'B' was for getting your money back if your call didn't answer or if they were engaged.

Many times when the telephone bill came Mum would look at it and say, *"It's no good, we just can't go on like this, it'll have to be taken out."* Every time she uttered these words it turned out, for one reason or another, that something happened to prove that it was needed for some sort of emergency, so the phone always stayed where it was.

Derek Hargreaves lived opposite at No 4 and he was about the same age as our Muriel. When they were about fifteen he walked past me one day as we turned the corner into our road and made a very derogatory remark to me about Muriel, something about what she had been doing with some boys. Now as you have guessed I did not really like Muriel, but never the less she was my sister. Whether it was true or not, I wasn't having him saying it. I flew at him. The next thing I had him bent over backwards on the Ashcroft's garden wall. Although he was older he was only the same height as me.

Another problem with having an older sister was that I had to put up with her music; nearly every home had a wind up gramophone that played our records. She would drive me mad as she played Ella Fitzgerald, Geraldo and his Orchestra, The Ink Spots, Duke Ellington, and the Glenn Miller orchestra. Then there was Frank Sinatra and Bob Hope with the songs from the Road Films, Lena Horne, Diana Shore, and Danny Kaye with all his silly songs.

There was one or two I liked. The best of all was Carson Robinson with his ditty "Life Gits Teejus, Don't It?" The verses I remember go like this:

The Sun comes up and the sun goes down,	My shoes untied but I don' really care
The hands on the clock jus keep a going around.	I ain't a-figured on goin' nowhere
You jus' get up and it's time to lay down,	I'd have to wash and comb my hair
Life gits teejus, don't it?	That's jus' wasted effort.

Our wireless came from Uncle George's factory; what today we would call a 'freebie'. Muriel and I would listen to Children's Hour (it only lasted half an hour) with Uncle Mac (Derek McCulloch). That was until Muriel thought it was below her age to listen to it anymore. This was also the case with The Ovaltinies that was broadcast about seven o'clock. She would say to me *"Still listening to that silly programme then?"*

When I was older I enjoyed 'ITMA' with Tommy Handley, not that I understood most of the innuendo. ITMA stood for "It's That Man Again". Coming in a close second was 'In Town Tonight'; the presenter would shout, "STOP" during the signature tune, and then say, *"Once again we stop the roar of London's traffic to bring you,"* and name the night's guests. Mum's favourite programme was 'The Brains Trust', with a panel of four prominent, clever people to answer questions. Mum said it gave her brain some exercise trying to get to the solution before the clever so and sos. We had to keep quiet during this or we got into trouble.

On Sunday, Jean Metcalfe presented a programme called 'Two Way Family Favourites'. From a studio in London she played requests, sent in from loved ones for their men and women who were serving King and Country overseas.

Among the comedians who came on the wireless to try and cheer us all up were Arthur Askey, Max Wall and Rob Wilton. Rob always started off with his famous *"The day war broke out, my misses said to me."* And how could anyone forget the toothless antics of Norman Evans. He performed his renowned 'Over the Garden Wall' sketches with wit and accuracy!

I remember Al Varledell for two reasons; first his excellent news reading, and second, his ghostly voice as he told his late night spooky bedtime stories - *"This is your storyteller, The Man in Black."* During the 30s and 40s everyone who performed on the wireless had to be dressed smartly. The big bands and the presentersall wore dinner suits.

After Carole was born I became rather fond of my little sister, and I was quite protective of her, as you would imagine. One day I was sounding off about her to some boys at school and one remarked that all babies were red, wrinkled and funny looking, just like prunes, and they never stopped crying. I was having none of this, my baby sister was a nice pink colour and had no wrinkles at all and hardly ever cried.

One day I pushed Carole in her pram to the shops on Riddings Road. Mum wanted me to go to three shops, Nelson's, the ironmonger, Howe's, the greengrocer and Meadowcroft's, the bakers. The first had been accomplished and whilst I was getting served in Howes I heard a kerfuffle outside and I looked and saw that people were in the area of the 'Pram'. Oh my goodness, somehow the pram had tipped forward, and the handle was on the floor. My baby sister, had her forehead on the footpath. Hell and damnation passed before my eyes, tears were streaming down my face. Mrs Howes was trying to console me. She took charge of the situation; she released Carole from the harness and took her to Kay's the chemist. Mr Kay cleaned and dressed a graze on her forehead then phoned Mum to tell her why I would be a little late getting home. She had already given my list to an assistant who was completing Mum's order and she told me to go to the bakers. So off I went to get the bread and that completed the list. I met Mum halfway up Acresfield Road, and she consoled me saying it wasn't my fault. Phew, what a relief.

Mum's old vacuum cleaner was like a Dalek out of *Dr Who*. It was called a 'TELUS'. and was shaped like the Russian dolls that were very popular then. It had a big belly and chest area for all the dust and a small head that was the motor and carrying handle. The long tube went in a hole near the base and it had various attachments. Sometimes she would resort to hanging small rugs over the washing line and beating the living daylights out of them with a carpet beater. Her mother, she told me, would throw wet tealeaves on the rugs to keep the dust down, and help to clean them when they were brushed with a stiff brush.

Mum was very pleased when the 'TELUS' was finally retired onto the Rag and Bone man's cart and Dad bought her an upright Hoover after his demob from the Army.

'Gumption' was a popular paste then for cleaning baths and cookers. Washing up liquid had not been thought of. When we washed the pots, a chore Muriel and I had to share, Mum sprinkled in washing powder and frothed it up by swishing her hand in it.

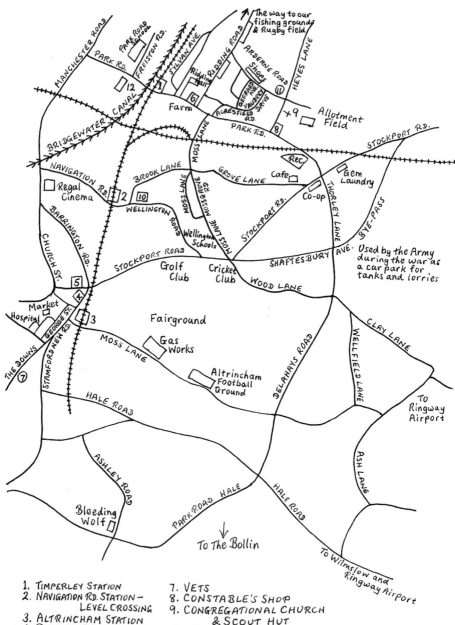

1. TIMPERLEY STATION
2. NAVIGATION RD. STATION –
        LEVEL CROSSING
3. ALTRINCHAM STATION
4. PICTURE THEATRE
        & SWIMMING BATHS
5. THE HIPPODROME
6. HOUSE WITH AIRPLANE

7. VETS
8. CONSTABLE'S SHOP
9. CONGREGATIONAL CHURCH
        & SCOUT HUT
10. BAND PRACTICE HOUSE
11. THE CROFT
12. JOHN SHERRATT & SON

My childhood Timperley

13. Frozen Ponds

The leaves on the trees were changing to their autumn golds and reds. Soon they would be thick on the ground, when I loved to walk through the thick carpet that rustled and crunched.

Summer days were always bright and warm, when it never rained, and when you never had to wear your gabardine. But summers had their down side; like dodging those sticky flypapers hanging down from the light fittings.

Winter came in fast, with lots of rain and winds that cut through your clothing like a knife through butter. *"It won't be long before were having snow."* I heard Mum say to Mrs Smith, and low and behold a few days later down it came. It fell very deep. Soon we had another visitor; old 'Jack Frost'. He would be nipping at our fingers and toes, and it wasn't long before we were inside the house to play - well on the days our mothers let us.

When the snow was on the ground most of us would play out in it. We didn't want to get our gloves wet, so they would be swinging from beneath our coat sleeves as your Mum had sewn the gloves onto tape and threaded it through the sleeves to stop you losing them. To keep your head warm, your mum had knitted you a Balaclava, a woollen hood, the face only exposed from the eyebrows to just under the nose. The area under the mouth got wet with saliva and hot breath and this made the wool go hard so the Balaclava had to be replaced on a regular basis. My Mum also knitted Muriel and me scarves. One year she made me one in the Park Road school colours, alternate green and yellow.

There was a 'posher' headgear made of soft leather with a fur or fleecy lining, like the skullcaps worn in the Middle Ages. To protect the ears they had flaps that fastened with a press-stud and if left undone, they flapped up and down just like the ears of Dumbo the elephant. These helmets were like aircrew wore - and I think the wearers often led a Walter Mitty existence. To complete the winter outfit, we had a 'heavy winter coat'. We looked the height of fashion as we clomped around in all this and our black wellies.

During the winter our kitchen/dining room and the living room, were used to their full potential; the front room hardly ever. Mum had to have the kitchen fire going to heat the water, and she would have to make full use of the oven for cooking and baking. I shall never forget the lovely smell when Mum made bread. Throughout the summer piles of slack (coal dust) were separated from the coal in the shed, for banking up the fire at night in winter, to keep it going for the morning.

The front room was used occasionally in the summer, but in the winter it was far too cold. If we were feeling musical, Harry and I would brave the elements and sneak in there when no one was in the house, because this room housed an upright piano. We would play duets of the entire piano concertos as we sat side by side sharing the wide piano stool. When we had finished our recital, we would turn and bow to the audience before playing an encore.

One day we had just begun our second piece when we were very rudely interrupted by someone in the audience shouting. *"What do you two think you're doing except making an infernal row? I've told you before not to bang on the piano like that. If it's too cold outside get in the living room and play"* and she ushered us out. We had been making so much noise we hadn't heard my Mum come in. For all the use we got out of the piano it might as well have been chopped up for firewood, and I am sure Mr Churchill would have been pleased to have received the ornate brass candlesticks that were screwed on it for the war effort. I can't recall anyone ever playing it except Harry and little old me. If anyone was able to play properly, they could have kept us amused with a sing-song during one of the many power cuts we had to endure. The only other furniture in the front room was a three-piece suit and the inevitable display cabinet housing Mum's best china.

During the war, whenever there was a shortage, people were very quick to spot an opening to make some money out of it; and it was not long before coal rationing was seen to be such. Before long we had men, sometimes women, coming round selling logs and peat blocks; and within a few years would you believe it, old tyres. The tyres had been cut up into small pieces, about six inch by three inch, and they burnt quite well but made an awful stink if the smoke happened to blow back. The other main fuel used to eke out the coal ration was coke, a bye product of making gas. It was lightweight and had a 'rustly' sound. The time to add it was when the fire was very hot, then it would give out a very good heat.

Whenever the chimney started to smoke due to heavy soot, it was common practice to save money by doing it yourself. This was achieved by pushing crumpled up newspaper into the chimney. When it was set on fire it would be drawn up into the chimney with a 'whoosh' and this burnt the soot off. Another way was to go and buy a product called 'IMP'. This was a three inches square small box containing chemicals. When it was placed on a glowing fire and as the chemicals burnt away, as if by magic it cleared the soot from the chimney walls. It was a great deal safer than the chimney fire, although it was a common sight to see a house with a chimney on fire in those days.

Another dangerous practice was the way people boosted a low fire. A hand shovel was stood on the ash pan cover or fret, and a newspaper was then stretched over it and held in place with the hands or the fire irons. You had to hold the paper tight to prevent it being sucked up the chimney. The blaze could be seen through the paper, and then you would smell it as it started to scorch the paper brown. This was the time to remove the shovel and paper; but often too late and the paper caught fire. A slight panic set in as you tried to get the shovel out of the way to push the fire ball up the chimney. Many a time my Dad or Mum singed the hairs off the backs of their hands.

One day a tile fell off the living room fireplace, luckily low down so it did not break. Mum just placed it to one side and every few days you would hear her say *"I'll have to fix that tile."* Many days later I was intrigued to see her go to into the living room with a tin of condensed milk. To my amazement she picked up the tile, smeared it with condensed milk and fixed it back. Do you know that tile never came off.

Old Timperley
Courtesy of 'Looking back at Timperley', Hazel Pryor

On a cold winter's evening there was nothing more Mum liked to do than get a pile of crumpets and sit in front of the kitchen fire and toast them. She used the wire toasting fork, made from two pieces of wire folded over in the middle, then twisted together, each piece of wire producing two prongs. Mum would sit there toasting and buttering - well 'margarining' - then hand them round. But she indulged herself by saving a knob of butter from the rations for her last mouth full.

Whilst we sat listening intently to the wireless, sometimes the fire decided to explode. This was caused by a piece of shale amongst the coal. Apart from the fact that we all nearly messed our pants, especially if it was a thriller we were listening to, you also had to jump about stamping on the volcanic hot shards that were burning the hearthrug.

One day Mum surprised us when she told Muriel and me that the carpet square in the living room had been over to Canada and back. Quite a few years after the birth of Auntie Babs, somewhere in the first few years of the 1920s, the Bagshaw family decided to emigrate but at the last minute had changed their minds. Grandad, and his eldest son George, must have been the expeditionary force as the photograph shows. Most of their belongings were on board the ship, ready to leave port, and they were almost on the gang plank when one of her parents got cold feet. The boat sailed off with their possessions and they had to await its return to reclaim them.

Grandad Bagshaw and Uncle George

Fitted carpets were hardly known in those days. For the likes of us the main floor covering was lino (linoleum) with a carpet square for downstairs. Upstairs it was lino with a small mat by the bed. If you missed it, the cold shock that shot up from foot to brain would wake you up as fast as a bucket of cold water. The nearest thing I saw in those days to central heating was a small gas heater in the hall of Auntie Babs's house.

Bedtime in winter was the start of a ritual, the filling of the hot water bottles. These were made from rubber or pot, some people even heated bricks in their ovens to put in their beds. They usually went into your bed about an hour before you plucked up the courage to jump between the icy sheets. Hot water bottles were definitely a necessity rather than a luxury - perhaps we were 'nesh'. As you can imagine, chillblains were very common, and I had quite a few, and one on my little toe turned septic. Mum would never ever let me fill my own hot water bottle, *'far too dangerous, especially for you.'* Mum scalded her hand a few times, but not seriously I am pleased to say.

In winter we put our clothes for morning under the eiderdown so they would be warm when we had to get out of that now cosy bed. Most winter mornings we woke up to find the windows all iced up on the inside, transformed by intricate ice patterns.

To help relieve the effects of coughs and colds Mum would make some special syrup by putting six onions into a dish, pouring honey all over them, then baking them in the oven. When the onions were very soft, she would squeeze the juice out of them into the honey syrup, and then drain the liquid off into a jug. After it had cooled it would be bottled. This was my favourite medicine, I don't think any house was without its bottle of a favourite homemade cure - 'Grannies favourite remedy' they were usually called. A must for nearly every household was a bottle of that very expensive stuff - no not whisky - olive oil - and not for cooking but for putting down the ears for earache, or wax in the ear. Before the oil was poured into the spoon it was placed in hot water, to warm it. The bottle was only about three inches high, and oil stained from being kept so long.

One good thing came out of Jack Frost's visits, he would freeze the pond at the bottom of the neighbours' gardens. One of our parents had to give the all clear that it was safe to venture on the ice, then those who had skates could show off. The skates were usually rusty from being in a garden shed and emery paper or a file was needed to clean and sharpen the blade runners. Most of the time they ended up sprawled on the ice.

For the rest it was a slide, made by the bigger boys and girls and far too slippy for us youngsters. We attempted to make our own - usually one of the bigger girls took pity on us and helped. Towards the end of the freezing period the big boys, without fail, always started breaking the ice up somewhere on the pond's edge. Guess who wanted to test if the water had re-frozen one day; yes I fell through. I nearly drowned, luckily for me a boy's father was in his garden and hearing the commotion ran down and pulled me out. Having wellies on did not help - the water in them must have doubled my weight!

During this period of the year I enjoyed frosty moonlit nights when the roofs of the houses shone like mirrors in the moonlight. I liked it when the roofs and the trees were covered in snow, and as it melted, nature-sculptured icicles which froze and re-froze. The telephone wires had walls of snow perched on top of them. When it started to thaw, soon someone would get caught with an avalanche of snow hitting them as it slid from a house roof. On some roofs you would see as much as a two-foot or more over-hang just waiting to drop. When we had icicles hanging they were very dangerous, so these had to have the same treatment as the snow - with a brush out of the top window.

Soon the beauty would give way to slush and water, the traffic that included a few cars, mostly owned by doctors, and the horse drawn wagons, would make ruts in the melting snow. Then, when the frost came in the night, it would freeze the quagmire making it difficult to walk about.

Winter also brought the magic of Christmas. Before the war when Dad worked at Lewis's, Mum always took us to see Father Christmas, his grotto a wonderland in itself, and different every year. I am sure my Dad told us, that, at sometime in Lewis's history, they deliberately flooded part of the basement. and made it into a Venetian spectacle including imitation buildings and scenery, and gondolas for customers to take trips in.

One year we called to see Dad in the furniture department and he said to Mum,

Lewis's and, below, Tib Street.
Courtesy of Manchester Archives & Local Studies

"Nellie, when you take Peter to the toy department be sure to let him see what's up on the big stand, I'm sure he'll like to see it." Dad was quite right, I did like it, but I would have liked it even more if I was having it for one of my presents. It was a model car, like a single seater-racing car, with a proper engine. Some little boy with a rich father would be the envy of all his friends.

"Well come along then, we'll have to get to the lifts before everyone else decides to leave the store." No matter how young or old they were the men who operated the lifts in those days were all called 'lift boys'. They operated the lifts up and down all day, closing and opening the lattice metal gates as they announced the goods that were being sold on each floor. *"Mind the gates please; going up, first floor ladies wear, coats, hats, gloves and accessories, table wear and bed linen, thank you."*

When we arrived at the ground floor I knew Mum would succumb to my annual wish and take me next door to Wild's Toy Store - the quickest way was via the arcade. I was always fascinated to see the ladies walking up and down with very high-heeled shoes and deep red lipstick. Some had a fur round their neck with a fox's head on, just like the one Grandma Scott had had. There was an old postcard amongst others in the letter rack at home - and I never understood it: Two ladies stood talking, one wearing a fur coat, *"Oh my dear I've been struggling for years for a coat like that, however did you get it?"* Second lady, *"I just stopped struggling."* Whenever I had the card out I could sense Mum laughing to herself as I mused over this card. It would be many years before I understood the joke, then I understood the trade those ladies were plying.

We went to look in Wild's window first; it was THE toyshop, the very best for miles around. Lewis's had layouts of train sets, but nothing like these, these were very big, and always displays in different gauges. Once inside I never wanted to leave this store - Mum had to practically drag me out.

Somewhere in the arcade would be the Jumping Bean Man, a tray hung around his neck. On the tray were the beans, like liquorice torpedo sweets, but rolling and jumping about. On one visit Mum bought me one, to stop me mithering. I had great fun with it, I would hold it in my palm so the creases held it and when you showed it to someone you stretched your hand out and it would jump. Usually off your hand!

On the opposite corner to Wild's was the famous Tib Street, well known for all its pet shops. Here you could buy all sorts of creatures, from cute puppies and kittens, to tortoises, fish and rabbits. I can't remember seeing the snakes and lizards that are sold nowadays, but there were a few monkeys and the unforgettable squawking parrots.

Every week Dad had to visit the basement food hall before he caught his train home on a Saturday, for the thick tomato sausages for our Sunday breakfast. My word, he would be in trouble if he came home without them. It was a ritual up to the war starting and they would go into a frying pan on their own as Mum fried the bacon and eggs in another. *"Who wants some bread and dip,"* she would ask, taking it from the bacon frying pan. *"Yes please."* We didn't think about cholesterol in those days. We even enjoyed dripping butties. Another unhealthy treat was a sugar butty.

My bread van Xmas present

The Stonemason's Arms
Courtesy of 'Looking back at Timperley', Hazel Pryor

14. Christmas, presents and games

No sooner had Mum got over the Father Christmas trip, she had to start the preparations for the big day - Christmas Day.

"Well Nellie, I'll get the steps from the shed and go and get it down," Dad said as he got up from the tea table and walked out of the back door. Dad was soon on his tiptoes struggling into the loft space. Suddenly we saw the torch switch on. I remember there was no roofing felt under the tiles in these days. Then the silence was broken, Mum saying, *"be careful on those rafters, George, we don't want you coming through."* Seconds later the tree, wrapped in its brown paper shroud and tied up with string, was gingerly handed down to Mum at the bottom of the steps. Although Dad was careful, Mum still got half the year's accumulated dust over her face. Next to appear would be the box of glass baubles and tree decorations, and the pull-out streamers for the living room. We didn't know then that in a couple of year's time all this would fall on Mum to do while Dad was in the War.

Some weeks before Christmas you would hear Muriel shout to Mum. *"Mum, going carol singing with Winnie and Dawn and a few others"*. This was a good way of earning some money. I wasn't allowed to go until I was eight, when I went with my friends just like Muriel. The trouble was by then not many people wanted the trouble of opening their front doors because of the black-out.

Mum insisted on putting the baubles on the tree herself, *"I can't take a chance on them being broken by you two. We had these at home when I was your age,"* she said looking me in the eye. There was one tree decoration that would be frowned upon today, the small candles in their pretty clip on holders- and the tree was made of green paper wrapped round the wire shape and cut with a 'fringe' to make it look like a fir tree. In all honesty it was an accident just waiting to happen. The holders were clipped to the ends of the branches, the candles were lit, and the room light switched off. The flickering candlelight danced off the glass baubles and cast reflections around the room.

To keep me quiet, Mum gave me the job of opening up the big balls and bells; they fascinated me, the way the intricate cut-out coloured paper would unfold from a flat half ball or bell into a lovely decoration. The streamers were anchored to a corner of the ceiling and stretched to all four corners of the room.

The Christmas of 1940 was a bit worrying. Only two nights before, into the early hours of Christmas Eve, Mr Hitler and his Luftwaffe had bombed the Manchester area. I suppose we had to be thankful that he left us alone to enjoy a few happy festive days, but they must have been nervous ones. Mum certainly did not want to have to leave our dinner on the table; neither did we. I remember her saying to Dad and us. *"That lot may be dropping bombs on us but I'll be dammed if he's going to spoil our Christmas,"* as she dished the spuds out. *"Come on George, get that bird carved up; even if we end up covered in dust he's not getting me in no shelter for the next hour."* Fortunately he left us alone until New Years Day 1941, when they started bombing all over again.

Within a few years the old pull-out streamers were the worse for wear and had to be thrown away. I was older now, so I could be roped in to make paper chains, made with any type of coloured paper we could get hold of. We cut the paper into strips, and, sticking the narrow edges together, made loops linked into the chain. Crepe paper was used to make bows and pom-pom decorations. Sprigs of holly were added, and mistletoe, if you could get it, or afford it. I don't think we ever had balloons; I think all the rubber was required for making other things in helping to win the war.

I was eight and it was the first year Dad was serving in the army. Some weeks before Christmas, Mum sent me to the Off Sales of the Stonemason's in the village, armed with a washed out glass pop bottle, to bring home some beer for the christmas pudding. When all the ingredients were in the mixing bowl, Mum would drop in some little parcels, two or three sixpenny pieces, each wrapped in greaseproof paper, and then we all had our stir for good luck and made a wish. Putting money into the christmas pudding was carried out every year without fail. Someone would be better off on Christmas Day and I really hoped it would be me. When the puddings had been steamed for a few hours and then cooled, they would be put in the back of the larder under the stairs for next year, and last year's would be brought out. They got better with keeping Mum said.

Christmas Eve was a very busy time for Mum. When she could corner Muriel she would give her chores to do; her cry would be, *"Mum, why can't he do this as well, it's not jolly well fair?"* *"How can I be of help?"* I would ask. How - *"sat on the chair in front of the fire"* - I was six before the penny dropped about the joke. But as I grew older I was able to give a little help and peel some of the potatoes.

Turkey, goose, duck and chicken were once a year luxuries in these days. I can't remember us ever having a turkey. Whatever unfortunate bird had been chosen to have its neck wrung would be hanging out in the coal shed. It was Dad's job to pluck and clean out the bird - I found it fascinating to listen to Dad explaining the poor bird's various organs. *"This is a girl bird,"* he would say. *"Look you can see some of the eggs she was preparing to lay."* I remember one year, Dad was sat in the scullery plucking the feathers from a bird and Muriel opened the back door - result feathers all over the place.

During the war years, Mum had some help from Babs, although I don't think she would put her hand up a chicken's bum if you paid her a king's ransom. Muriel more often than not would endeavour to disappear from sight, but if she hadn't, she would have to help Mum prepare the vegetables. The task began with the potatoes, carrots and turnip. Sprouts - you always had to have sprouts - were trimmed and kept dry. The peas weren't out of the freezer then; we didn't have one in those days, they were dried peas and very hard, and had to be steeped in water over night with a soda tablet added to help keep them green.

Soon the final touches would be put to the morrow's feast; getting the bird ready for the oven. Unfortunately for Mum, it would be many years before we saw the luxury of an oven that turned itself on, she had to get up early and do it herself. Mum always put a few extra shillings in for the gas meter; she would not chance the gas running out on Christmas Day.

The Christmas cake was retrieved from the depths of the larder where it had been stored. A week or two before I had seen Mum stabbing the bottom with a fork and pouring some brown liquid all over it. Out came the large cut glass bowl for the trifle. Mum's trifle was a trifle to look forward to - she always put extra sherry in at this time of the year, mixing it with the juice from the soft fruit and the jelly before pouring it over the sponges. Plenty of fruit followed this before it was taken to the coal hole to set over night in the frosty conditions, ready for the custard on top first thing in the morning.

Jellies and blancmanges had the same fate; out into the cold they would go, to keep company with the bird. We had to make the most of winter, it was the only time these goodies set. Mum retrieved a special piece of equipment from the depths of the 'under the stairs' larder on Christmas Day and high days - the cream maker. An ingenious item if ever there was one; a glass bell shaped bowl, the base six inch with a two-inch top opening, onto this screwed a cup shape, about three inches high. Fixed through the centre was a tube and piston, like a boat's bilge pump. Full cream milk, no cissy stuff like skimmed, was poured into the cup a little at a time as the handle was pumped up and down. Through a couple of holes in the bottom of the tube came the cream. Magic! This was how the cream for the trifle was made. Mum spread it all over the top before decorating it with little snowmen and reindeer.

Mum would also, if she could get one, cook and press an ox tongue a few days before the festivities. The pressing took place in a basin with a small saucer placed over the meat, leaving enough space for it to press down. Then it was the smoothing iron or some other heavy weight on top to compress it. During the war you always tried to keep 'Spam' in the larder and the other popular tinned meat, corned beef - 'bully beef'.

Only a few people could afford refrigerators, the price was prohibitive, so perishables were kept in the meat safe, a wooden cabinet with the door frame covered with fine metal gauze, to let air in and keep flies out. It was placed onto a thick marble slab and it was a must in larders to keep food cool. The larder during the war was also utilised occasionally as a makeshift air raid shelter - well it was under the stairs.

Whilst all the work was going on, the grown-ups were washing down a few mince pies with a little sherry. I had a drink of milk sat on my chair by the fire, in a world of my own, dreaming of what Father Christmas might bring me.

From my early years a few Christmas mornings spring to mind, but one stands out above the rest. I would be six at the time; I had emptied my sock,which always had a few little presents on top of the stalwarts of an apple, an orange and a sixpenny piece hiding in the toe. Then I tackled the pillowcase with the proper presents in; would it be one of the things I had asked Father Christmas for? Some of the favourite extras might be in the pillowcase, like the Post Office, the John Bull Printing Outfit, and the annual.

The exploring over, I crawled down my bed to open the curtains. It had snowed during the night and everywhere was crisp and clean. I felt cold, but before I dived back into bed I wiped the condensation a little from the window to see if anyone was out in the road; there wasn't, but something below just caught my eye. I couldn't believe it, there was a smashing new pedal car, blue, and with a long bonnet, red steering wheel and black seat. I didn't feel cold any more. I couldn't contain my excitement, and went bursting into Mum and Dad's bedroom. There they were sat up in bed - and expecting me.

After I had dragged them into my room to look through the window at my new car, I then dragged Dad down the stairs so he could bring my new car inside for me. It turned out that Uncle George had sent it for me. *"Wow! What a beauty!"* *"Well we had to be up early anyway,"* Mum remarked. *"I'll go and put the kettle on and get breakfast started although you won't be eating much will you,"* she aimed at me. *"Didn't Father Christmas bring you any other presents then?"* chided Dad. I am ashamed to say, I can't remember what Mum and Dad bought me that year.

Mum told us that Grandma, Grandad and Auntie Dorothy would be here about eleven o'clock and she wanted to have the table set before they arrived. So, she gave Muriel and me our instructions, telling us to get on with it without the usual falling out. Most Christmases the 'Scotts' would come to our house and Auntie Babs and Uncle Geoffrey usually 'popped over', as Mum called it, just for half an hour, if they hadn't gone away somewhere.

When the weather improved and I could take my new car outside, all my friends had a turn. We would push each other up and down the avenue, sweeping from one side of the road to the other. Some years later, when I had outgrown my pride and joy, Mum gave my car to Geoffrey next door to play with. A few days later Mrs Long told Mum that it had been stolen from off her drive. Mum suspected her of selling it. It was believed by some of the neighbours that she sold a lot of their rations as well.

On the run up towards Christmas, as well as carol singers doing the rounds, we had many a choir, stopping every few hundred yards. They did it just for the love of the festive season. Then the Salvation Army could be heard playing carols and hymns outside the shops on Arderne Road. I would ask Mum if I could go and listen to them, then after calling for Harry we would run up the road before they could disappear somewhere else. When we saw the collection box coming round, that was our cue to disappear.

There was one Christmas when I can remember what Muriel got; she was twelve. I remember it so vividly because a week before I went into the kitchen whilst Mum and Aunt Babs were wrapping up a bicycle basket, and on the table there was a bell, front and rear lamps and a leather tool kit. *"Don't you say anything to Muriel or you'll spoil the surprise,"* Mum said to me, with that 'or you'll be in trouble my lad' look in her eyes. The bike was in part for her passing the entrance exam to go to Sale High School.

Winter meant more than just long nights, cold weather and snow; it also brought the pantomime season. I recall going with the family to see what must have been Mother Goose with 'look out behind you' spluttered loudly through jaw-bulging boiled sweets.

From small toys to big ones, games of all types filled my toy box or the shed. Besides toys for Christmas and birthdays we could always rely on some relative sending a postal order, anything from 6d to 2/6. I thought it very grown up to go to the post office and hear them bang the stamp down to cancel it, and then hand over the money to me. I was a lucky little chap, although I didn't appreciate it at the time.

Many presents I received remain as fond memories. The car Uncle George sent and another, the bread and confectionery cart from Auntie Babs and Uncle Geoffrey, that had imitation loaves, cakes and jam tarts made out of papier-maché. Another papier-maché item that found its way into many homes at the time was a model of a country cottage, from Sunday school, for putting spare coins in for Barnardo's Childrens' Homes.

One of my pride and joys was the clockwork train set; the engine was rather heavy, about eight inches in length and painted black with a sloping front like the famous Mallard. It had three carriages and an oval track with a branch line that went into the middle; I practically wore the wheels and track out. Other favourites were Meccano and Lego construction kits; and one called Bayko which has now disappeared. This had a base plate with small holes half an inch apart to hold the support wires for the bricks. These had grooves in their sides that slid between the wires until you had built to the height required. The kit also contained doors and windows - especially bay windows - and tiled roof panels.

One of our neighbours, Mr Lightener, gave me a large kaleidoscope - fascinating, a different pattern every time you looked in. When I was thirteen he gave me a large stamp album and stamps which are still in my bookcase.

There were many different board games then including ludo, snakes and ladders, and draughts. In an effort to keep cigarette customers in their clutches, tobacco companies came up with a great ploy, in printing sets of cards - what became known as cigarette cards - in sets, usually of fifty. These were in many guises, football, cricket and tennis stars to name a few. Children of the smokers would be sure to want to collect them. Of course the big stars were kept until the last, and if you think that 'dad' just had to buy 50 packets you would be wrong - they were randomly inserted so you doubled up many times. There was an advantage to this, though, in that it created great swapping fun.

They quickly found their way into a favourite game of being flicked against a wall. Holding the card between the index and middle fingers the hand was curled towards your palm, then with a quick flick you sent them skimming through the air. The object was to see who could throw nearest to the wall, and whoever achieved this kept all the cards on the ground in that session.

Many 'things' were collected in those days. Train and car numbers were big enthusiasms. When Harry and I were quite young we weren't doing very well with our collecting. There weren't many cars around and we were too short to see over railway bridges. One of us had a bright idea. So off we went, pads and pencils in our grubby little hands. We had quite a lot of numbers on our pads rather quickly; in fact we were well up Vaudrey Drive. We were half way up a driveway and just about to write a number when all of a sudden the front door opened. A lady stood there, *"I've been watching you two from the bedroom window; what do you think you're doing?"* After the shock had died off, I stammered, *"W-We're just collecting h-h-house numbers,"* holding out my pad for her to see. A look of what I know now to be total disbelief took over her face, as she said, *"You stupid boys - go home this minute and don't leave the gate open on your way out."*

If for any reason we couldn't play out, one of our homes had to take the brunt of our presence inside. If it was our house I would get the bagatelle table out - we watched the half-inch ball bearings chasing round the table and bouncing off the pins after a hefty push with the cue. I believe Uncle George bought me the table skittles. It was a shallow tray with skittles on it. Half way down on the right hand side there was a pole with a ball and chain swivel on the top. The idea was to hold the ball out to the side and swing it in a circle to knock as many down as you could. The game also came out when the family wanted some entertainment on winter nights as a change from hangman, beetle and other card games.

Tops and whips were very popular, mostly with the girls though. Tops were made in two popular shapes, one looked like a mushroom with a long stalk; this was called a window breaker, as it could fly up in the air when it got going at high speed. The other looked much like an upside down walnut whip. Both had steel button studs in the bottom. Of course we all played the various games of marbles and it turned out to be quite a social event when we had swapping sessions.

Another favourite was the field telephone, a couple of empty baked bean tins and a hole pierced in the middle of the bottom of each with a nail. A string was threaded into each hole, some 20 feet in length, and when it was pulled tight between the two cans it became a two-way radio. The first mobile telephones?

In the autumn conkers were the thing for the boys - a few girls as well. We armed ourselves with heavy sticks, to hurl into the trees to knock the conkers down. When we had collected enough we would set off home discussing all sorts of things that were supposed to make them harder, like soaking in vinegar, even putting them in the oven for a while. After we had strung them, we would walk about with our biggest and strongest looking dangling from its string. It wasn't long before you were challenged to a duel - *"What's yours, mines a fourer, do you want to fight?"* *"OK, but mine's only a oner, so baggy I go first."* Some you won, some you lost, but it always puzzled us how it always seemed to be what you thought was a good one went into little bits the first time you put it to the test.

When we had had our fill of conkers, we would make a boat to sail in the bath. A small flat piece of wood, with a keyhole shape, about an inch long, cut into it, was sat on the water and you would put a drop of camphor oil in the round part of the cut out. As the oil expanded on contact with the water it was forced out and in doing so pushed the boat forward - very scientific!

My Uncle Geoffrey was very good at making paper aeroplanes; one looked like a large dart, another was in two parts; the fuselage about eight inches long and pushed into the main body, intricately folded in a way that I could never grasp.

15. Cubs and Scouts

The weeks had been dragging by; I had been counting the days, and now at last it was here my eighth birthday and old enough to join the cubs. The pack met every Tuesday in the scout hut at the back of Heyes Lane Congregational Church where I attended Sunday school.

Some weeks before Dad had come home with his brand new Home Guard uniform, but Mum said I would have to make do with a secondhand cub's uniform whenever she could lay her hands on one. Mum couldn't spare the valuable clothing coupons - which had started in April 1941. Money was tight, as well, with Muriel having just started at the high school, with her new school uniform, and a few schoolbooks.

We did not have to wait long. A lady whose son had moved up into the scouts had things to sell. The jersey was dark green, made with that hard scratchy woollen material; you had to wear a vest under it. Having tried the shirt on, Mum decided it would do - but now she had to take the badges off for the lady's son. I wondered how many badges I would earn.

Both of Mum's men were now in uniform, but we didn't know at the time that Dad would be swapping his for that of a real soldier in a month's time.

For some months I had to wear my every day school trousers, the usual short grey ones. Sometimes I wore my brown leather sandals and took my pumps to run around in. Mum now had to buy me three important items though, a 2nd Timperley yellow neckerchief, a leather woggle, and a green cub cap, which had yellow braid from the centre button down to the rim, like the segments of an orange.

The lady who led the cubs, 'AKELA', was very nice and I fell in love with her. Her name was Helen Gemmell. Mrs Harding took over as second in charge about a year later. I earned a few badges and I attended an award ceremony along with many others. Mine were for knots, first aid, tracking and something else. One thing I could never get to grips with was the nightmare of 'signalling with two flags' - to give it its proper name semaphore. Philip tried to teach me on many an occasion. My Mum said I was as 'thick as two short planks' as far as some things went.

To get onto Heyes Lane I had to walk over the 'Croft', a piece of waste ground at the end of Arderne Road. On the way home a small gang of older boys led by a snotty-nosed boy called Bradshaw would chase us if they were around. This always caused me to have an asthma attack and when I got home I would have to go and lie on the bed until I calmed down. I would have to fight for breath; it was terrible, it was as if I was being suffocated. We did not have the inhalers we have today to give relief. Towards the end of November, every year without fail, I would have an attack of bronchitis, and this put me in bed for about a week. I was given a bowl of hot water with Friar's Balsam and menthol dropped into it, then a towel over my head and I was left to inhale the pungent steam for ten minutes, five times each day. Mum had to take me to the Manchester

Our cub pack and scout group

Children's Hospital every six months to see a doctor who specialised in chest conditions. I always went home with a bottle of medicine, unfailingly the same horrible black stuff which smelt and tasted awful. When I reached puberty, I am glad to say, I grew out of my chest complaints.

We would all sit round an imitation log fire made of red paper and a few logs with a light bulb under it. Akela would teach us the cub songs, and tell us cub stories, but most important of all we would learn cub law and the cub promise. When we had learnt them, we had to stand in front of her and make our vows. Now we were given the first badge to sew on our jerseys, the cub's badge, over our left breast which signified our heart.

I enjoyed being in the cubs. As well as being taught how to do all sorts of things there was the interaction of the team games that taught us to enjoy the thrill of winning, and to accept defeat with honour.

On the anniversary of joining you would be given a star next to your cub badge. Subsequent years, you would get a star, but this had a 2, 3 or 4 embossed in the centre, with different coloured backgrounds.

As you entered Heyes Lane from Park Road, there were two shops set back from the road, and it was on this frontage that we all assembled on a Sunday morning for church parade. Most of the cubs, including me, would look at the scouts with admiration, envying their Canadian Mounties' style hats and the different insignia of rank, along with their badges. I thought the white lanyards worn around their necks and wound round their neckerchiefs looked very smart. The more senior scouts wore daggers in scabbards pushed into their socks just below the right knee. As a cub, if you were chosen as a patrol leader or a seconder (I became a seconder in the second year), you would carry one of the two flags, the troop pennant or the Union Jack. After we had formed up in twos, behind the scouts, the troop leader would shout, *"Shoulders back, right foot forward, quick march."*

One meeting started with Akela getting us all seated and saying *"I'd like you all to be very quiet as I have something very sad to tell you. Last Saturday the Upton brothers were on a day out with their mother and father and they visited an outside swimming pool. A terrible accident occurred in which they both drowned."* The room became more silent than silent; the impact of what we had just been told slowly sank into our minds. Then she told us, *"We will all attend their funeral if your parents agree; this will take place next Saturday and we will form a guard of honour."* She gave us all a note to take home and we attended their funeral. It was a very sad occasion for us.

A few years later, and after waiting impatiently, Thursday arrived and I was on my way to my first scout gathering. There were other organisations that boys could join; the Boys' Brigade and The Church Lads' Brigade, both had church parades and bands that could be heard from time to time playing them on to their church. Then there was the Air Training Corps, for those wanting to make a career in the RAF. There was the Sea Scouts, I suppose they wanted a seafaring life when they grew older. As they got into their late teens they went to help the lifeboat crews.

Eventually we arrived at the Co-op outfitters in Altrincham to buy my new gear. It was a large corner shop on Stamford New Road opposite the railway station, which is not there any more. In we went but when the lady assistant brought the trousers, I didn't expect them to smell like they did. It was like a farmyard and being a dark brown colour didn't help! *"Stop being so ridiculous, it'll soon go when you've worn them a few times,"* said my Mum as she pulled me close and held them up to me. When the socks and trousers had been wrapped in brown paper and tied up with string they were handed over for me to carry home. No Sellotape then!

"Mum can I go and look in the scout shop window and have a look at the staffs?" *"Yes, just as long as you're quick, I'll go next door,"* she said. I knew I had to wait to get a staff, but what I really wanted to goggle at was the scout knives in their leather scabbards.

As we entered the railway station the ticket collector looked at our tickets and waved us through on to the platform. It wasn't long before the train came in on the opposite platform,and when the passengers had got off, it went up the line towards Hale. Just under Moss Lane Road Bridge you could see the train swerve to the right as it crossed over the points, and soon it was on its way back to our platform ready for the return journey to Manchester London Road station - now Piccadilly station.

We had a few parcels in our hands and Mum was carrying her purse. As she stepped up into the carriage the purse fell, hit the edge of the platform and fell on the line. The porter told Mum that the next train would be very busy so it would be best to make our journey now. He would retrieve the purse after the train had cleared the station and put it on the following train. On the short journey I noticed that the two light bulbs in the compartment were blue. The fountain of all knowledge -my Mum - explained, *"because they're not as bright as the normal ones, for the black out."* The house key was in Mum's purse, but the next train was soon in and the guard had it.

I had been playing with Peter Davies at his house and on my way home I met the young man who lived opposite Peter, Charlie Ward. He was an apprentice in a factory that made things out of metal - brainwave, would he make me a knife? Seizing the opportunity I asked him. A couple of weeks later, he shouted me over and handed me the blade. *"Wow thanks a lot, but there's no handle."* *"Oh we don't have anything to make handles with; you'll have to make your own."*

I walked home with the blade in my hand wondering how on earth I could get a handle on to the four-inch nail type thing sticking out of it. In my mind I could picture the knives in the shop window, all shapes and colours and design. How could I achieve one for my new knife? Putty, I'll use putty! With some pennies in my pocket I set off to Nelson's Ironmongers on Riddings Road.

When you're full of enthusiasm you can't wait to get started, so taking the putty, as Mr Nelson had explained, I started to knead it. I moulded it onto my knife and tried to put a bit of shape to it, then left it to dry. A few days later it was still soft underneath, and about a week later I learnt that such a job was not what putty was intended for - so much for my brainwave - and Mr Nelson was right after all. Next I tried nailing two bits of wood on to it and to whittle it into shape. This did not work either so I abandoned my homemade knife.

'Bob a Job Week' had arrived and we were to go around in pairs offering our services for the minimum price of a bob, twelve old pennies, or in today's money 5p! Many people were looking forward to our call, their hedge was due for its annual trim, there were lawns to mow, vegetable patches to dig, rose gardens to weed, and hundreds of windows to clean. Sometimes you got lucky and were asked to wash and leather a car, or even give it a polish. Most people were fair and gave you a fair rate for the job for scout funds. Others were very mean and took advantage of the situation, getting as much work as they could and only giving the minimum 'BOB'. We had to take it with a smile, give them a scout's salute and say thank you before leaving. We made mental notes not to call on them the following year.

I went on three scout camps, 1945 Chapel-en-le-Frith, 1946 Delamere Forest and in 1947 to Beaumaris on Anglesey. Auntie Babs had told Uncle George that I needed a ground sheet and that he should buy me one. The week before my departure it still hadn't arrived so she had to remind him, but on the Thursday, just a couple of days before we set off, a parcel arrived; Uncle had sent it by registered post, all the knots sealed with sealing wax, and the man at the post office had been busy with his blue wax crayon, and put the lines that followed the string. Now I would sleep dry.

My first experience of camping would be tinged with a great excitement, for when we arrived at the camp site at Chapel there was a Girl Guide company already in the field. This was a situation that had to be sorted out without delay, the rules clearly stated: *'guides and scouts would not under any circumstances occupy the same field at the same time over night'*. Someone had slipped up very badly! When Dick Harding and one of the senior scouts came back from seeing the farmer they told us to pick up our kit as we were to sleep in the barn, but would be back to the field to prepare our meal.

This turned out to be fun and after we had set out our blankets on the straw we headed to the other side of the field from the guides to make our lunch. Eventually it was back to the barn but when we saw our beds, horror of horrors, we discovered lots of creepy crawlies had laid claim to our sleeping quarters. Our intrepid leaders set forth again, back to the farmer and the guide leader.

How high up in the scout hierarchy they had to go I don't know, but whilst we waited for the outcome we had to collect up all our gear and take it outside. There we had to take a partner and shake our bedding very well before the senior scouts inspected it all.

An agreement was reached and we were allowed to pitch our tents. Whether this was the first time that scouts and guides had shared a field for the night I'll never know - perhaps we made scouting history that day.

After the guides had left on the Sunday morning, the field became a hive of activity. The troop's hierarchy was busy organising the patrols in things that had to be done. One of my jobs was to help make one of two latrines and put up the sacking screens, which always had an earthy smell.

Then it was into the woods to help collect kindling and logs for the fuel store. Some time later we saw some of these lashed together making tripods to hold wash hand basins near the kitchen and a tripod contraption to hang a big cooking pot on.

Just a short walk through a copse led us to a small lake where we could bathe and swim. Yes, by now I had learnt to float and swim, but only on my back, and only for a short distance. But I gashed my foot on some broken glass hidden amongst some pebbles, which put paid to my splashing about and it was back to camp, using Alan Sheldon for a crutch, so I could have it attended to. Our knowledgeable leader inspected my wound, *"Aah, mm, no tendons severed - you'll live,"* as he put a field dressing on.

To the right of the camp, on a hillside, was the wood, and a senior scout took our patrols on a trekking exercise. I didn't realise just how high the hill was, it was more like a mountain. Then about half an hour into the trek it started to go a little dark, and, looking up, we could see a mist sitting on top of the trees. It was all very quiet and starting to feel a bit scary; we all just stood looking up for a few seconds, until our leader blew his whistle that brought us crowding round him.

Soon he was explaining that the mist was in fact low cloud and that we were to walk back down in single file. If anyone lost sight of the scout in front we were to shout out and the crocodile file would stop so that they could catch up. The low cloud was in a hurry to get even lower; it was very frightening. It had started to swirl around a bit lower down and in a few minutes we found ourselves walking in it. *"Don't worry lads, it'll be alright,"* said our intrepid leader. All of a sudden there was a *"whoopee"* from down in the front; they had seen the wall around the field. Soon we were all over the wall and into the safety of our colleagues. Very soon the whole camp was shrouded in the pea souper and you could hardly see a hand in front of you. Being a scout was certainly helping to develop my character.

I was one of a chosen few who were to take part in a tree-felling lesson. The felling axe was three-foot in length, nearly as big as some of the boys who would have to wield it. Off we went into the woods again, our senior scout leader shouldering the axe with its leather shield protecting the cutting edge. We soon found the trees with the yellow cross on that had been allocated to us by the landowner and gathered round our leader to listen to a lecture on safety, then on deciding where the tree was to fall and how to accomplish it. The senior scout made two V shaped chalk marks one on each side of the tree, to show the areas to be chopped. If done correctly, the tree would drop in the place intended. He then made the first few cuts, after which we took it in turns with a few blows each. Both sides had been cut through enough, so he took the axe and told us to stand clear while he finished the job. It dropped just where he had predicted, to a round of applause.

The day after, two other scouts and me had a pow-wow with the scoutmaster and were told that we would be each chopping a tree down all by ourselves and that this would be for our Woodsman's badge. In the afternoon the senior scout took the three of us to our trees and we proceeded to chop them down. I was second to take the axe, how long it took I don't know, but it seemed like an hour. He told me that I had made a good job of it, and it dropped more or less where I had predicted. When we returned to camp we also had to make various items from branches and string or rope.

As well as cutting my foot on every camping trip it always seemed to fall to me to catch the brunt of the night rain. At Delamere we had to dig a trench around the tent to take the water away as we were actually camped on a slope. The previous night our tent was flooded by a torrential down pour in the middle of the night, and I got wet through yet again.

At Delamere the senior scouts built an aerial runway. One end of a stout rope was tied high up to the trunk of a very large tree. The other end threaded through a pulley with a log seat suspended from it, and was attached to a large tripod lying flat on the ground in the field. Then the fun started as we all looked on wondering what was happening. All the senior scouts and the assistant master took hold of a rope we hadn't seen, and said, *"Right lads, heave, heave, heave,"* and slowly the large tripod rose as the stout rope tightened. When it was fully taut, large stakes were hammered in the ground to hold it all.

It was great fun sitting on the log seat as it travelled down. It must have been about my third or fourth turn during the week when Norman, the Harding's evacuee, got hold of the rope to start me off, and pulled me very fast. The seat with me on it was turning this way and that as I travelled very fast with no hope of stopping. My back hit the tree, knocking the breath out of me, I couldn't breath, how I held on I'll never know - it was probably seeing the big roots of the tree growing into the brook way beneath me that made me hang on. It must have been twenty-five feet up if it were an inch. The pain frightened me, had I broken my back? Luckily, no I hadn't, but it was badly bruised. Perhaps it was a small price to pay for being excused duties for a couple of days!

I got home from my first camp full of enthusiasm; I couldn't wait to show Mum how to make dampers with flour, salt and water, mixed into firm dough. This could be cooked in two ways, first it could be flattened into a thick pancake or, second, into a sausage then wound on to a stick to cook it over a hot fire. Having no camp fire to hand I had to use a gas ring. I don't think she was very impressed, especially when I ask her to taste it. *"Right me lad upstairs for a bath; I think you're in need of one."* I must have been up there for some time, I could hear Mum shouting me from a distance, the shouting getting louder and louder, slowly my eyes opened and through the haze Mum's face appeared. *"Come on*

you silly boy, you could have drowned if I hadn't been in the house. Sit up, I might as well scrub your back." I stirred my near frozen body; the water was that cold.

Beaumaris camp had its mishaps as well, but not just for me. Dick Harding had purchased a small push and pull bacon slicer for cutting the bread, and he nominated two other users beside himself. No one else was to use it due to the danger. *"Mind your fingers!"* He warned. A few days later Bill Gordon, the assistant scoutmaster, walked up to Dick Harding saying *"I've done it Dick." "Done what?"* He put his hand out with a finger end missing, and blood pouring out like a tap.

We were allowed some time to ourselves, so a few of us went into Beaumaris. After a little while we went to see a small church that had gone down in the local history records. This little church had been turned into a morgue for the bodies of twenty poor souls who lost their lives when a ship sank in the treacherous waters of the Menai Straits, way back in the 1800s. We next headed for the castle. We soon found ourselves going up one of the towers, emerging on to the ramparts. The view we saw was quite stunning, over the town and looking down the Menai Straits.

The troop leaders also organised a one-day trip. They booked a boat, like a big rowing boat with an engine, for a sail round Puffin Island, a natural home for these funny little birds with their large heavy and brightly coloured beaks.

A few years after the end of the war we had our first Gang Show, staged at the Regal Cinema, and it was a huge feast of entertainment performed by different scout troops from all over the area. The evening was rounded off when the cast sang the first verse, then all the audience joined in the old favourite, *"We're Riding Along on the Crest of a Wave."*

Word came round that, now the war was over, the region was to form its own band, so anyone who was interested in joining could apply through their troop leader. Those who wanted to be considered were to present themselves at a large house, situated on the corner of Brook Lane and Wellington Road close to Navigation Road Railway Station. This was my chance of fulfiling one of my life ambitions to be a drummer. On the appointed day I presented myself full of hope. Alas my dreams were to be shattered, yet again, when I was chosen to try out the bugle.

Band practice was attended religiously for weeks and weeks, a few dropped out for one reason or another leaving the rest of us to soldier on for many months. One night the bandleader gave us the date for our first public appearance - a big church parade in Bowden, sometime in the late autumn of 1948. We had about six weeks in which to polish up our act before the big day. The band had been going for well over eight months now and we thought we were very good! But something now took over in me that I didn't have a lot of control over. Yes it was that girl that I had met. So I left the band after all that hard work. Soon I gave up scouting as well; Mum said it was down to me, she supposed I knew where my priorities lay. She put it down to my growing up!

So there would be no more marches to the 'Rec' and good-bye to the dreaded semaphore, but I was taking with me happy memories.

16. Hobbies and Interests

"M-u-u-m, can I have a pen friend?" I shouted to her in the scullery. *"What have I told you about shouting like that, come in here! I've told you before; you don't shout to me like that, I won't have it."*

Not a good start I thought. *"Now what's all this about?"* Mum was at the sink peeling the potatoes, so I held the article up for her to read. She nodded her agreement, *"But you'll have to pay for your own stamps."* That's all I needed to hear and I didn't stop to listen to any pearls of wisdom Mum might utter. I had a letter to write!

Some of the magazines during the 1940s were Picture Post, Tit Bits and the Weekly Telegraph. The latter had a children's section that I never missed reading. This week my eyes were drawn to an article with the headline 'USA - PENFRIENDS WANTED'.

Six weeks went past - a very long time to a now impatient twelve year-old. The first thing I couldn't help but notice was, in the top left-hand corner of the long envelope, a lovely coloured picture of a sunny and deserted beach, with a curving palm tree dipping its long leaves into the crystal clear water. We had never seen anything like this in England. The paper inside was printed in the same way. The letter was from a young lady in Hawaii; to be honest I didn't know where the Hawaiian Islands were. As usual I had to ask my tree of knowledge, Mum. *"They used to be called The Sandwich Isles many years ago,"* Mum informed me. *"Thanks Mum, but where are they please?"* *"Now why don't you get the atlas out and look it up for yourself."* *"OK."* I said, in a fed up way. I took the atlas from the book case and found they were in the middle of the Pacific Ocean.

Over the next few weeks I couldn't believe it, I received twenty-two letters from these islands and only one was from a boy. As I had to pay for my own stamps there was no way that I could support this many penfriends - I don't think Mum would have either. I soon reduced the number to just two, girls I might add, and I wrote to them for about three or four months before it became just the one, Nancy Yamaguchi.

Nancy lived on the island of Oahu, where the Japanese bombed the USA fleet on the 7th December 1941 at Pearl Harbour. She must have thought that we were still in the middle of the war - I suppose we did still have the dreaded rationing which they didn't - because she sent me many parcels of fruit, pineapples, coconuts and breadfruit, and chocolate bars. I learned that pineapples grow in the ground like turnips. One time I upset her by asking her, in all innocence, if she and her friends wore grass skirts. She wrote back quite indignant but I must have been forgiven as I still continued to get my candy ration from her. I would send her comics and Muriel's Girls Own Magazines.

As I had received so much 'candy' from her, it was only fair that I sacrificed some of my sweet coupons to send her some of ours. I bought a selection from Constables on the corner of Heyes Lane and Park Road, our favourite shop for sweets. It was a landmark for miles around. They also sold newspapers and magazines, cigarettes, toys and games. Mum said it must be a little goldmine. I bought gobstoppers, sherbet dips, pouches of tobacco made from coloured shredded coconut, toffee cigarettes, bubble gum, and lucky bags. Mum threw a lot of them out saying they were cheap rubbish. So, along with different types of chocolate bar, I sent her some love hearts, cherry lips, liquorice in many shapes such as a pipe and shoelaces, Catherine wheels with a toffee in the centre, liquorice torpedoes, dolly mixtures and fruit pastilles and gums.

We swapped letters for over two and a half years, but it fizzled out when I started going out with a girl at home when I was fourteen.

I was presented with a bicycle on my eleventh birthday. I seem to remember Mum subscribing to Provincial Checks, a sort of credit club, a collector came round once a week. How Mum managed to eke out Dad's private's pay, I honestly don't know, but I do know she did worry over money. I remember her saying about Muriel, *"Thank goodness, she'll be leaving school next year in June, and get herself a job."*

As I was still in short trousers there was no need for cycle clips, but you had to have a cape and a southwester, a large waterproof hat. Those days they were made from a black waterproof material, later yellow, possibly for safety. The cape was like a bell tent with press-studs down the first twelve inches in the front of the neck. If there was a headwind it was very hard to make progress, sometimes it was better to get off and walk.

One day a pal at scouts by the name of John Dobson asked me if I would like to go cycling with him and his dad, so I arranged to meet them the following Sunday at their home, remembering to take my packed lunch as instructed. Off we went into the country, where to I haven't a clue, but it was a nice sunny day. I got a bit breathless from time to time but they didn't seem to mind stopping so I could get my wind back.

They lived on Grange Road, off Park Road just before getting to the railway bridge near the Rec. They were building new houses nearby. Somewhere around Dunham Massey there was a prisoner of war camp; we were told they were Italians. These men were brought to this site every morning and it was their job to dig the foundations and all the trenches for the services. If we were passing this way about 4.30, we would stand near to where the lorries came to pick them up. We would watch as they were marched out in columns guarded by armed soldiers. The prisoners all wore squares of cloth of various colours sewn onto their trousers and jackets. We watched them get into the transport; all with our thoughts as to where they were captured, who they were, and where they came from. I never heard anyone shout any kind of abuse at them.

My favourite ride with the gang was to Ringway Airport; here they had various warplanes. Exactly what they had stationed here I don't know, but in a field on the corner of Wilmslow Road and Pinfold Lane were parked up a few squadrons of Beaufort Bombers. They also had Spitfires and Hurricane fighters and some more types but can't be sure which ones. We had various ways of getting there, but whichever way we chose we had to go up Park Road and eventually pass Timperley Church. Due to the war all the road signs had been taken down so if you didn't know the way to any place one could get lost very easily. We turned left into Clay Lane, and we now had three choices that would take us into Hasty Lane that skirted this part of the Airport.

One of the routes took us past an old barn where an old man sold delicious ice cream, a choice of vanilla or chocolate, we would only go this way if we had money to buy some, the trauma of passing without was too much to bear. I think it was called Butteryhouse Farm. We would often see this old man during the school holidays on George Street in Altrincham carrying two boxes, one of cones, the other wafer biscuit, for his weekend trade.

As there was no traffic on these lanes, we would ride 'no hands'. Putting our arms out to the sides, they became our wings - we were fighter pilots. If you lent over to one side, then the other, your bike would weave, and we would engage with the enemy in a 'dog fight'. Inevitably we would crash, but never any bones broken, just plenty of grazes and bruises.

As you would expect, during these arduous war years, gardening was not very high on Mum's list of things to do. Inevitably the garden went to pot so to speak. Of course I was very busy doing important things with the gang. The flowers that dominated the garden were Michaelmas daisies and lupins. The annual bedding plants were a thing of the past.

Dad always enjoyed doing 'his' garden as he called it. Before he was called up he would do some 'DIG for VICTORY' for an elderly couple at number two Leicester Avenue. They couldn't do any gardening, because as well as being old they were in poor health; he always sat in a chair coughing a lot and spitting into a glass. The first time I saw it I was very close to being sick. He had great difficulty with his breathing and Dad was happy to do what he could for them in their garden. I bet it turned into a large weed bed when Dad had to leave it when he went into the army.

"Nellie-e-e, have we any string anywhere?" Dad shouted from the back door. *"It's under the sink in a jam jar,"* came Mum's reply from the living room.

"What are we going to do now Dad?" "You'll see in a minute," he replied, and he dived into the new lavatory come garden shed. I stood and watched as he tied some of his gardening tools together in a bundle. *"Come on, go and get your wellies, you can come with me."*

Putting his tools on his shoulder we set off, up the avenue and down Arderne Road, over the croft, across Heyes Lane and down a path that led to a big field. Here we found men digging and raking all in different places. I was puzzled, until Dad told me it was called an allotment. The Government had asked the people to 'Dig for Victory', to help the war effort by growing their own food to eat. The local council had allocated fields and designated them 'allotments', so each person who wanted to, had a small section to grow food for his family. Dad set to with his spade; first he took all the grass off a small area, turned it over then raked it all nice and level. Then he planted some potatoes.

He cleared the rest of his plot and sowed various seeds - and then he was called up to go into the army. It was the field near John Dobson's home that houses were built on.

Farmers had to clear and plough all land that was not being used and cultivate it to grow food, and the Government introduced Land Army Girls. These ladies did a

Barrage balloons and, below, a local Ack-ack gun

fantastic job, they ploughed fields, planted spuds and then harvested the crops when they were ready. They grubbed out a lot of hedgerows on the MOF's (Ministry of Food) orders. This was to make sure that every available piece of land was farmed to its full potential.

A lot of women were made to go on what was called 'munitions', working in the factories, making things from bullets to tanks and aeroplanes. The BBC visited the canteens of the larger factories to entertain the workers with well known acts of the day - the programme went out at lunch time every weekday and was called 'Workers Playtime'.

Harry called for me one morning but before playing I had to give the hens some fresh water so we carried the watering can between us and this must have been a distraction until the job in hand had been completed. Leaving the hen pen we were part way back to the house, when we both saw it, whatever it was, lurking in the plants and hanging from the trees?

"Looks like something off a Christmas tree," I said to Harry. *"Yes, it does,"* he replied and we both looked up into the sky. We started to collect these ten inch by half inch strips that look like hard silver paper. When we had picked up all we could reach, we decided to go and seek help. Looking up and down the avenue no one could be seen, so we walked towards Harry's house in the hope of finding someone to ask. Round the corner came a man who we knew to be an ARP Warden. With me holding the intriguing items out to him, Harry said, *"Please, can you tell us what this is please?"* *"Oh that's something the Germans drop from their aeroplanes."* *"Why?"* We asked in unison. I think he was in a hurry, as he took a couple of steps, before he stopped and said, *"To try and confuse our Radar"* *"What's that"* we asked. He opened his mouth as if to speak, looked up to the heavens, shook his head and walked off.

In a field near Ringway Airport, inside a large fenced-off area, was an army lorry and some kind of trailer, with a hut at one end. At the other end was a raised platform with a big drum of wire and at the end of this wire, floating in the sky, was a silver balloon - a barrage balloon. These were part of the defences against enemy aircraft. There were also searchlight and anti-aircraft gun (ack-ack) stations around the area. When the strong beam of a searchlight caught an enemy aircraft other stations would direct their beam onto it as well. This made it more difficult for the plane to escape the wrath of the ack-ack guns. Mum bought me a toy searchlight and ack-ack gun; it was good being in a darkened room with it switched on. I would fly one of my toy planes through the light and if a friend was with me we would take it in turns to try to shoot it down - the gun fired little shells by spring power.

I joined the Church choir where my cub pack was based. On my third attendance I was asked to sing on my own. I had sung two verses when the lady held up her hands and stopped me. She turned to one of the other boy, *"Go and ask Mr Burgess, to come in please; he's in the garden. I want him to listen to Peter sing."* The vicar came in, taking his gloves off, and he stood in the entrance with his muddy Wellington boots on. I was told to sing the hymn again - and in future I would be singing descant and a few solos. It was a surprise for me - and a surprise for Mum when I told her.

Many a time Harry and I would be heard singing something like, *'I'll take you home again Kathleen'* as we walked along. Why we chose Irish songs to sing I don't really know. It could have been due to the romantic sounding words and melodies. Without doubt our favourite song was *'Molly Malone'*. We could imagine this sweet young lady pushing her barrow around the streets and shouting to attract people to come and buy her fish produce, but we were very sad when no one could save her from the fever that befell her.

To say we were musical in the true sense of the word would be stretching the truth, but we did try to drive our parents demented by attempting tunes on a variety of instruments. These included comb and paper, bones, spoons and the inevitable mouth organ, a Jew's harp and the favourite kazoo. What on earth was that you may ask? It was made from tin and imitated the shape of a coffin, about six inches long. At the end that went in the mouth, about an inch in front was a round turret. You hummed or sung; with the mouth shut and two or three fingers regulating the tone over the gauze covered turret.

One hot summer's day Peter Davies and I were playing at Gestapo. I had acquired some paraffin and into this we pushed sticks and set them alight. Thus armed we went around our garden pretending to set fire to imaginary buildings, the Michaelmas daisies being the buildings. None caught alight, but I was soon to wish they had. Auntie Babs had brought her swinging garden seat with her, and it still had the winter cover on. The cushions were still in place and an old blanket protected them from any possible oil from the lawn mower that was stored on top of them.

"Dis ist a gute howsen to be bern-ed ya?" Nods from Peter gave the required approval, so it was done with a pretend touch of the blazing stick and we carried on with our game. *"Look at that,"* shouted Peter pointing in the direction of the house, with a tone of terror in his voice. I turned and saw the corner of the swinging seat blazing.

WATER! was my first thought, and I rushed into the house and got pans. In turn we filled them and rushed out to throw the water on the blaze. How much hit the right target I'll never know, but we worked like mad with the thought that the lawn mower would blow up. The fire was out but I could now fully realise what was in store for me. Oh blimey! The worst part was that no one else went into the garden; it was up to me to tell my tale of woe. Of course the strap came off the back door and I couldn't sit down for a week. We never played that game again.

We didn't have gangs that were always at each others throats, just play gangs, made up of boys who lived close together. But one day during the summer holidays we were playing cowboys and indians and someone had a bright idea. We had a pow-wow with that lot on Leicester Avenue, and the other lot from Arderne Road and we divulged our plan. A coin was tossed and my side were to be the indians. Battle was postponed at first due to some of the boys having to go out with parents or some other matter - so the battle of Little Bighorn didn't take place for a few days.

This gave us time for strategic plans to be put forward by our gang Harry, Philip, Geoffrey, Ian and Peter D and I. Luck was on our side, under the bench behind the coal shed we had a pair of wheels, off Muriel's old doll's pram, and these gave me an idea. The plan got the required approval and was put into action. We found a piece of wood, like a small railway sleeper, in Harry's garage, and we attached the wheels to one end. We managed to fix a sturdy upright of about three foot in the middle of this base, and using big staples left over from the wire netting on the hen pen, we now fixed a bow, made from a long garden cane, on top of it. We made about a dozen arrows from all manner of small branches and canes and now declared ourselves ready for battle.

Our scout reported that the cowboys were hiding round on Leicester Avenue. *"What guns hava da gota?"* I asked in an Indian voice. *"Two men da haf cap pistola, wun he haf bigga pop rifle, sum haf potato shoota and one man he hava da pee shooter, Bigga Cheef."*

Well it all turned out to be a complete waste of time. As we rolled our secret machine out into the road, and set the first arrow, the look of horror on the faces of our opponents was a sight I will never forget. We only managed to fire the one arrow; before it had time to leave the bow the cowboys had fled, hell for leather up the avenue. When Mum saw our triumphant machine she said, *"You can take that dangerous thing to bits right now"*.

One day during the school holiday, Miss Statham, who lived at number 21 next door to the Tattersall's, shouted to Harry, Ian and me to come into her front garden. She went into her house and came out carrying a large black bird. *"Do any of you know what type of bird this is,"* she asked, and before any of us could answer, a blackbird, she told us. *"Well it's a Jackdaw, we...."* as she looked down at her little brown dog. *"... we found him in the garden, didn't we Beauty.?"*

Miss Statham told us that they were very naughty birds. *"They steal things, especially things that are shiny and bright. Here Harry you hold him,"* and she thrust the bird onto Harry's arm before he had a chance to agree or not. We were all surprised that the bird stood there looking around quite happily.

After that, if we didn't have important things to do, like boys have to, we would visit Miss Statham and take turns to have the bird on our hands and feed him. As he recovered, from whatever injury had befallen him, he took to jumping onto our shoulders, even onto our heads. When we called one day, she told us that 'Blackie' had decided to fly away. *"He must have got better mustn't he"*, she said, and shut the front door leaving us stood there.

Harry's garden had a privet hedge on the side bordering Leicester Avenue, which shielded us from the prying eyes of Mrs Tattersall on the opposite corner. One day we were interrupted by hysterical screaming, *"Blimey, what's that?"* We all said together and rushed to the front gate to see who was being murdered.

Miss Statham was running and jumping up and down as she chased after her little dog, Beauty. *"Stop, stop, oh what can I do, what can I do?"* Someone had tied Beauty underneath a bigger black dog and Miss Statham was trying to catch them both. Poor Beauty, she was being dragged around, her head hitting the road. We heard someone shout, *"Throw some cold water over them."* *"What would that do?"* I said to Harry, but he couldn't enlighten me - it was a few years before we realised what the dogs were doing.

When Dad finally came out of the army, he came home sporting his new demob suit and brown trilby hat. As I was now twelve years old I was able to give him some proper help in the much needed tidying up of the garden. Where the hens had been, he planted potatoes; this would sweeten the ground he advised me, it must have done because we had some lovely potatoes. Vegetables were planted towards the house, and Dad started a fruit plot around the apple tree. There were strawberries, raspberries and the inevitable rhubarb.

The big mistake we made was sowing all the lettuce in one go, we could have supplied the whole neighbourhood, and unfortunately we were not the only ones to make this error. Anyway we did enjoy this home-grown produce, although most of it came all at once. We did not have freezers then so a lot had to be given away - providing we could find someone to give it to. Dad's plans for the garden were now nearing completion, and he was very pleased with it. I am sure it helped him to adjust to civilian life again - a lot of men seemed to do the same. And it was nice to be able to work with him again; properly now that I was older.

Not long after this, oranges and bananas started to come back into the shops. Banana boxes were rather heavy and looked like small coffins, a foot wide a foot deep and about four feet long. Strong string threaded through the box and the lid in two places acted as hinges. These boxes had to be returned complete or the shop didn't get the £1 deposit back.

Orange boxes weren't returnable as they were made from cheap wood with gaps all round, about fifteen inches square at the ends and about three feet in length with a solid partition across the middle. They made great bedside cupboards. But more importantly, with the shelf taken out, and four wheels attached, they made a fantastic bogie, and yes we made one. They would be called 'go-carts' today.

17. After the War

Who would have thought, that when we went to bed on Monday night 7th May 1945 we didn't know that the war in Europe was over?

Mr Winston Churchill broadcast to the Nation with the official news immediately after Big Ben had struck 3pm on Tuesday May 8th 1945. He finished his speech by saying *"Although Japan remained to be subdued the war in Europe would end at midnight. Advance Britannia! Long live the cause of freedom! God Save the King."*

When Mum heard the news, like thousands of other people she started to cry with relief and of course when we were all together we all had a very big hug, and it set us all off with a mixture of tears and laughter. Everybody was ecstatic. The war's over, the war's over, people were shouting to one another. Neighbours were hugging and kissing, shaking hands, patting people on the back. The first thing Mum did was to get rid of the blackout curtains; they were all outside in a pile near the shed when I got home from school.

On my way home from school sometime later I saw a bill board outside the newsagents on Moss Lane 'MANCHESTER LIGHTS SWITCH ON PLANNED'. As soon as Mr Smith arrived home I dashed round to ask if he would check in his evening paper when this was going to happen. When I got back home, with bated breath I asked the question. *"Mum can I go into Manchester to see them switched on?"* The night arrived and I was on the electric train going to London Road Station, on my own!

I always enjoyed the train journey into Manchester but somehow tonight it seemed different; then it came to me, it was the buildings, only half of them were still standing. When the train passed rows of bombed out terraced houses I could see children playing amongst the rubble, it was odd seeing parts of walls covered in wallpaper. One house still had the chimney standing, like a pinnacle of defiance. It made me think, just how lucky we were to be twelve miles away.

I walked down the station approach and on into Piccadilly Gardens. This would be the first time since war began, nearly six years ago, that the centre of Manchester would be flooded with electric lights. Without warning I was stood in a flood of light from the streetlights and all the shop windows; they must have arranged that they were all to come on at once. Well you should have heard the cheering, it was quite incredible.

I saw people with tears running down their cheeks, not just the ladies either; even I shed a tear or two. It was awe-inspiring, the whole place seemed to be overflowing with people, and still more were pouring into the gardens.

As you would expect, the crowds included a lot of service men from different forces and different nationalities. They were cheered and slapped on their backs along with remarks such as, *"Well done mate, thanks chum and hope you'll soon be out of that mob."* Cigarettes were being handed out, not just the *"here mate, 'ave a fag,"* but quite a lot of full packets as well.

It was odd to see all the buses and bikes; along with the few cars with the petrol

Gerrard Avenue VE street party.   *Courtesy of Mrs Ruth Smith*

Shaftesbury Road development at the end of the 1930s and after the war

to spare by their owners, all with their un-shrouded lights blazing and blowing their horns, and bike riders tinkling their bells.

I stood near to Lewis's building and had a good look round; I never imagined it like this, although I had seen the cinema news of Coventry and London. I made my way, with a big lump in my throat, to the shop window of my favourite store, 'Wild's Toy Shop'.

A few days after the war ended the Gang were soon all reporting that they had seen mums talking up and down the avenue. They were arranging to have a big street party, a V E Day celebration. All the children had a job to do as their contribution; to collect anything that would burn for the bonfire. It was to be built in the junction of Gerrard and Leicester Avenues. Where the wood came from was amazing. We all kept the fruits of our labours in our own gardens and on the appointed day it was dragged to the site. On the appointed Saturday, the borrowed trestle tables were erected and covered in anything that resembled a tablecloth. Over the previous few days bunting and flags had been hung out, from windows, between lamp posts and between two houses.

Around five in the afternoon Mums started to disappear and return laden with all manner of food; plates of sandwiches, cakes, buns, jellies, blancmanges, bottles of pop and big pots of tea. Where it all came from I don't know. The back shelves of larders and cupboards had been raided; many items had no doubt been saved in the hope of such an occasion. We were all seated and tucking in to this feast with many a Mum hovering around with a jug or teapot and passing round plates of food of every description. Why is it that mums find it so very hard to sit down?

Ronny Holland worked his gramophone on the Smith's garden wall; he was kept busy winding it up and changing the records.

The time for the bonfire to be lit was fast approaching. At the end of the applause for his magic show Mr Tattersall made a little speech. He said how we must all be glad that the war in Europe was over and how we must all be looking forward to the Japanese defeat. *"Now who better to light this bonfire than someone who has risked his life putting fires out for the last few years* (laughs and big cheers), *and who has been injured many times? More cheers. Ladies and Gentlemen I give you none other than our own Fireman Mr Jim Allcroft."*

He got up a big round of applause and shouts of *"Thanks a lot, well done."* He came forward a little bit embarrassed to take the torch, a stick with paraffin rag on, to light the fire. Mr Tattersall, still wanting to be in on the act so to speak, just had to strike the match. When the fire got going properly it made a magnificent blaze.

At about ten o'clock, people started to put potatoes in the embers of the fire to bake. Some people had had a little too much to drink and started singing and dancing around the fire. Everyone had a very good time; some went off home to sleep off the drink, some stood around and talked, and others, like most of us young ones, ate the potatoes.

No one gave much thought to the fact that we would all be doing the same thing again in four months time when the Japanese were defeated. Our party had a slightly smaller bonfire as we had used most of the fuel in May. There was a spate of bonfire wood raids all over the place, but it was all taken in good fun. I did notice quite a few gaps in the local trees though. As before, Mr Tattersall performed his same tricks and still got a good ovation. What puzzled most was where on earth the food came from in such a short time since VE Day - by gum there must have been some hoarding.

Looking back I am sure that nobody fully comprehended the devastation those two Atomic bombs caused, although we understood that it had brought a quick end to the War and saved thousands of allied lives.

During the 1945 election, Derek Hargreaves's Dad used their house as the local committee rooms for the Conservative Party. Being nearly twelve I had no real interest in politics; we had the Daily Herald delivered every day but it was many years later before I knew it was a Labour paper. But just because it was Derek's house, Harry and I spent about 20 minutes of our precious time, walking up and down past his house, holding our noses.

For the first few months, after Dad had come home, he went back to work at Lewis's in his old job of furniture salesman. Some time later he came home one Saturday with a parcel. He had been presented with a chiming clock for over twenty years service - and a goodbye present. It looked rather well sat in pride of place on the mantle piece, although I never liked the thing. He had decided to leave Lewis's because the train fare to Manchester had gone up, and he had acquired a similar position selling furniture at the Altrincham branch of the Manchester and Salford Co-op. Now he could cycle to work.

Tragedy was to hit the avenue at this time. Derek Hargreaves's parents owned a belt making business and Mr Hargreaves was secretary of an association to do with the clothing industry. One day Derek and his Dad set off to an exhibition in London. In mid afternoon news started filtering through that there had been a very bad crash on one of the roads leading into London, and a coach was involved. Later we heard that Mr Hargreaves had been killed and Derek was very seriously injured.

Many weeks later, when we got home from school, Mum told us that Derek had come home in an ambulance that afternoon. He had been carried through to the living room where his mother had had his bed put for convenience. Past conflicts were forgotten; Derek never seemed short of company and Mrs Hargreaves now left the door off the latch. Even Harry and I condescended to go and have a look at him a couple of times, we had to agree that we felt sorry for him laying there with a leg and an arm in plaster and, at first, his head bandaged up. The scars were still visible from the many cuts from flying glass. But within a few months he was back on his feet - well crutches.

After Mr Smith was demobbed he resumed his job with the laundry again, and one day he called me over to him when he arrived home and told me that if I wanted to I could go with him on his rounds during the school holidays, if mum would let me. So as soon as the school holidays started I accompanied him. Although I enjoyed helping him there was a down side; I had to be up and out early. Today this would be called work experience, wouldn't it?

During the rounds we called at very big houses in Bowden and Hale on the outskirts of Altrincham. At one particular house the staff would give us a drink, tea for Mr Smith and homemade lemonade for me; this was always in a glass jug that was taken from the fridge - very posh! Some days we would be collecting the dirty laundry, usually tied up in a big bundle. When his round was finished and we were heading back to base I would ride inside the van, climb on top of the big pile and make a little den amongst the bundles.

Back at the laundry Mr Smith would reverse the van into the bay and a couple of men would come and throw all the bundles into large baskets on little wheels and take them into the works. We would go to the canteen for another drink and he would leave me there finishing my drink while he went to the office. When he came back he had a leather hip bag slung over his shoulder. *"What's that bag for Mr Smith?"* *"It's to put the money in when people pay for their laundry."* I felt a right fool, but it was nice to be told an answer, instead of *'you'll see!'*

The first time we went back and opened the back of the van up, what a difference, the clean laundry now in neat brown paper parcels tied with string, and some in big laundry baskets that belonged to the customers. Mr Smith told me he was glad of my help when we had to deliver these; it was quite a struggle up some of the big stone steps. Some ladies would give me a penny or two from the change - always well received with a polite 'thank you'.

During the winter months, especially if it was chucking it down with rain and there was no one to play with, I would be in Mr Smiths. Just before five o'clock, on a Saturday evening, he would switch on the wireless, to give it time to warm up ready for the football results. *"Now sit quiet and don't talk!"* I would sit still, usually on the arm of his chair, while he checked off his coupon to see if he had won a lot of money. I'm still trying some sixty years later.

Mrs Smith came round to see my Mum sometime in about 1945. She was very excited about something and they went into the lounge and had a chat. When Mrs Smith had gone I heard Mum tell Muriel that Mrs Smith was going to have a baby, something they had wanted for a very long time. A baby boy whom they named David was born some months later.

During the summer of 1946, Muriel had just turned seventeen, and she was up in her bedroom getting ready to go out. Mum, Dad and I were still sat at the table having our afters and a drink of tea, all was quiet and tranquil, but a car horn blasting loud and long, out in the road, soon brought us to our senses. Dad slopped his tea with a splutter and Mum practically shoved cake up her nose.

The next thing we heard was the mad dash of Muriel charging down the stairs. By this time we had all recovered and I was in front of Mum and Dad going down the hall towards the front door being opened by my 'in a hurry' sister. I followed her outside with Mum and Dad close behind, and outside our gate was an Austin Seven Coupé. It was a four seater, already with three boys and two girls crushed up inside. She's never going to get in there I thought, just at the point when Mum had also sized up the situation.

"Where do you think you're going crushed up like that?" she demanded, just as Muriel's backside squirmed into the back seat. *"Blackpool"* one of them shouted as the car lurched forward and was off down the avenue like a rocket before Mum could say another word.

As we walked back into the house Mum was mumbling to herself, but I heard the words, *"She'll wish she'd stayed in Blackpool when she gets home, you mark my words George."* *"Mum, why did she sneak out like that?"* *"You'll understand when your twenty-one,"* she said, and left it at that. I often wished that I had remembered all the questions to ask again when I was twenty-one!

I got myself a job delivering evening papers for a newsagent called Tomlinson's, situated on our side of the station approach, on Park Road. All went well for quite some time, from late summer, all through winter and into the following summer months. It was June 1947, and we were breaking up for the summer holidays, and at the morning assembly we were told school would be closing an hour early. With a bit of time to kill, Ian Watkins asked me if I fancied going with him to see his Auntie. It was only a short walk from school, over to Wood Lane, across Thorley Lane and into Clay Lane where she lived.

Was I surprised to find that she owned and lived on a strawberry farm? We walked round the side of the house into a schoolboy's dream. We were met by Ian's auntie, a homely buxom lady, to be honest a bit like my Mum; then we saw them, row upon row of juicy red ripening fruit. She told us we were welcome to go and pick ourselves a small punnet to take home - we didn't need telling a second time! We were having such a good time in all the little sheds and the big hut where the punnets were filled before being sent off to market. In no time we heard his auntie shouting *"Ian, it's quarter to five, hadn't you better be getting home."* I thought how pleased Mum would be with the strawberries, then like a bolt from the blue it hit me. In a panic I shouted out, *"My paper round! Oh heck, I've forgotten all about it!"*

The shop must have been about two miles away; I would never make it - which way would be the quickest. I tried to run all the way, but I couldn't run without the asthma kicking in. I rushed into the shop and stammered out *"I'm sorry I'm late."* But he was not a happy man at all - he said he had got the morning boy to do my round - and my services would no longer be required. Although getting the sack hurt my pride, it had its compensations, no more getting home soaked to the skin or cold winter evenings walking round pushing papers through ice cold letter boxes.

One night Mum and Dad went out leaving me in charge of the house; I had to promise to be grown up, after all I was nearing my thirteenth birthday. All was well and I came inside as my pals had now all gone in - it was starting to go dusk. The time was about seven thirty and all was still and quiet. The half hour programme I'd been listening to on the wireless had ended, so I sat reading, or perhaps looking at a comic. A sudden eerie noise made me jump out of my skin. *"What was that?"* I shouted to myself. Whatever I was reading was now sprawled on the floor. A noise upstairs; yes there it goes again; and yet again. A distinct creak now, just like one of the stairs makes. I wasn't waiting around for any introductions. I tiptoed into the kitchen, opened the knife draw, picked up a carving knife and was out of that back door before you could blink an eye and stood by the garden gate, ready to dash up to Harry's if necessary.

A few people passed and said, *"Hello Peter, what are you doing?"* Hiding the big knife behind my back I answered, *"Just waiting for Mum and Dad."* I was still stood there about an hour later when they eventually came home.

"Hello son, what are you stood out here for, it's going cold now?" *"Waiting for you to come home,"* I replied. Mum wasn't stupid. *"Well why wait outside then."* I made no answer, but I had turned slightly and she must have seen the knife - *"and what's the carving knife for then, come on inside and you can tell us when I've put the kettle on."* They didn't half laugh when I told them. Dad said it would have been because of contraction in the wood after the sun had gone down. We live and learn!

Not many weeks after my thirteenth birthday Mum had to go into hospital for an operation, I don't know what for exactly, but I heard someone say *"it's a ladies' thing"*. I remember going on the train to London Road station then finding my way to Ancoats Hospital. When I eventually found the ward, I think I had about 20 minutes of the hour's visiting time left. As I walked towards Mum's bed she was sat up and looked quite cheerful I thought. *"How's Carole, are you all coping alright?"* *"Yes Mum we're fine, Dad says you're not to worry about us, all we want is for you just to get better quickly."* I think I managed to convince Mum her baby daughter was OK - even I had managed to change her nappy a few times without sticking the safety pin into her little tummy. A half smile appeared on her face and I took this to be an acknowledgement of my prowess.

Suddenly the vicious ringing of a bell shattered the calm of the ward, and I looked to see a nurse with both hands waving a brass bell up and down.

I was at a loose end and thought I would go for a cycle ride. It was getting cooler now in the early evening and not having a proper jerkin, I said to Dad, *"You know your battle dress; well could I borrow it to go cycling in please?"* *"That thing, I should have burned it months ago, I need to forget all about that. It's hung on the rake in the outside lavatory; yes go on and get it."*

I hoped that Harry would come with me, but when I told him I might go over to Wilmslow to call at Auntie Babs's he declined my invitation. So, off I went alone and soon I wasn't far from my destination, at the point the road went down hill to cross the River Bollin. Taking my feet off the pedals and holding my legs out straight in front of me was great, coasting down at ever increasing speed, it was very thrilling.

But then I had to go up the hill - I went up for the first 20 yards with little or no effort at all, then I started puffing and panting until I couldn't turn the pedals any more, and I more or less fell off onto the narrow pavement. I had to push my bike up the rest of the hill which appeared twice as high as the coming down part. When the road flattened out, I got my breath back and rode the rest of the way, ready for that refreshing drink at Auntie Babs's.

Leaning my trusty steed at the side of the house I walked round to the back and knocked on the door. No answer, so I peered through windows in down stairs rooms. Perhaps she didn't hear me knock? I went to the front and rang the bell - still no response and I was really parched, I would have given my eye-teeth for a drink of water. Oh well, better head for home.

Back home Mum met me with a wry smile on her face. *"Been to Auntie Babs's have you, you should have heard the tirade I got from her when she knew it was you. Knocking on the doors and peering through the windows, and why on earth had I let you go to her house, of all places, dressed like some navvy in Dad's old battle blouse."* Then Mum had a good laugh. It turned out that Uncle Geoffrey had got them into debt by borrowing money from his mother's estate before she had inconsiderately died inside the seven-year period. So now he had to pay tax on the money and he didn't have it. Babs thought that I was from the bailiffs, and she was hiding upstairs.

Early in 1946, I asked Mum if I could have some long trousers. *"I don't know just yet, I'll have to see,"* came the stock reply. Some days later Mum came in from the shops, *"The house opposite the Post Office has some long trousers for sale, I've just seen a card in the shop window. Here, there's a ten shilling note, go and see if they fit, and ask if they'll take nine bob for them if they do fit."*

"Hmm, just a bit off the leg will do it," the lady said as she held the trousers up to me. *"My son's growing like no one's business,"* she told me. *"My Mum says will you let us have them for nine bob please."* *"Mm, I don't really know, OK then, nine bob will do,"* as she handed me the trousers and a couple of sixpences.

A couple of years later Uncle Geoffrey gave me a very smart pair of light grey DAKS he'd grown out of. They also wanted a bit off the legs - this 'bit off the legs' has followed me ever since childhood. One day I will have a new pair of long trousers that don't require a bit off the leg, I thought.

One of the reasons I wanted long trousers was because I had discovered the Milk Bar in the village. This was the 'in place' to meet friends, and to sit and look at the girls. Oh yes, they even had tables and chairs outside, very continental. The owner had two daughters who were keen pony riders and took part in gymkhanas all over the county. Their photo was in the local paper quite a lot along with the two Palomino ponies he had bought them.

The daughter of the Wild family, who lived opposite to us, had a little girl called Sheila, who was five years old. She played with my little sister Carole on a few occasions in our back garden. One fine summer's day in 1947 - Carole would be two and a half - Sheila came across to play and she carried a little pink handbag. Now Mum didn't altogether trust little Sheila by now, so she said, *"That's a nice little handbag, did your grandma buy it for you, I bet you've got lots of nice things in it haven't you?"* "Yes," she replied as she skipped into the garden to join Carole.

Not what Mum had hoped for; Sheila was not showing her secrets! A very short time later Mum went into the garden to see if all is well. It wasn't. Carole was sat in her little wooden chair holding a little mirror and Sheila was behind wielding a pair of scissors and cutting - or should I say chopping - her hair. Mum had just got her hair long enough to curl up a bit and she went absolutely ballistic at the sight. *"So that's what you were up to with your bag, wait till I see your mother, pick your things up and get back home. You're a very naughty girl."*

The Wild household had moved into their house around 1942, they consisted of Mr and Mrs Wild, their son aged about thirty and their daughter, with her illegitimate daughter, Sheila. Now father and son liked a drink, but on certain occasions it didn't appear to like them, and you could hear them having a row quite often. But it was on the night of a full moon, when the old man used to go really wacky, every full moon night ended up in a serious fight. In anticipation quite a few of our neighbours would position themselves in ring side seats looking out of the bedroom windows.

Father and son wouldn't have been home from the pub for more than ten minutes, when they'd be in their drive shouting at each other. First one would threaten the other and put his fists up, and then it would escalate into a punch up that eventually would end in the middle of the avenue with them trying to beat seven bells out of each other.

Then the old woman would appear with her wound up towel at the ready to do battle in trying to return them both into the house. First one, then the other, would be unlucky and connect with her flailing baton; she didn't seem at all fussy who copped one of her blows. Eventually both men got fed up of not knowing who they were fighting and lost concentration until one of them would be caught by his shirt collar and dragged through the gate. She would push him down the garden path, still hitting him with the wound up towel and eventually fling him into the house. With his opponent ensconced inside, the other would run or stumble past the old woman as dodging her blows.

You either looked forward to this entertainment or dreaded the time of the month coming round. They certainly lowered the tone of the neighbourhood.

As I have said, the first things Mum did, when the war was over, was to take down the black-out material from the windows. The second was removing the paper blast strips from the windows, and this turned out to be rather a hard job. After soaking with soapy water, many sharp implements were used in an effort to remove the awful sticky mess. Mum said she wished she lived in a tent. Eventually it was down to the last window, the one in the toilet. *"Peter, you'll have to do this one, I can't climb up and stand on the seat like you can, go on, up you go."* After the crosses were on the window sill, Mum passed me a cloth to wipe the water up. *"I don't know,"* she said with a sigh, *"you've used as much water on that little window as the rest of us have to do the whole lot."*

Then the piano went. What would Harry and I do now on rainy days. Mum had to pay someone to take it away, but she got something for the three piece, and some time later another three-piece arrived.

When Dad came out of the army Mum gave him about a week to get acclimatised to civilian life. Then it was, *"George, we could be doing with some re-decorating being done, it's not been touched for over six years."* Wallpaper? Now this couldn't be bought anywhere so they purchased some of the new decorating medium 'Rufcast'. This was a sort of emulsion paint that contained sawdust and small chips of wood which gave a rough texture to the finished painting job.

They worked hard at every opportunity, stripping the paper off the walls of the hall and stairs and landing. Dad must have been swearing a lot - I would come in from the important things with the gang, and would hear Mum say, *"And you can stop that army talk in this house, George Scott, what if the children heard you?"*

Some years later when wallpaper became available again, Dad wished he had never put the stuff on, it was near impossible to remove, and it certainly took the skin off any part of hands and arms that happened to brush against it.

Most people had the same idea of freshening up their homes after the gloomy days of the past six years. As they did it, wanting to preserve their privacy, whitewash would be painted on the windows; it was that or sticking newspaper up. But to save on electricity and let light in during the day, the small top windows were left as they were meant to be.

We were sat having our tea one night and Dad started talking about what had gone on in his store that day. Muriel looked even more bored than usual and gave a big 'I'm fed up' sigh and I saw a little grin on Dad's face. *"Yes, one of the bigwigs from Hoover called to see us, he and I had quite a long talk as he was quite taken with the photograph I sent him of Muriel."*

A stunned silence followed, and then she dropped her knife and fork in shock. *"What's it about, why did you give him my photo, what's it for, oh tell me please?"* *"Thought I was boring you,"* said Dad. *"Go on George, stop teasing,"* said Mum. *"They want a young lady to help make a sales training film."* This was right up our Muriel's street, and it was a while before she came off cloud nine again.

After a few meetings she actually got the part; anyone would have thought she had landed the lead in a Hollywood movie. Learning the script was hell for us, but eventually she had it off pat and the day of filming arrived. Dad told us that they were very pleased with Muriel's capabilities. We never saw the film, but to be honest, I was a little bit proud of my big sister.

The various visitors who frequented the streets before the war were now starting to return. The first to arrive, was the Rag and Bone man, with his small two-wheeled cart and brown pony. You could hear him calling out when he was a mile away; he certainly had a voice that carried, no doubt a requirement for the job - *"Raa-hag-abowan"* he would shout, or something very similar and equally unintelligible.

These carts always had fat tyres on the wheels and the man would always be sat on the front of his cart, with his legs dangling over the right side and the reins held loosely in his hand. Both man and pony looked as if they didn't want disturbing. If anyone gave him old clothes or metal items they would be given various rewards: donkey stones to whiten the steps of terraced houses, balloons and goldfish for the households on the new estates. That is probably how we got our goldfish, come to think of it.

The re-appearance of the 'Pop' man was a welcome sight; he had a horse and cart before the war, now he had a small lorry. It was fitted with sloping shelves from behind his cab, like a big 'A', partitioned into boxes just big enough to hold one of the large stone jars. He sold ginger beer, sarsaparilla, dandelion and burdock, as well as lemonade and cream soda. Mum would treat us sometimes when funds would allow and she would buy ice cream so we could have cream soda with a dollop of ice cream in it.

Mum had often swished the carving knife across the back step in her attempt to put an edge on it, but now a thankful sight again was the mobile knife grinder on his specially adapted bike.

We had a new visitor. This man had a brown face, a black beard and a bandage all over his head. When I ran in to tell Mum, I was informed that it would be a turban he was wearing, a sort of religious head dress. He eventually knocked at our house and he must have opened his suitcase as he waited for Mum to open the front door, because its contents were already spilling over its sides. *"Gud mawning tu yu kind lady, are not we lucky to be 'aving such luveely weather today. I am vanting me tu be shooing yu sum loveely material, or vill it be sum new tee towels yu'll be vanting?"*

As his patter unfolded he would of course have half emptied the contents of his case all over the front step. Mum was a soft touch so she purchased a tea towel or two. He must have been very strong because his case was nearly as big as our garden shed.

Then there was the gypsy peg seller. What a colourful sight these ladies were, with long billowy skirts that would move in rhythm with their walk. They wore colourful embroidered blouses with a shawl round their shoulders; and their dark skirts were embroidered with a wide band of floral design near the hem. I always thought them a picture to behold. Some people seemed to have a fear of these ladies and wouldn't open their door to them. They carried their basket of pegs in the crook of their left arm with it resting on their hip, their gold and silver bangles making soft music as they walked. They would read palms if the lady bought some pegs, even tell your fortune if you crossed their palm with silver. Mum always handed over a silver sixpence for a dozen pegs.

The parents of that snotty nosed kid who chased us over the croft when I was in the cubs, a Mr and Mrs Bradshaw, purchased a small lorry and started coming round selling fruit and vegetables. Mum would go out and buy from them until one summer evening she thought they twisted her out of some money. Mum gave them a pound note, and they said it had been a ten bob note. They said they would phone after they had checked the till (an old box). To give them their due they did phone back, saying the till was correct. Mum was positive - but it was only her word against theirs - and she had an empty purse.

One Friday when I arrived home from work - yes I had started in September - Mum asked me if I would go to Hathersage with her the following day. She had been speaking on the phone to a very old friend from her childhood days. She happened to mention that one of their farm dogs had puppies, and if Mum wanted one, she was to go over for it. Mum just couldn't resist the temptation, whether it was the thought of seeing her old friend or getting a puppy, I shall never know. I can't remember what happened to Towser?

We travelled to Hathersage by train; I think we had to travel to Stockport to make our connection on the Sheffield line. On the walk up the hill to the farm, Mum was reminiscing about when she was a young girl. She spoke fondly of how she helped her friend to deliver milk all around the Hathersage area in the pony and trap.

When we arrived at the farmhouse door it was a meeting of old friends, hugs and kisses and *"Come in, come in, oh it is lovely to see you after all these years, the kettle's on."* After some tea and cake I asked if I could look round the farmyard at the animals, leaving them to reminisce without me sat there.

Eventually Mum appeared with her friend who took us into a little room off one of the barns, *"this is where she is with her puppies."* She shouted to me. Mum and I had a good look at them all and finally decided on a cute looking one, with black and white markings. Mum put it in her shopping basket on top of some old towels in the bottom to act as a bed, then covered it up for the journey, leaving its little head poking out.

Good-byes said, we set off down the hill to the station. On the way down I was telling Mum about the pigs wallowing around in the mud and she started to tell me the following true story. Her friend's father, the farmer, had a prize boar whose services were required by a neighbouring farmer to service their sows. No way could they persuade the animal to walk up the plank into the trailer, farmhands tried pushing and pulling, but it refused to budge one inch. One had an idea, and suggested using a sort of dumper for moving bales of hay, to lift the pig into the trailer. With more push and shove the operation was successful. The process was repeated the day after, with the boar again being manhandled into the dumper and into the trailer. On the third day they came out ready for yet another struggle, only to find the boar already sat in the dumper.

When I think of it now I have a smell 'up my nostrils'; washday Mondays. It was a hive of activity. Mum would fill the copper boiler with water, light the gas then wait for the water to boil. Whilst waiting I would see her sorting the clothes and putting the hand washing to one side. Then she would sit down to take the stays out of her pink corsets ready for being washed. I remember the times when she would come home from wherever she had been and the first thing she would say was *"Oh I'll have to get these blooming corsets off"* as she climbed the stairs to her bedroom.

When the water reached boiling point she would turn the gas down, open the lid and tip in some Rinso or Oxydol washing powder and perhaps some bleach called Lanry.

One day I heard her say, *"Oh good Lord I've put too much in, what a mess."* I just had to go and look what had happened, froth was pulsating down the sides of the tub as Mum was frantically trying to mop it all up. I beat a hasty retreat.

Other pieces of equipment were the dolly tub; a galvanised rib sided barrel with a small tray welded to the top rim for holding the washing soap, usually Sunlight or Puritan. With the tub came the dolly stick which looked like a three legged milking stool with a spade like handle for twisting and turning the clothes through the water. Then a 'posher' - now this always intrigued me, it was like two copper bells stuck inside one another that had holes in and around it and stuck on a handle of about eighteen inches. When this was pulled up and down in the wash tub or the sink, it caused a vacuum that sucked and pushed the water out of the clothes helping to clean them.

Then the corrugated scrubbing board - you may know them as skiffle boards, used in skiffle bands in the 1950s. Any stubborn dirt or stains were rubbed with bar soap then gathered up in a handful and rubbed up and down the board. Sometimes Mum had to resort to a scrubbing brush as well. Some items such as loose collars and table cloths needed starching, and Mum always used Robin. This had the cheeky little fellow's picture on the packet. Mum had to make a paste with the powder then she would add the hot or cold water to make the required amount. Whatever she wanted to starch was put into this gooey liquid then put through the mangle and hung out to dry. When she had some items that required hand washing the favourite would be Lux or Sunlight Soap Flakes.

The mangle was quite a big thing, with two eighteen inch long wooden rollers, six inches thick and a large wheel with a handle which I turned when helping. Within a few years, Mum obtained a more modern one with thinner rubber-coated rollers - the modern world of high technology. These old mangles had a dual purpose; they were a scullery table when not in use, the large wooden tabletop folded back when two levers were released. All this was on a cast iron frame with a shelf to catch the water.

If it was raining and the washing could not be hung out to dry we had to suffer the clothes horse in front of the fire and the merry-go-round of all the clothes taking their turn to be dried. This was followed by the masses of ironing, not Mum's favourite chore - with her bad legs standing wasn't a good thing. When finished, the clothes airer was lowered, all the things were hung over the four rails and then it was pulled back up near the ceiling to fully air the clothes off. After this process sheets and towels went into the airing cupboard, and all the rest into draws.

One Friday, in August 1949, Dad came home from work and announced during tea that someone from work was going to call at about seven o'clock. No matter how much we mithered him to divulge why, he would not tell us. I am sure Muriel was dying to get up to her bedroom to get ready for going out but her curiosity glued her to her chair.

The knock on the door came at just before seven, and Mum jumped up, *"No I'll get it,"* said Dad as he rushed to the front door. After a few minutes two heads bobbed past the kitchen window, one walking backwards and they pushed through into the kitchen and put down a big parcel. We all stared in anticipation.

"Right George, best of luck," he said, nodding at the 'thing'. *"I'll see you tomorrow, Bye all."* After he'd gone Dad said to Mum, *"It's all yours love, so come on, get it undone."* Soon Mum realised it was a Hoover washing machine; Dad had got it on the nod, interest free, from his work. When Mum took the lid off and took out a small wringer, she said *"How the blazes am I supposed to get double sheets through those things? Stupid if you ask me."* Dad told her not to get excited, as he would show her all about it, when it was fixed up. It would not be true to say that Mum was not too pleased, she was very apprehensive and had many reservations as to how clean it would get the clothes, and *"where's the paddles"* she asked.

You should have seen her face when Dad pointed to the four-inch agitator on the side; it only stuck out one inch. *"How is that thing ever going to clean clothes?"* Right she said, seizing her chance; you'd better prove it then. So whilst Mum was finding some washing, Dad man-handled the washer into the scullery. We spent an enjoyable evening watching Dad do the washing for a change and listening to him expound the virtues of this modern miracle.

One thing that always accompanied washdays, and appeared to be universal, was the tradition of the cold meat from the Sunday roast. This was served just cut up or put through the mincer, in which case we had shepherd's pie. Then milk pudding for afters - rice pudding, or if you were unlucky, sago, frogspawn we called it.

Dad's wartime pal Fred Townley, was back cleaning windows in Cheadle, and they kept in touch after the war. One day his wife called round to see Mum on the off chance. Auntie Babs was due any minute to take Mum out. Uncle Geoffrey and Auntie Babs had recently acquired a Jaguar, with the large headlights on the wings, in which Auntie now arrived. Mum could not leave Mrs 'T', as she called her, so they took her along for the ride. Later, I heard Auntie Babs say to Mum *"That bloody woman, she was driving me mad with her 'what a lovely car you've got Mrs Jones', every few hundred bloody yards. She was lucky I didn't stop and strangle her."* Not always a nice lady, our Auntie Babs.

18. Secondary School

We left Park Road School one year early. We bade farewell to the boys and girls as we walked through the school gates for the last time. After the 1943 summer holidays we would be going to Wellington Road Secondary Modern School.

The school holidays seemed to fly by; all too soon it was the first day at our new school. Being a big building, it was very daunting for us ten year olds. We played in the playground - well to be honest we stood about in small groups, we felt just like intruders. After what seemed hours, a teacher came out and the noise ended as they all formed into their form lines, and we followed suit. *"Right, you new boys, hold it there, the rest of you to your form rooms."* *"But Sir, what about?"* *"No assembly this morning Jenkins, come on there boys, get along, quickly now."*

He walked up our double line of boys and we wondered what was going to happen. Halfway along he stopped and said, *"Will you all face this way please."* He welcomed us and explained that we were to be put into a class with no name, a sort of holding class for the year. *"Right face the front again and follow me - and no talking."* He escorted us from the playground to a classroom and when most of us had found a seat he said, *"Just think you're still at Park Road for another year, and next year you will be known as form 1 A/B and 1C."*

Then he took a sheet of paper off the desk and told us that, if and when our name was called, we were to go and stand at the front of the class. I was left, still sat looking at a lot of other boys I had never seen before, with a few from Park Road dotted amongst them. Addressing the ones stood out at the front, he told them that they would be in group 'C', and to go outside and stand in line until a teacher would come for them. A few sighs were heard when we realised that we were in the A/B group.

Both groups were overflowing with pupils; how large our A/B form would be next year depended on the results of the grammar school examination next year. This would be our form room for the year; he introduced himself and told us he was the deputy head. *"Well I'll be leaving you now, your new teacher is in a meeting with the headmaster, so talk quietly amongst yourselves but no noise please. Well, good luck,"* then he walked through the door.

We were all jabbering away in hoarse whispers until one of the boys shouted, *"Here they come".* A few moments later they entered the room, so we all stood up. I wasn't able to see them properly, but when we sat down I couldn't believe my eyes - it was Miss Henshall.

The Headmaster introduced her to us all and explained that Miss Henshall had agreed to come as a relief teacher before leaving to get married - that news blew one of my ambitions. But it wasn't all doom and gloom as she recognised me, so that was a consolation. Then she said 'hello' to the few others she remembered - oh well, so I had to share her! But it was a very nice reunion.

Wellington Road Secondary Modern School
- and me when I went.

Below: Looking towards Navigation Station and the level crossing
with houses of Timperley beyond
Courtesy of 'Looking back at Timperley', Hazel Pryor

Miss Henshall left after the six months and a dumpy lady took over, but she had a good sense of fun and always had a happy face. Boys being boys, we tried to take advantage of her good nature. One day whilst we were waiting for her, a boy put a drawing pin on her chair, she came in, sat down, and we all held our breath, but she didn't even notice - either that or she was as good an actress as she was a teacher.

At the end of our first year at Wellington Road we all had to make our way to Altrincham Grammar school to take the examination to see how many of us were 'grammar school material'. It turned out that I wasn't. Peter Davies, David Critchton and quite a few of my friends were. Quite a few who had come from other schools passed as well, so our class numbers were now reasonable.

The disappointment of not passing soon passed; to be honest, I think the fact that it had proved Muriel to be better than me in the academic stakes, upset me somewhat - a blow to my ego! However I accepted the fact and soon settled into my new school life.

I had been at Wellington Road for just over a year, when one day our teacher informed us that the school leaving age was to be changed from fourteen to fifteen years of age. We held our breath. *"This new law will take effect for all children born during 1933 and after,"* he advised. We were all given a letter to take home. This was a great blow to a lot of the boys and a bone of contention with many of their parents. Why? Because they would not be able to rely on the extra money that their offspring would have earned in that year. As it turned out I would benefit from this change in the law.

One day, during school holidays in 1944, we were all playing out in the road, and just before our mid-day meal we had ended up playing football against our garden gates. Acting as goalie had become a hazardous affair now, our talent at kicking the old tennis ball had increased with age. You had to be mad as a March hare to try and stop it with any part of your anatomy. So the gates had become the goalkeeper. Still the tennis ball was better than the old tin can we sometimes resorted to.

Our game was interrupted as the post van pulled up to deliver a parcel to our house. I ate my bit of lunch in a hurry, concentrating on getting out again as quickly as possible, but then as I got away from the table Mum called me back. *"Not so fast me Laddo,"* and she handed me a parcel, which had my name and our address on it. That it had a lot of foreign stamps on it was in itself a mystery, especially when it turned out it had come from India.

For a few minutes it never struck me that there was a war on, and this parcel had come half way round the world to ME! All this time I was of course opening the surprise. What could it be? Putting the enclosed letter to one side, I unearthed and held up, would you believe it, a deflated leather football. I thought I must be dreaming. The panels were in the shape of the famous letter 'T' of those days. Boy, oh boy, beyond my wildest dreams, I was now the proud owner of a leather T ball. But where had it come from?

We discovered that Margaret, the daughter of Mum's best friend from Sheffield, had arranged for her fiancé, Eric Thompson, to send it over for me, while he was serving with the RAF in India. He had written all the instructions on how to look after it in the letter.

The Linotype factory
Courtesy of 'Altrincham, Past and Present', Gillian Fitzpatrick, Trafford Leisure Services

Print room at Sherratt and Hughes in Timperley
Courtesy of 'Altrincham, Past and Present', Gillian Fitzpatrick, Trafford Leisure Services

Footballs in those days had a bladder; a heavy rubber balloon that was forced into the case through a two and a half inch slot which had to be closed up using a leather lace. Eric had even enclosed a football friend, a device for blowing the ball up with a bicycle pump. I dashed out like mad in the hope that my pals would be waiting for me. Harry and Ian were sat on the wall. *"Look what I've got,"* I shouted; *"it's come all the way from India. It must have cost a fortune."* .

Well they were like me, we couldn't wait to push the bladder into the casing and blow it up. After we'd tried to push the bladder tube in for what seemed half an hour, our joint efforts finally accomplished the job. Harry pressed the lace up hole together as I battled with lacing it up. By the time we had finished, sweat was pouring off us and Peter D had arrived, and was quite rightly impressed with my present. *"Are you going to dubbin it before we play with it?"* he asked. We looked at each other, and then we agreed that we had better - well Eric had said it should be. *"I've only got a bit left,"* I volunteered, as Harry was saying *"I've got some."* He was out of the kitchen door like a bullet from a gun. When he got back, seconds later, I had started smearing my bit on. *"We'll soon have it finished,"* said Harry, *"and then we'd better go to the rugby field."* *"If we kick it about on the road it will spoil it,"* said Ian. By then the rest of the gang had gathered.

We all rushed off to get our footie boots, then off we trekked to Sale rugger field, across the bridge. We marched onto the hallowed ground and sat between the goal posts to change from our pumps into our boots. Soon we were kicking my new possession around. Philip and I soon got puffed out and had to rest for a while, and we sat and watched the other four as they scored goals.

Harry sent a high ball over and Ian who was stood waiting near the goal headed it between the posts. Oh dear, he was none to happy as he held his head, and a little trickle of blood appeared. The leather thong had cut his forehead. This and the fact that the ball picked up water from the ground meant we soon avoided heading - it was like a cannon-ball hitting you. That's why we had to use Dubbin - to waterproof it just like football boots. The only other place I ever saw footballs in those days was at school, and these were kept under lock and key when not in use.

In my second and third year I was milk monitor. I never aspired to Prefect, but I am glad to say I was not on ink duty - powder had to be mixed with water then you had to refill all the form's ink wells. The boys' hands after, were filthy with ink stains. If the ink spilled out over the little white pot, well, it ended up all over the brass fitting, with its sliding cover, and that was a job and a half to clean up. We didn't have modern paper wipes; just an old cloth that just seemed to push the mess around.

My job in this elevated position of milk boss was to make sure that the correct number of crates and bottles had been left by the milkman. I also had to make sure that all the empty bottles were collected and left in the right place. Should there be any milk left over, then at the end of playtime I could give out seconds. Some days when the janitor was very busy, and hadn't time to carry the crates of milk down to the cloakrooms, I had to get another boy to help me with them - he would definitely demand and get an extra bottle.

All went well for the first year, but sometime through the second I had to show my authority; one boy thought it was his right to take extra. *"No way,"* said I. *"Put it back please."* *"Who's going to make me?"* He said with a snigger. *"Just put it back."* I said. *"Make me."* That was enough. Being in the cloakroom was not a very good place to engage in fisticuffs; the big coat hooks sticking out from the steel tube partitions made it a dangerous arena.

A short fracas took place until he gave up with blood pouring from his lip. Well one cannot have one's authority flouted, can one? The teacher on duty had been summoned but when he arrived it was all over. We both had to go and see him before going into our separate classes, but he sorted us out and I had no more trouble for the rest of my term in office.

The milk bottle tops during my school years were made of cardboard and had a perforated push-out in the centre. In school we pushed this in and stuck a straw through the hole. Girls and mothers used these tops to make woollen pom-poms that could be sewn onto scarves and hats.

The relationship with the janitor gave me the opportunity to go down those concrete steps into the forbidden glory hole of the boiler room. There, painted black, with gleaming copper pipes and brass fittings, with the pressure gauges looking like eyes, was the boiler. At feeding time, when he opened the boiler's mouth, the extreme heat knocked you back. It took some feeding as well, with shovel after shovel full of coke; a greedy monster. When the supply of coke was delivered by a tipper lorry, I remember the noise it made was a rustling sound.

A lack of teachers, because most able-bodied men were serving King and Country, meant our schooling was badly disrupted. Temporary teachers came and went, but there were a few stalwarts, like the terror Mr Waywell - 'Washer' Waywell, who would wash the floor with you. A very strict teacher indeed. The door of the staff-room would only have to open slightly, and quiet came upon us as if by magic. He would stand in the doorway for only a second or two, but in that time he knew if he would have to take action with any boy he saw messing about. Should it be another teacher emerging, normal service would be resumed immediately. It was a general consensus of opinion that although he was strict he was a fair disciplinarian. He earned respect for the great teacher he was.

Other teachers, who were not called up, were Mr Hart, who taught arts and crafts, Mr Torrence, science, Mr Salt and Mr Ashurst, woodwork, and a history teacher called Mr Norris, who also taught music. We had periods when there wasn't a teacher available, but a solution was soon found to keep us out of mischief. A boy from class 3C had a talent for story telling, so for two one-hour periods, once a week during my first year, we assembled in the arts and crafts room. He came to enthral us with his tales that he made up as he went along. His timing, bringing the story to its conclusion with our next lesson or home time was incredible. We must have been the best-behaved class in school whilst he was in charge - with the exception of Mr Waywell's class of course. Quite a few of us wondered if he would sometime in the future make his living from writing. I remembered his name for many years, but it's gone now.

Mr Waywell was the maths teacher for the whole school, but all boys eventually ended up as 'his' class for twelve months in their third year. This was a perilous journey into the unknown. One heard stories - but were they true? So much mystery surrounded him in the first two years, and no one was letting on. Was he really as bad as they said? I remember quite a few instances. The first was when I was actually in his class in 1946.

Once or twice a week after assembly, we had Bible reading. Now, besides me, there was one other boy in our class who had a bad stammer. The half hour lesson usually started off with Mr Waywell reading the first few verses, and then at random he would indicate, by pointing his finger at a boy. It was wobetide anyone who could not start without a pause from where he had left off. After the boy had read a few verses you would hear "NEXT", and the boy to the right took over. Now came the turn of the other stutterer, the first verse went a bit slow, the second a bit slower - he knew what was coming. Already a few titters, then came the line, *"And they drank their own piss and ate their own dung."* When this line is spoken properly, it is bad enough in a class of boys, but hyphenated by a bad stammer, I ask you? As you can imagine, a few boys just could not hold their mirth and laughed out loud. Mr Waywell's face turned red; he pointed to the perpetrators. *"Come out here you, you, and you, you as well."* The four sheepishly went forward into the lion's den. They each got two strokes of the cane; when he was really cross he could lay it on and this was one of those occasions. The four boys where shaking and nursing their fingers for quite some time. The only time I got a couple off him was for really untidy and blotchy work and for not paying attention.

The other incident was more serious. It occurred during my last term. He was attempting to teach us logarithms, and half way into this particular lesson he set us a short test. Whilst we were concentrating he suddenly decided to walk round the class in his usual quiet way. Suddenly, from the back of the class came a mighty explosion, we thought the heavens had opened and God had declared Doomsday. He stormed across the classroom like a cyclone. His voice boomed, the whole school must have heard. *"You...you... get out to the front,"* he roared as he helped the boy to his feet.

We knew he was madder than mad; he had been injured in the First World War and he had a silver plate in the back of his head. When he was annoyed this part of his bald head turned various shades of red and the plate appeared to protrude more than usual. His head was near to purple and his plate appeared to throb. Quickly he took up his cane as he shouted at the boy, *"Hold out your hand."* The cane came down with a loud 'swoosh', you would have thought the boy's fingers would have been chopped off and fallen to the floor. He lifted the boys other hand with his cane. 'Swoosh' again and then three and four, we all sighed with relief. But then another two hard blows landed. Six, yes he had given him six of the 'very' best. We had never witnessed such punishment before, we could hardly believe what we had just witnessed. Tears were streaming down this big boy's cheeks. *"Get back to your seat, you disgusting creature."* When class was over we found out the reason for Washer's outburst. The boy had been masturbating.

Oh yes, I nearly forgot, you never went home and told your mum or dad that you'd had the stick or been punished. They would ask you what it was for, and then they would give you a slap to go with it - then another for telling them in the first place.

I always enjoyed Mr Hart's classes; two of my favourite lessons were lino and potato cuts, and marquetry. For the linocut work he would issue us with a three-inch square of thick brown lino, but we had to bring our own potatoes. We were given three or four cutting tools for both jobs. After the pattern had been cut, we coated the surface with poster paint and printed the design onto paper.

Ever so often Mr Hart would throw us a snippet of information, such as, *"Now boys, does any of you know why we chew our food?"* There were a few answers, such as *'it would hurt if you swallowed it in big chunks'*, and *'it makes it taste better'*. *"No, no boys, to make sure your body gets the best out of the food, it is very important that you chew every mouthful at least twenty times or more. This will make sure that the mixing of the saliva with your food is done properly; this is the first important part of digestion. Now you boys, remember that won't you."* *"Yes Sir"*, we replied in unison.

On the first floor, above the classrooms, were the Biology and Science rooms and a Music room. For the first two years we didn't have a biology teacher, but then he was demobbed and came back to try to teach us all about the miracles of life. Amoeba was the starting point and the school had a microscope. The most interesting part for me was when the teacher brought some fresh pond water in. We took turns in studying the amoeba dividing. It was fascinating to see how quickly they multiplied.

During our last year, the lessons were based on human biology and reproduction. I really enjoyed these lessons and I would have loved to have had the brains to enable me to train to become a doctor. Three years later, when I was called up to do my National Service, I did become a nurse and also trained as a chiropodist.

Dad asked me one day what I was doing at school, and I told him human reproduction. *"Do you find it interesting?"* he asked. On my way out, I shouted over my shoulder, *"It's alright, I think I already know it all."* I heard him say to Mum, *"Clever little sod that one."* The truth of the matter was that I hardly knew anything at all.

Science was not a strong subject of mine, but I was very interested in some aspects. The classroom had four or five three-foot high benches, split into 4 or 5 sections, each with four drawers and a Bunsen burner. One lesson I recall was why white bread turned brown when toasted. It was a question in a test paper some months later and when Mr Torrence gave us the results he used my answer as an example - but my pride didn't last long. He asked me if I had listened to the lesson as the answer was completely wrong.

Mr Torrence had two metal blocks on his desk one day, and he started balancing one on top of the other, holding them in such a way that he let the bottom one fall before catching it. This was getting a bit boring until he was holding the top one and the bottom block didn't fall - now he had our full attention. *"Can any of you bright sparks explain why this block hasn't fallen off?"* One piped up. *"Please sir, magnets sir."* No this wasn't the answer he informed us, but we weren't convinced. *"John, you come out here and try to pull it off."* John couldn't. Then he showed us, he slid the bottom block sideways. *"That, boys, is precision engineering, both of these two surfaces have been ground and polished perfectly flat."* He explained that even a fingerprint on one surface would prevent them sticking together. We were amazed.

One-day as he was nearing the end of the lesson, he asked if anyone could bring an empty gallon oilcan for next week's lesson. These were very scarce and only one boy, Peter Frazer, said, he would ask his father, but felt sure he could bring one. True to his word on the appointed day, Peter turned up with the can and handed it over. Now you would expect an oil can to be rather grubby, but no, this was in pristine condition.

"This lesson is about contraction involving water and steam," advised Mr Torrence. He explained about the power of steam and vacuums. Whilst he was telling us this he put an inch of water in the can and placed it over a lighted Bunsen burner. He ignored the can as he talked, but when he heard the water boiling he screwed the cap on and placed the can on his bench. Then he started talking again, ignoring the can completely. This puzzled us all. Suddenly there was a loud bang and the tin just crumpled in; we couldn't believe our eyes. Peter could - with a wail of disbelief, he shouted out, *"Sir, what have you done? My dad wanted that tin back...."* He couldn't carry on, tears were welling up in his eyes, he was so upset he had a lump in his throat. He said his dad would kill him. I don't think anyone of us would ever forget what contraction can do.

We started having woodwork lessons in our last two years. Luckily I ended up in Mr Salt's class for woodwork. We were soon to learn that all the stories we had heard about him were true, he was a jovial character, but also a very good teacher. He very quickly earned our respect. One day, at the end of an afternoon lesson, he disappeared into the stock room. When he eventually appeared we couldn't believe our eyes, we hardly recognised him. He had on a very large brimmed hat with a black veil hanging down over his shoulders. On his hands he wore big gauntlets and he was holding a tin can with a spout that had smoke coming out of it. We were all helpless with laughter as he walked out like a zombie. He announced that after we had all gone home to the safety of our mothers' arms, he was going to see to his bees. His timing was impeccable - as soon as he had finished talking the bell went and we left him in peace. There was a serious side to this as well; he looked after the beehives in the school garden and collected the honey. From time to time he showed us interesting things about bees. One important thing was that if there were no bees to pollinate the plants we would all be dead as mutton within three years, because no pollination meant that nothing would grow.

'Dig for Victory' was one of the slogans of the day, so one of the lessons in our curriculum was gardening. Guess who took us, yes Mr Salt. He taught us how to grow many vegetables, but one in particular was to stand out in my mind for ever; celery! We had to dig four trenches, each a foot wide and one and a half spade spits deep, then a layer of farm manure was laid to a depth of 6 inches, followed by soil to fill the trench to within six inches of the top.

After they were established more manure had to be administered. Near to the trenches were two big tubs; we had never taken much notice of these until now - we thought they were water butts. On hearing the word manure quite a few boys started wandering to the back of the class, but you couldn't kid Mr Salt, he wouldn't allow anyone to skive out of a job. Pointing to the back, *"Right you four, over here, you two, take off that lid, you two, that one."* Oh no, what a stink.

Mr Salt fell about laughing, and then he told us that it was farmyard manure with water added; left over winter it was now liquid manure. Phew, it did stink something awful; we all held our noses as he tried to convince us that the smell would be more tolerable in a few minutes.

As if by magic two buckets suddenly appeared, it dawned on us then what was coming. *"Form two lines, one here and one there, now spread out and form two chains."* Lifting a bucket he explained that he would fill them and hand them out. We had to pass the full buckets down the line, share a bucketful between three plants and pass the bucket back. Some of us went home with stinky boots that day; I don't think our mums were very pleased, mine wasn't for sure. We were told that it would be an on-going part of the class's responsibility - if we wanted, we could bring our wellies next week.

Soon everything in the garden was growing very well, but when Mr Salt brought a pile of old newspapers out a wag remarked that he'd forgotten the deck chairs. Well we were soon to find out what the papers were for. We were soon knelt down with our noses barely out of the manure as we attempted to wrap up the celery plants in newspaper. *"Right you lot stop fooling about and do the job properly, you won't be going home until it is."* We all knew that we had tried his patience to the limit. *"Sorry sir,"* came from every quarter, and we settled down and left on time with it all well wrapped and tied with string. We learnt that the paper was to keep the sun off the celery - if the sun was to get at it, photosynthesis would turn it green with chlorophyll, making it inedible.

In woodwork, yes we did do some, the first item we were let loose on was a pan stand, to teach us the simple cross joint. We had to master the tenon saw, learning how to cut in a straight line. Quite a few of the boys kept me company in finding that chisel work was a lot harder than Mr Salt made it appear. We were allowed to take our first attempt home, but I don't think a lot of mothers were pleased to receive their son's offering! After about a month in the kitchen it seemed to disappear. I often wondered if my spiteful sister had disposed of it.

After more practice with chisels and planes and their care and how to sharpen them, came the ultimate test, a dovetail joint. We were shown various examples; all this did was to spread more doom and gloom over the task ahead of us. I can guarantee that we never went in for a lesson from Mr Salt without we all had a jolly good laugh. Every time he went into the stock room for a long plank of timber he always staggered out with his knees buckling under the exaggerated weight that was resting on his shoulder. He would pretend not to be able to negotiate the doorway without the antics of a circus clown, and when he did eventually get into the workroom well, we had to look out for ourselves, that's if you didn't want a crack on the head. He would twist and turn, and we'd all duck, but I'll guarantee he always managed to hit someone on the head.

One day a boy cut his thumb, and on showing the wound to Mr Salt he examined it at great length with a few 'ums and 'ars and a very serious expression. He looked the boy straight in the eyes and said *"You'll die after this you know."* Tears started to well up in the boy's eyes, and Mr Salt had to explain very quickly that he couldn't have died **before** he'd cut his thumb now could he? Very slowly it dawned on the boy that it was one of his jokes. Instinctively he gave Mr Salt a slight punch on the chest. *"Sorry lad,"* Mr Salt said as he ruffled the boy's hair. Another one of his remarks in a similar situation would be, *"That will turn into a pig's foot by morning."*

My Dad went to a winter's night school, but he wouldn't tell us what he was making. When I asked Dad what Mr Salt was like he told me that he did joke with the adults but he didn't do silly things like he did with the boys. Eventually he came home very proud of his standard lamp with marquetry in the square wooden base. Mum allowed him to put it in the living room, so it must have been all right.

Mr Salt was well liked and respected, so much so that when it was made known that he would be getting married to one of the dinner ladies every one was delighted. Without much prompting the top form started to organise a collection throughout the school for a wedding present. Some of the boys tried to pull his leg with remarks such as, *"Have you been getting second helpings Sir?"* The Friday before they got married Mr Gouch sent a note round to all forms that the teachers had to assemble all pupils in the hall at 3:30. He presented the gift from all the staff; the school prefect was to make the presentation of the wedding gift that was from all the boys.

After the war a Mr Gilmore joined the staff as our permanent English teacher. We soon got to like and respect him; he always tried to make the subject very interesting and fun to learn. He was a very good shot with a piece of chalk at talkative boys. He could knock a flea off a parrot without ruffling its feathers. Sometimes the blackboard rubber would come your way, to be fair he aimed to miss, but the breeze parted one's hair.

It was the beginning of my last year at school. Why anyone would wish to learn about boring history, I don't know. All those kings and queens, different battles on land and sea, it was all in the past so why on earth bother? This was my thought as the class entered Mr Norris's room for some more boring history. *"Settle down, settle down now. Right, who can tell me who Louis Pasteur was and what he was famous for?"* Blimey, here we go again. One or two hands went up. I braced myself for some uninteresting guess. *"He discovered germs sir."* I sat up - if he was right I could get interested in this. *"Quite right, this year we will be covering amongst other subjects, the pioneers of modern medicine."* Now this was really of interest to me; I would be enjoying history lessons from now on.

Microbiology turned out to be the terminology for germs, and Louis Pasteur did a lot of experiments on anthrax and rabies. Vaccines for both these diseases were developed and a few years later immunisation against diseases became commonplace. He also advocated changes in sanitation and sterilisation, especially in hospitals. Pasteurisation of milk was his discovery. We also learnt about Joseph Lister, a British surgeon who pioneered the use of antiseptics. Queen Victoria allowed him to operate on her, and later she made him a baron. We learnt about the great leap forward in diagnosis by the use of X-rays due to the discovery of radium by Madame Marie Curie and her physicist husband Pierre. She died on July 4th 1934 from leukaemia due to her exposure to radiation.

We learnt about the discovery of pain relief, as early as 1799, by the British chemist Sir Humphrey Davy with nitrous oxide, which became known as laughing gas, because when the effects were wearing off the patient became engulfed in uncontrollable laughter.

We learnt about the discovery of the wonder drug, 'M&B', the first kind of antibiotic in the 1930s, and of Alexander Fleming, whose teardrop fell onto a mould growth that he was working on, and the accident led to the discovery of penicillin. Yes, I really did enjoy the history lessons during my last term. I came from near the bottom to just over halfway up during this last year.

Physical education was a mish mash of lessons in the first couple of years, as if someone thought, give them a ball on a cricket or football pitch and that will keep them fit. That was until 1945 when a new teacher joined the staff, to teach us geography and physical education. He was a bubbly man about five feet two, and quite young, who had been in the RAF in aircrew. We enjoyed an exciting afternoon during his first games lesson. But our first geography lesson was a howler. It all began when he reached up into the Scottish Highlands. Within minutes he was reminiscing about a war time experience. *"Ah, I was posted up to the Shetland Isles during the war, I was in the RAF you know."* As there were no camps up there he had been billeted out to one of the cottages, this was inhabited by an old crofter and his wife. The first morning he came into the kitchen-cum-living room for breakfast, he told us he couldn't understand half of what they said to him.

The conversation went something like this, *"Yul biharvin sum purrage nay doot 'a fel ur bellie."* He didn't have the opportunity to say yes or no before the lady 'ove the noose' slopped a big scoopful into a dish and smiled at him. As he could now smell bacon frying he decided to give the porridge a go in case he would forfeit the bacon. Looking around the table he spied the sugar pot and, not being fond of porridge - and in this case the look of it either - he liberally sprinkled sugar all over it. Taking a deep breath, he went for it. He told us he had no choice but to spit it back into the dish, the sugar was salt. We all fell about laughing. Well that was our first lesson over, but where exactly are the Shetland Isles?

We had a happy time as he taught us about other countries, their people and their cultures, their flora and fauna. Peru stands out in my memory, the picture of the man with his very ornate and colourful clothing wearing his tall hat with a wide brim and stood against the back drop of high mountains, holding a llama at the end of a rope.

One day he told us that in a few weeks he would only be teaching us geography, and after the *"Oh, sir why sir?"* chorus had died down, he informed us that a new teacher would be taking over our PT and games.

Mr Garside wasn't liked very much by the boys; it was his superior type of attitude. Outlining the importance of physical training took up most of our first lesson on PT and games. How they would be beneficial for our general health and how games would teach us how to work together with a team spirit that would help to build confidence in each other. Just like the scouts - I thought I'd heard that somewhere before. He was going to arrange inter-house cricket and football matches, and if possible he would try to arrange some inter school matches. But we were all very relieved because we had heard rumours that he was going to change over from football to rugby. Phew! That would have been bad news.

I have mentioned that I had asthma, but it wasn't going to stop me playing footie. I was always disappointed if I was not picked. As a player on a scale of 1 to 10, I suppose I would have been a value of 3 to 4, not very good, but a tryer.

"Sports day. Who wants to be in for the high jump?" After a few seconds a little laughter came. *"A bit slow there boys; let's hope that's not an omen for the hundred yards then."* A few titters followed his attempt at wit. Most of the PT lessons in late spring of that year were given over to selection and training for the forthcoming sports day. We all had to try different events as an elimination exercise under the teacher's beady eye. I had a go at the long jump, but knocked the air out of my lungs - I just sat there, unable to breathe or move, until the teacher realised what was happening. That feeling of complete helplessness was really frightening as I fought to get air into my lungs.

Both Riddings and Arderne Roads had been tarmaced, but most of the other roads on the estate had not been made up yet. I don't know whether the builder went bankrupt or the war prevented them being done. We did have kerbstones, grids and trees - the trees were replaced within a few years with lamp-posts. The road surface was alright for playing cricket, just as long as we used a tennis ball. The neighbours must have dreaded the arrival of the summer months; we must have driven them all mad. No doubt they were worried about their windows; I believe glass was hard to come by during the war years. None were ever broken as far as I can remember, but we did rattle a few panes. Playing cricket in the road was easier than when we went to the rugby field, because the garden walls would act as a fielder, and this saved a lot of 'puff' especially for Philip and me.

If any of my pals could acquire a tennis racket and I could manage to sneak Muriel's out of the house, without her knowing, it gave us the opportunity to imitate the pre-war stars of Wimbledon. Fred Perry was the British and Wimbledon champion in those days.

When I was approaching my fourteenth birthday Muriel was going out with a young man called Ian Barber, who happened to live opposite our school gates. He stayed at our house one night and he had to share my bed. I had just fallen asleep when I was disturbed - Ian was getting out of bed. *"Where are you going,"* I asked. Putting his hand in his pyjama jacket pocket he pulled out a little packet. *"Have you ever seen one of these? It's a French letter,"* he said. He told me about them and then said he was going in to talk to Muriel. From previous remarks I had heard about her and boys it didn't surprise me; anyway I kept my mouth shut.

A day or two later when he came round to see Muriel he was carrying a suitcase. I think Mum was worried, but unfortunately Muriel wasn't running off with him, in fact the contents were for me. He passed the case over to me saying, *"These are for you, pal."* He'd given me some cricket gear, two sets of pads, a wicketkeeper's glove and a cricket bat. It wasn't in very good condition he told me, and so it would require some attention. There were also the six stumps and bails; a lot better than the old sticks we usually used. From that moment, to me he was the best of Muriel's many boyfriends.

Armed with some tape for wrapping around the point of impact with ball, sandpaper and a bottle of linseed oil, I set to work. When I had finished the restoration work I noticed that the thread binding of the handle was coming undone. I managed to secure this with some glue after asking Mr Tattersall for advice, hoping he'd have something to stick it with.

Next day when all the gang was assembled and loaded up, we set forth to the rugger field - with a quick look at our old fishing and swimming pool as we crossed the bridge. We all sat in a circle and chose who was going to bat first. *"Eeny-Meeny-Miney-Mo, Sit the Baby on its po, when it's done wipe its bum, Eeny-Meeny-Miney-Mo,"* or the other one that is now politically incorrect. The winner put the pads on whilst we knocked the wickets in and set the bails.

It must have been a year later when I took my bat to school. What a mistake this turned out to be. I had had my innings, out for a duck, with a ball that hit the ground then rolled under the bat and hit the wicket; I just could not believe it. *"Let's have a go with that bat of yours Scott; I'll show you what it's used for,"* said the teacher. I was none too pleased about his sarcasm, I can tell you. *"Don't break it, Sir,"* I said, handing it over grudgingly. The bowler had another five of his over left; the teacher had a few runs off him and ended up on the receiving end of the new bowler - the crafty so and so.

It so happened that the new bowler was a big strong lad who played for the school first eleven, and I could sense these two squaring up to each other. The first three or four balls were delivered harmlessly enough, but the next one down bounced to a nice height, the teacher stepped out, squared his shoulders; the bat came back, an almighty swipe, and he hit a six. What was that splintering sound of wood that came to my ears?

"Sorry Scott seems your bat's broke," he said handing it back to me. Perhaps it was a good job that I was rendered speechless. Just like a teacher, he never even offered to try and have it mended or to replace it; the only thing left for me to do was to see if Mr Tattersall could help me again. He did.

One day during the school holidays I went to watch Lancashire play. Mum made me some sandwiches and packed them up with other goodies and a drink. I booked my ticket to Warwick Road station, where the train stopped right outside the Old Trafford ground. I also watched cricket at Timperley just along the road from school. It was not a very big ground and one day I remember a batsman hitting a six and the ball came down over the wall hitting a car parked on Wood Lane.

During the summer months of our last year we were informed that some Manchester United players would be visiting the school to coach us in the skills of football. Messrs Jack Rowley and Charlie Mitten arrived. Dixie Dean also turned up one day - I'm not sure who he played for. They made up two teams from our form and the United players joined a team and changed over at half time. Our school goalkeeper, Colin Warburton, who was only a little lad for a goalie, but very agile, was praised by both men, and as a reward they gave him some tickets to go and watch Manchester United at Old Trafford.

Unfortunately for me, PT now included swimming, and I was not very keen at all, for one reason I could not swim; I got panic attacks and asthma. We had to walk to the public baths; we would be marched in threes like soldiers, over a mile to our water torture, our swimming trunks rolled up in a towel. We were separated into three groups, those who could swim, those that thought they could, and the other half of the class who could not.

One afternoon a mysterious couple descended on our school. He was tall whilst the lady was short and stocky, and she wasn't dressed like other ladies - heavy tweed

Altrincham Swimming baths - inside and out
Courtesy of 'Altrincham, Past and Present', Gillian Fitzpatrick, Trafford Leisure Services

suits, shirts with collar and tie, brown brogue shoes. Her hair was cut short like the man's, and to look at them put the fear of God into us. Who on earth were they? If anyone dared to ask a teacher, it was the same answer I would get at home. *'You'll see!"* The sight we saw in Class 4 frightened us to death. Word spread around the school like jungle fire. It was a black dentist's chair. Next to it was the dreaded drilling machine. The flywheel looked like it had come off a bike, and was operated by a foot peddle like Mum's sewing machine. Attached to this on a swivel arm, was a white tray; no doubt for the instruments of torture.

After the first class had had their teeth examined, the rumour was rife - *"they're Germans"*. Well, she did speak with a foreign accent, and anyone who spoke with a foreign accent during this time had to be a German. We had only seen the news at the cinema so we hadn't a clue that the countries near to Germany spoke a similar language.

Some reported that there was a cauldron bubbling away on a small table. I was thinking about my broken tooth, and I could feel the drill already. In I went, shaking like a leaf; I was very relieved to have only one filling. Oh those treadle drilling machines, the vibration nearly shook your head off. These days it's nearly a pleasure to go to the dentist.

During the early years at Wellington Road School, we would stop on the railway bridge on Moss Lane and watch the trains as they puffed their way underneath us. They were mostly goods trains pulling ballast wagons, which were quite long. As the engines came under the bridge, they were always 'puffing' with great force, and making huge clouds of gritty smoke, and we tried aiming small road stones down the chimney just as it came into view to see if the power was strong enough to shoot them back up again. If we took physics at school we could have claimed we were doing a scientific experiment, then it may have had some meaning. We didn't even have the brains to realise what we were doing could have been dangerous.

But I was getting a little more mature; I had been elevated to the senior echelon at school. We used the senior gate in and out now, and the girls' part of the school also used this if they lived on this side of Timperley.

One day as we crossed the junction of Grove Lane we saw a man lying on the pavement. Just then someone recognised Dr D'Acuna's car, a Rover, so they flagged him down. He got out of his car put his stethoscope to the man's chest and said, *"He's dead"* just that, got back in his car and drove off. We all stared at each other in utter amazement. One of the boys ran up and asked an houseowner if they would telephone someone for help. Soon he was running back shouting *"The amb'lance's coming and a cop car,"* so we all hung around for the excitement. Soon we heard the 'd'ring-d'ring-ing' of an emergency bell. *"Bet it's the police car"*. *"Bet it's the amb'lance"* said another, and the ambulance came down the road. The doctor's ears must have been burning the day after, as we were all talking about it at school.

Pushing through the school gate on my way home one afternoon, I spotted a girl that I liked. She rode her bike very slowly, as another girl walked at her side, deep in conversation. After they had parted, instead of riding off, she rode over to me and said,

"That girl's called Elvera Jones; she wants to know if you'll go out with her." I was dumbfounded; I stuttered, *"I'd m-m-much rather go out with you."* *"OK then, but I've got to get home now so I'll see you tomorrow; bye."* So began a two-year relationship.

During assembly, a few weeks prior to the summer holidays, the Headmaster made an announcement - boys who wished to go potato picking should obtain their parents consent then give their names to Mr Salt before the end of the week. Spud picking, great news. Mum eventually gave her consent. Next morning I handed in my name to Mr Salt who allocated me to a farm in Warburton, not far from Lymm. Then he told us the bad news, we would have to start work at 8am. A few boys withdrew their applications!

The farm was reached easily by cycling, about five miles along the side of the canal and then a short distance up a country lane. The first morning dawned and it seemed to be the middle of the night; oh blimey 6.30, what have I done. Mum was very kind, she got me up this first morning but then told me I would have the alarm clock tomorrow - and I was to wake Dad up at seven o'clock before I left. I got my bike out of the shed and set forth on my adventure. It didn't take as long to get to the farm as I had predicted but I wasn't the first there; another boy was already waiting in the farmyard.

We stood there in the early morning sunshine, watching the last traces of the early mist disappear from distant fields. When all the pickers were assembled a farmhand led us to the field, the tractor had the potato-lifting machine coupled up and large baskets were set out about twelve yards apart. We were given a few instructions on safety rules and soon we were hard at work filling our baskets as the tractor passed our stretch. Another tractor towing a trailer came along and someone emptied our baskets for us so we would be ready for more spuds. We had a mid morning break about 10 o'clock, and a needed rest, but we were even more pleased to hear the shout, *"Break for lunch, break for lunch, be back at 1 o'clock'*. Mine wasn't the only back that seemed as if it were breaking - we all wondered if we would survive the afternoon. My lunch inside me, we set off to the field with a little more enthusiasm. At lunchtime we had a little time to ourselves, so into the second week I promised to take my prized football the next day, so we could have a kick around after we'd eaten our lunch. We had got used to this hard work by now, and the energy was flowing back. We enjoyed our four weeks picking spuds, we all agreed that it was hard work but enjoyable. Getting paid at the end of each week was even more enjoyable, and I must admit that I for one felt a lot fitter for the experience. We had just two weeks holiday left before we started our final year at school and ten days of this was spent at scout camp in Anglesey.

I arrived home one afternoon to find my Mum in the front room with the mother of my girlfriend. I just said hello then beat a hasty retreat up to my bedroom; whatever could they be talking about - I didn't know if I wanted to know. *"Bye Peter,"* drifted up the stairs. *"Bye,"* I replied and saw her walk off down the avenue.

"Peter, I've something to talk to you about," Mum shouted up to me. My stomach was full of butterflies; *"whatever's happened?"* I thought. *"Sit down,"* she commanded. I felt sick, but managed to say *"What's the matter Mum?"* Did I want to hear this, I

thought? Why do we always think there's something wrong? *"Mrs Downs came to ask me if I would let you go away with them and Inez next week, that's if you want to."* I couldn't believe it. *"Well, would you like to or not, we thought you'd be pleased about the offer."* *"Oh I am, and I do Mum, honestly, I just didn't expect this."* *"What did you think she'd come round for then? Go on then clear off, I told her you could go if you wanted too."* As I left the room I saw a wry grin on Mum's face. We went to North Wales and had a smashing time.

In the years of 1947 to 1948 I realised that I would have to pull my socks up. It was my last chance to take advantage of the education I was receiving; better late than never. We were taken on a few factory visits. Last year's visits had included the Gas Works at Altrincham and the Electricity Generating Works at Old Trafford. Our first visit this year was to Weaste and Salford Docks. One warehouse that was to stick in a lot of our minds was where two floors had been stacked high with sacks of coffee beans and cocoa beans.

The Linotype factory at Broadheath was intriguing. This is where the machines that cast the lead strips to print the newspaper pages were made. This was followed up by a visit to the Daily Express newspaper printing works at Ancoats, where we saw the use of these machines; the noise and the speed they operated at was rather frightening. The paper was called newsprint and came in on large lorries, some by horse-drawn wagons. It was interesting to watch the large Shire horses backing the long flat wagons into the unloading bay.

Then it was to the bacon slicer and weighing machine works of ASCO at Broadheath. First we went into the foundry where the iron castings were made; blimey it was hot. All the castings were left outside where they went a bit rusty, but a few minutes in the sandblasting soon had them shining. In the engineering shop the machining was carried out and then they were stove enamelled. Soon all the parts were married together on the assembly line, the scales shining white, the bacon slicing machines red.

At the end of the tour, much to our surprise, we were taken into their canteen for tea and cakes, super! Now this really was our best trip; we had to agree that seeing something made from start to finish was fascinating.

What turned out to be our last visit, and one of the most intriguing for me, was with Mr Norris our history teacher; he took the class to Altrincham General Hospital to see the X-Ray apparatus in action. The technician promised to keep it as simple as possible, but most of the information went over our heads. Then we were introduced to a doctor who said that he would show us how to find something wrong with a digestive track. *"Who's been X-rayed before?"* he asked. Up went my hand! - and I was called forward.

He explained that I was chosen because I was still living after being X-rayed before! After I had taken my shirt and vest off, he stood me at the back of a screen, and handed me a glass of white liquid which I had to sip on his command. He explained to the class that it was a solution of barium, a chemical that showed up on X-ray. The experience lasted about twenty minutes as the class saw my 'innards'. *"You may be a little constipated for a few days, but don't worry"*, he said. I decided there and then never to volunteer again.

In the last month of our school years we had to sit through a lecture about China by an ex-army Major. We trooped into the assembly hall, and like all boys, I was thinking I couldn't wait to be out of there again. How wrong we were; we were enthralled with his accounts of the civil wars that had raged throughout the 1920s and 30s and up to the present day, 1948.

Mum arranged an interview for me with the manager of a bookbinding firm, Mr Nightingale who lived just round the corner on Leicester Avenue. Some months previously he and his wife had suffered a tragedy when their young son had somehow managed to fall in to the pond at the bottom of his garden. I remember Mum being terribly upset; she said she could not understand why a little so and so like Sheila Wild opposite, with parents and a family like hers, wasn't taken instead of a lovely little boy with loving caring parents.

Towards the end of February, Mr Gilmore announced that the headmaster had agreed that the school could put on a concert in the last week before the summer holidays. Our class was to perform a play. After a few weeks, and a lot of deliberations, Mr Gilmore arrived at his decision. Some hoped that they would be chosen whilst some hoped they wouldn't. It was rather a shock as Mr Gilmore announced *"Scott, you'll play Mrs Wilson."* Well after all the derisory remarks and wolf whistles, was I surprised? I had the lead role, playing the mother.

It was quite hard work. Sometimes Mr Gilmore asked us to stay on after school to rehearse. Dress rehearsals brought another dilemma, what clothes to wear? Muriel lent me one of her skirts, a jumper and a cardigan, and a pair of shoes. Dad came up with a rolled-up pair of socks. Embarrassed I asked in pretend innocence, *"What's the socks for, Dad?"* *"You'll want to look like a proper lady won't you?"* Mum said. When I got to school, I still couldn't make up my mind about the socks; they were in and out like a yo-yo during the final dress rehearsal, especially when the lads started giving me wolf whistles. Mr Gilmore said to keep them in, but just before my entrance, I am afraid I chickened out. On the way home, Harry asked me if I would go to the pictures with him. I hit him over the head with Muriel's clothes in the paper carrier bag.

The day after was prizegiving, the last but one day at school. During the previous week, a small number of boys had visited the headmaster's study to select a book for a prize for good work. You can imagine my surprise when I was summoned to his inner sanctum. There were not many left but in the eight or nine books there was one on bookbinding, my chosen career decreed by Mum; but I chose a book on gardening.

"Peter Scott" boomed from the platform, and off I went wondering what it would be for. With book in his left hand and shaking my hand with the other, Mr Gooch announced, *"For the best all round progress during the school year."* You could have knocked me down with a feather. I still have the book, and refer to it often, during the season, and anyway, I gave up bookbinding when I was demobbed from the RAF in 1954.

It is inscribed in the Head's writing: *Progress Prize, July 1948, Wellington Boys School.*

I have to admit; I had mixed emotions about the challenges facing me. I received a letter to say that the bookbinding job was mine if I wanted it. I did; so Mum and I had to go to the factory for the signing of that special document called an indenture, an agreement that I would stay with the firm for a period of six years and during this time they would teach me the trade of bookbinding. The trouble was, like many I did not know just what I really wanted to do. But the time had arrived, whether I liked it or not, and I went to work for the princely sum of £1. 2s. 6d per week - 64p in today's money.

Harry, Geoffrey and me now went on cycle excursions to the River Bollin, to the same spots we had visited with the cubs and scouts. One place had a dam which allowed the water to form a natural pool in which we could all swim. It was deep enough for shallow diving and attracted quite a few bodies during a school holiday period. If you walked towards Hale you could see a field from the bend of the river. From this vantage point we could look across to the other side and indulge in a bit of spying. It was a favourite spot for the Yanks to bring their girl friends to do a bit of kissing and cuddling.

The Bollin. *'Courtesy of Altrincham, Past and Present', Gillian Fitzpatrick, Trafford Leisure Services*

In this my final year at school, fate must have decided to take me full circle and give me another broken arm. As I stood with a few friends on top of an air raid shelter watching the girls' inter-school hockey match - watching them run round with their skirts tucked into their knickers - all of a sudden, a boy charged up behind us in horseplay and managed to push us off. I had broken my left arm again.

Scarborough in the 1940s
Courtesy of 'Vintage Scarborough', Bryan Berryman.

19. Holidays

"Cor Mum, this case is heavy!". It was the late summer of 1944 and Mum was taking me on holiday to Scarborough. I did not know if Mum was looking forward to the train journey, but I certainly was, I hadn't been on a long journey. *"Do you think you'll be able to carry that case up to the station Peter?"* said Mum with a worried look. *"Course I can, Mum."*

Soon we were walking up Park Road towards the station. When we arrived at London Road station, (now called Piccadilly) we had a short bus ride over to Victoria Station. Wow! I hadn't seen a station as big as this, there were about twenty platforms. I set off for a bit of exploring, but I didn't get very far as the ticket collector would not let me off the platform.

From where we were sat, I could see across a few platforms, and there was a train coming in, *"Look Mum that train's a 'namer'."* The platform was double sided, so passengers shared the usual two waiting rooms, a general one, and one for ladies only. In cold weather you would open the door to be met with the welcoming warmth of a blazing fire and newspapers on the table.

The main railway operators that I remember most were LMS standing for London-Midland & Scottish, LNER for London and North Eastern Railway and GWR, Great Western Railway.

"Clunka, clunka, clunka, clank", down the platform came a porter pulling a large four-steel wheeled flat truck, some called them bogey wagons, and sometimes they had a trailer linked to it. The truck was piled high with an assortment of brown cases and the odd large trunk with bands of heavy bamboo and steel corners for protection. Most of the cases were battered, as ours was!

On the platforms at the small stations along the way I saw groups of two or three milk churns from the local farms. The porters just tipped them over to one side and rolled them on their bottom edge towards the guards van, shouting *"Mind yer backs please."* There were bundles of newspapers and magazines. A Post Office van came driving down the platform and the driver off-loaded a dozen bags of His Majesty's mail next to the parcels. And no station platform would be complete without the coo-coo of racing pigeons, waiting in their baskets to be transported to the various towns for their race home.

When the train's departure was imminent, the porters would walk down the platform closing all the carriage doors, shouting, "MIND THE DOORS PLEASE, mind the doors." Then people would start hanging out of the windows as they waved farewell to their loved ones who had come to see them off. They would have to buy what they called a platform ticket,which cost 1d.

The arrival and the departure of these magnificent steam trains was surrounded with a magic I cannot explain. During the journey, when I had grown tired of reading the pictures to the left and right of the mirror telling of 'Bracing Skegness' or 'Lovely Llandudno', I went and stood in the corridor looking out of the window. To my joy the engine suddenly came into view as we went round a long curve, and there were two of them. I could see the steam hissing out between their wheels, and clouds of grey smoke puffing out of their chimneys. Looking back I could see the guard's van - and I counted fourteen coaches.

When I was tired of standing, I went back and sat with Mum. She told me that one time when Dad was home on leave, he told her the train seemed to talk to him when he was coming home; the wheels said *"I'm takin' you home, I'm takin' you home, I'm takin' you home"*. But it was a different message going the other way; it said, *"I'm takin'yer back I'm takin'yer back, I'm taki..."* Mum said she had something in her eyes, and she wiped one with her handkerchief.

The boarding house was down a steep, narrow road, leading to the south promenade and the beach. The part of the beach nearest to the sea had large concrete blocks set in it and posts with barbed wire coils spread between them. You could not forget there was a war going on. At night I would lie waiting for sleep to overtake me, as I listened to the waves crashing onto the shore.

One of the highlights of the week was when three lorry loads of soldiers descended onto the prom. About ten minutes later I was thrilled to see the arrival of a tank sat upon a transporter, just like my Dad drew for me in a letter to Mum. The engine of the tank was started up with a thunderous roar, and a great belching cloud of black smoke from the exhaust tubes. After it had warmed up it was driven off the trailer and onto the beach, where it went up and down a few times between the ranks of soldiers.

It was as good as the Punch and Judy shows that took place on the beach, and the religious meetings every Sunday. Best of all I loved going to the underground amusement park called Gala Land. It first opened in 1877 as 'The Peoples' Palace' and held one of the largest aquariums in the UK. It was purchased in 1928 by the Scarborough Council and after a few alterations it was re-opened as Gala Land. The aquarium was transferred to an old ship in the harbour, the ship was later used in the making of the film 'Moby Dick'.

There were many small side shows like dart throwing, a shooting gallery, a coconut shy and many more. One stall Mum had forbidden me to go on was the 'win a goldfish' by throwing a ring over its bowl. *"Don't come back with a goldfish or it will end up in the sea".* There were rides for young children and for us bigger ones a 'big dipper' and dodgem cars. I spent many a happy hour down in this wonderland of fun.

An older boy who lived on Leicester Avenue had made me a three-sectioned fishing rod, and Mum made a case for it out of black-out material. It had lain safely on the net luggage rack at the back of the case in the compartment throughout our journey. Now I was going fishing off the harbour wall. Unfortunately I speared a man on my way, but after a lecture on how to carry such a weapon, *"Upright my boy, upright like this,"* I was on my way again. But I didn't catch anything. I don't think I could cast out far enough. My luck turned when I went on a sea fishing trip. We anchored quite a long way off shore, and I caught a couple of mackerel - the landlady very kindly cooked one for me.

Dotted along the prom were many small seafood stalls and I would often stop and look at the various dishes - dressed crab, mussels, clams, scallops, whelks and winkles.

Amongst the guests at the boarding house was a family, and their eldest daughter of about 14 years could sing. One night the father came round the tables telling us that

Gala Land. *Courtesy of Mr. Max Payne MBE*

Sports Roller inside Gala Land. *Courtesy of Mrs Lillian Short*

his daughter had entered a competition at the amusement park and would we all go to offer her some encouragement? The big night arrived and most of the guests went along to cheer her on. The Master of Ceremonies made a few witty remarks, and then he said, *"With no further ado, please welcome....."* A little boy of about eight performed a rendition, followed by many other contestants of all ages. And yes, our girl sung 'There'll be Blue Birds over the White Cliffs of Dover' - and she won.

For a day out, one summer, Mum took Muriel, Winnie Monks and me for a day out at Blackpool. I remember that special smell - my sister put me right that it was known as ozone - and in the background the sound of the bells around the donkey's necks as they took girls and boys up and down the beach, led by a young man with no shirt on.

Grandad Scott died on January 14th 1947, and Mum said to Dad that she thought it would be a good idea to take Grandma and Auntie Dorothy on holiday with us. Next time we visited Park Avenue, Mum put the idea to them; they thought it a good one and Mum said we would be going to Bridlington.

Dad had hired a car. He had a problem starting it after he had picked Grandma and Auntie Dorothy up, but he told Mum it was probably because he was not used to it. From the outside, the large six seater Austin looked very well, but it had hidden talents that Dad was going to get rather fed up with. Luckily he spotted a garage when it started to give more trouble, and in those days they were not just for getting petrol; they always had a work shop and a mechanic if not two. Leaving the ladies in the car, Dad and I trudged off to seek help. Soon we arrived in Bridlington without further trouble.

After a fun-filled day on the beach - Grandma slept all day in her deckchair - we packed up and headed for the car to go back to the digs. Dad put the key in the ignition and said, *"Well here goes, hold your breath"* - and the car purred like a kitten - well until we got to some traffic lights! Dad called at yet another garage on the way back, the mechanic had a fiddle about under the bonnet again and all seemed fine.

Next day it took a lot of starting and it was cutting out whenever Dad had to stop. We took it into yet another garage. After a look under the bonnet and a bit of fiddling about the mechanic opened a rear door. First the carpets were flung out from between the back and front seats. I could tell Dad was thinking, *"What ever is he doing now?"* Then two trap doors were flung out and there was a *"Good God! I've never seen anything like this in my entire life! It's a wonder you've not all been killed."* He beckoned Dad closer to show him the thick cables that linked the two batteries; they had worn half way through as they were rested over the drive shaft. *"Whoever rented you this death trap should be prosecuted."* After he had fitted new cable, he advised Dad to take all his bills to the renter and also to claim inconvenience payment for all the trouble.

The car was alright for the rest of the holiday, until on the way home. Driving through Leeds the engine decided to have a rest again and Dad coasted to a stop outside a row of houses. Believe it or not at that moment an AA patrolman rode up on his motorbike and sidecar, just as Dad was lifting the bonnet. *"Good evening sir, can I render assistance?"* *"Yes please. By gum we're lucky you were passing,"* said Dad.

The AA man dived under the bonnet, but whilst he was umming and aahing, a man came out of his house. Dad thought he was annoyed that we had stopped outside his house; but no, *Good evening, I'm a motor mechanic, can I help?"* After rolling up his sleeves he invited the ladies into the house where his wife gave them tea and cake. He told Mum to use the phone if she wanted, so she rang Auntie Babs and Uncle Geoffrey to come and pick the three of them up. The mechanic soon found the cause of the trouble, the high tension leads to the sparking plugs were rotten and would have to be replaced. As it was now Saturday evening there was nothing he could do till morning. We went into his home for some tea while he phoned some a bed and breakfast for Dad and me to stay at.

About an hour later Babs and Uncle Geoffrey arrived in the Jag and whisked Grandma, Auntie Dorothy and Mum off back home, leaving Dad and me to see the job through. The man now took us to our digs and said he would pick us up in the morning.

He came for us about 9.00 in the morning, and when we arrived back at the car, Dad naturally expected him to start work on it. But no, he handed Dad the car keys and told him that the car was all ready to drive away. Dad just couldn't believe that the man had got up early and done it. After a bit of 'argy bargy' he finally agreed to take payment for the cable he had bought - and not a penny more! A true knight of the road.

On the way home Dad told me some of his experiences in the Army. In 1941 when he was called up he was thirty-nine and one month, just months away from being exempt. He had to do his entire square bashing and training alongside men that were as young as eighteen, mere lads he said. That alone nearly killed him, never mind a Jerry bullet!

He told me about the invasion, when he was driving in convoy through Belgium. He said it was very hot, so hot that they were nearly passing out with the heat. During one stop, that just happened to be near a farm, Dad noticed a group of men all stood looking at a bonnet of one of the lorries. Being curious, he walked up to look, and there they were cooking eggs on the hot bonnet.

When they drove into Hamburg, some weeks later, it was almost flat; Dad told me there was hardly one brick standing on another. He had recalled then how, when they were waiting to embark on the invasion, the sky went black with the bombers going towards Germany. Wave after wave passed over, hundreds and hundreds of planes. They all said, *"someone's going to cop it"* but he didn't realise he would see this result of it.

He said one of his pals had a near miss one night as he slept under his truck. He got up to spend a penny and when he got back he found a lump of shrapnel from an exploding shell embedded into his makeshift pillow. It had come right through his truck's bonnet.

20. The Wedding

I was never surprised when I saw Muriel walking down the avenue on the arm of a different boy, but I had to do a double take one late August afternoon in 1948 when I saw her walk into the house with her latest, a Jamaican.

Muriel

It was obvious that Mum and Dad were expecting the visit because Mum had set the table with a few sandwiches and cakes. Muriel introduced him to us as George Altamonte Rodney, or just Rod. *"Peter, get something off the table and go and carry on with whatever you were doing, there's a good lad."* said Mum. About an hour later I saw Rod come out of the front door and as he walked out of the gate he shouted *"Cheerio then"* to me.

During the next week or so I got to like Rod a lot - although I was only fifteen we got on very well. A few weeks later he came and joined me in the garden. *"Peter I'd like a little talk, if you wouldn't mind."* *"Sure,"* I said. We walked down the garden and he got his cigarettes out and offered me one. The gist was to ask me if I had any objection to his becoming my brother in law. Well I didn't expect that, did I, but I told him I didn't mind one bit. They were to be married in a month, at Timperley Parish Church.

A man who lived on Leicester Avenue ran a private car hire business, and he was to supply the wedding car. The gang often stopped playing outside the house to let him purr past in his shiny black Packard. Whoopee! At last I was going to get a ride in it.

When we arrived at the church, Rod was stood with his best man and a small band of guests. *"She's coming,"* shouted someone. We all turned and started to walk down the path towards the church but when we were halfway down, the church doors opened and solemn music hit our ears - a vicar, followed by pallbearers and a coffin, were coming out to the graveyard. We all about turned, leading the funeral party up the path, and Muriel made a dash for the car again until we got the thumbs up from the verger.

The reception was held at home. Babs had come over from Wilmslow early to help Mum prepare, and she took charge of setting the buffet table. She made a lovely job of it with vases of gladioli of different colours, and Mum and Babs made a very good spread.

A month later Muriel had a baby but it was stillborn. Over the next few months Rod told me something about himself, and we got quite close. He had come over to England to study constructional engineering at Manchester University. He must have been older than Muriel because his studies had been interrupted when he joined the RAF to serve King and Country. He had been a Warrant Officer and a Navigator flying in

Mosquitos with a pathfinder squadron, directing the bombers to the targets by dropping flares or fire bombs. He described hair-raising exploits over Germany - sometimes they had to change theirs trousers when they got back to base.

Mum and Dad got on well with Rod; he helped Dad to paint the outside of the house - or was it the other way round. One night Dad and Rod were sat at the living room table in a studious manner, looking at what appeared to be a gardening book and many leaflets. It transpired that the literature was about 'How to Grow Tobacco'. Some weeks later the seedlings were ready for planting out.

The tobacco plants turned out to be a success; the leaves were collected and tied in bunches at the stalks and hung up to dry. When dry they took them down again and guess what, they wet them again. *"Whatever is going on with my pans?"* asked Mum as she found the two tobacco barons at the gas stove. *"Just making a concoction for our baccy,"* said Rod. *"Well, make sure that that pan's clean when you've finished, and don't leave a mess!"* On the cupboard top there was a tin of black treacle and salt petre, and next to these two milk bottles of clean cold water. Hiding behind this little lot I spied a half bottle of Navy Rum. Squeezing past them I stretched out my hand and picked the bottle up. *"Thirsty work then?"* *"No clever clogs, we're putting two tots into the mixture for flavour, now clear off."* Dad replied. After the leaves had been soaked for some time, half a dozen were rolled up together like giant cigars, and then all the bundles were left to mature for a few weeks.

The time arrived when the 'baccy' was ready for its fate. Rod shredded his to make roll your own cigarettes, whilst Dad crumbled his up to smoke in his pipe. What was it like? I think 'alright' was the concensus, but it smelt like burning cabbage.

Some months later Mum told me that Rod and Muriel were going to live in Jamaica. Rod gave me a small drawing board and two 'T' squares, to save carting them over to Jamaica, and I have still got them.

Muriel wrote to us all about the trip over to Jamaica on the banana boat and how Rod had made a swimming pool for the passengers. He used a large tarpaulin sheet, some packing cases, and a few steel scaffolding poles, then the crew pumped water from the sea to fill it. She said it was a godsend for everyone to cool off during the hot days at sea.

Muriel wrote telling us that Rod's father owned a banana plantation, and that Rod had done some designing and overseeing of building work for him, and he was now involved with the design and building of a rum distillery.

At first Muriel wrote to Mum on a regular basis, but this soon wore off. I am sure Mum was upset but she didn't say anything to me. Six months or so later, Muriel wrote to tell us that their marriage was ending in divorce. The next we heard from her was many months later, when she wrote to tell Mum that she was enjoying the life of a receptionist at one of the island's best hotels, Frenchman's Cove. She had spent Christmas day on the beach, swimming, and sun bathing, drinking and eating roast suckling pigs. Just the life for our Muriel!

21. Riddings Hall Social Club

Striding up the long drive to the big house my fortitude was beginning to waver. In days gone-by this was a sort of manor house. Next to the house I found a large modern single story building that had been erected to provide a meeting hall, with a stage for plays. I was informed that I would have to see the club secretary, and after waiting for about 30 minutes he eventually arrived. It was Mr Clark, known as 'Chippy' Clark to everyone, because he owned the fish and chip shop on Riddings Road.

After some questions he handed me a form. I had to get it signed by two sponsors who had to be members. I thought, that's killed it. *"I don't know anyone."* I told him. *"Well you come and buy fish and chips at my shop, don't you?"* "Yes." *"Well then, you know me don't you, and we'll go and ask someone else."* Within five minutes I had the required signature. *"Welcome to the club, but you'll be a junior member for two years."*

The club only had one table tennis table, but I had another reason for wanting to join this club; it was because they had an amateur dramatics society. The problem for me was my stutter. It took me sometime to pluck up the courage to go and ask if I might join them, but the night of no return arrived, and with my heart a flutter, into the lion's den I went. Mrs Amy Sheldon was the producer, a middle-aged lady with a slim build. I stammered *"Hello, m-y...m-y n-name is P-p...eter S-sc.-Scott and c-could I p.-p-please join th-the group as I-I enjoy am-am-amateur dra-dramatics?"* I thought, well that must have scotched any chances I might have had - I fully expected her to show me the door. But no, she said she was pleased to meet me, and, yes, I could join. From the amount of people in the room she wasn't short of potential thespians. She advised me they were in the process of casting for the Christmas pantomime, and my eyes lit up.

At the next meeting I was allocated the part of one of the children in 'The Old Women who Lived in a Shoe'. Just one line - *"What's that?"* But even this worried me, as 'w' was one of the letters I had trouble with. With only this one line I was able to follow the parts of the rest of the cast, and I was soon quite familiar with the characters. Then many weeks into rehearsals the man who was playing the lead part as the dame, came to see Amy to tell her for personal reasons he would not be able to continue with the part. This was a big blow for Amy and the rest of us. Where I got the nerve from to ask if I could take over the lead, I will never know. But ask I did, in my usual stammering way.

She was very kind in the way she refused my offer. But I really wanted to prove to everyone that I could do it without stammering, *"I never st-t-a-am-mered in t-th-the scchool p-p-play,"* I told her. *"Just give me a chance please."* So she did.

For the performances we had a proper make-up lady; she needed quite a lot of paint and expertise to make me look the part of an old woman. The smell of that grease paint, it reminded me of a disguise set I had when I was a lot younger. The paint, the excitement of waiting for the transformation from me to somebody else, it wove its own magic for me, sat there in front of the make-up mirror. I must admit it gave me great aspirations.

Above: Riddings Hall

Right and below, the Regal

Courtesy of 'Altrincham: An Illustrated History', Pat Southern, Trafford Leisure Services

The moment of truth arrived. Was I going to let myself, and more importantly, Amy down? I was for running out then but, taking my courage in both hands, I made those faltering steps onto the stage. It's quite marvellous what the sound of applause can do for you.

Amy took me to one side when the pantomime was over, and gave me a hug. She said I had been very good. She then admitted, with a laugh, that she had kept her fingers and toes crossed for me until we were well into the second act. We gave two performances, and I did not stutter once, and the impediment became more or less a thing of the past. I put it all down to the trust Amy had put in me. It gave me faith in myself. Thanks Amy.

The club held dances on a weekly basis, so I decided to go to a dancing school on Hale Road near Altrincham. We were taught the samba and the rhumba, they even tried to teach us the tango, but the quickstep was my favourite. I was no Fred Astaire but the lessons did enable me to enjoy Saturday nights at Altrincham's Stamford Hall - once to Ray Ellington and his band.

Just a few yards up the road from the Stamford Hall, were two of Altrincham's three cinemas, The Picture Theatre on Stamford New Road and The Hippodrome on Victoria Street. The Picture Theatre was affectionately known as the 'bug hut' and this was where I spent most of my Saturday afternoons as a child; well it was cheaper than the Hippodrome where Muriel went. And of course I went to the children's matinee, far too childish for sophisticated Muriel when she was twelve.

One thing for certain, no matter which cinema you visited, you could always rely on the projector breaking down at least once. The other thing was that if it was a long film, it necessitated a change of reel halfway through. These forced interludes were met with derision - all hell would be let loose during the children's matinees, with a lot of booing, and if it was at a tense moment in the film, a near riot would ensue - you were likely to receive an empty ice cream tub or empty toffee bag on the back of your head. The usherettes would be dashing up and down the aisles trying to restore some semblance of order.

At evening performances a little more decorum was shown, especially when the manager came out on stage to apologise and explain the reason *'for the delay in your evenings performance'*.

Our Saturday matinee programmes were made up with about three films plus the news. There would be the inevitable cowboy film, usually 'The Lone Ranger' and his trusty steed Silver and Indian friend Tonto. Tonto always called his master Khima Sahbee. Then there was 'Flash Gordon in Space' - if anyone in the 1940s had said there would be a man on the moon in 25 years time they would have been branded a half-wit - and probably despatched to the mental hospital at Macclesfield.

We had to have a spooky one as well. Oh yes, while this film was showing we were at our quietest, except for the shrieks of fear and the screams - from the girls, of course. One scary serial was called 'The Clutching Hand'. The opening screen was all

The Hippodrome
and The Picture Theatre

*Courtesy of 'Altrincham: An Illustrated
History', Pat Southern, Trafford
Leisure Services*

white, and slowly a black hand, followed by the arm, would slide up and across the screen, then all of a sudden move quickly as if attacking someone. No matter how many times we watched it, most of us would jump a mile into the air. The film was always accompanied by ghostly music; you were never ready for the crescendo when it came. There were incidents throughout the film that kept making us all jump and scream out in shock, like when someone opened a cupboard and a body fell out. At the beginning of the 1940s they released an Arthur Askey film called the Ghost Train which was great fun, although it scared the pants off us.

We did of course have the old comedy favourites as well; Laurel and Hardy, Abbott and Costello, Old Mother Riley with her daughter Kitty, and what about the antics of Donald Duck and Popeye, great fun!

One evening Mum surprised me by taking me to the Hippodrome to see Snow White and the Seven Dwarfs. Yes, it was 'posher' than the Picture Theatre. Some time later she took me to see 'The Wizard of Oz'.

Once or twice the air raid siren would sound when we were at the pictures. Then, it was shear bedlam as some couldn't get out quick enough. The rest of us just sat there and hoped that the projectionist did not get cold feet and switch off but he kept going until told otherwise by the manager. If the show really had to be suspended he would come out on stage and say, *"Ladies and Gentlemen, for your own safety and that of the staff, would you please leave the cinema and seek shelter. Thank you."*

Now I was older, working and courting, it was the time for me to indulge in the finer things of life. I could now afford to go to the third of the local cinemas, the Regal Cinema on Manchester Road, Broadheath. This was quite a classy establishment, and an added attraction was the large theatre organ which would rise up from the depths in front of the stage with the organist playing. When he had finished, and was on the way back down he would give us a wave as we responded with civilised applause. The Regal showed the better and recently released films. Here we would see films starring the water goddess, Esther Williams and the other swimming hero, Tarzan, the hero of them all, played by Johnny Weissmuller, with Jane, in 'Tarzan of the Apes'. The flamboyant Carmen Miranda wore very tall hats mostly made of fruit, and danced around in elaborate flowing gowns. We saw 'Gone with the Wind', staring Clark Gable and Vivien Leigh - the first epic we saw. As this cinema was not too far from home, just at the top of Navigation Road, I would guess just over a mile, we usually walked. Yes we got through a lot of shoe leather.

If we wanted to really push the boat out, we would take a bus ride and go to Sale Lido. Here they had a dance floor that came out and covered a large swimming pool. When the pool was in use there were windows at one end where spectators could partake in refreshments while watching the swimmers glide past. In 1953 a cinema was also added and the Lido was renamed the Lacarno.

The Regal at Broadheath burned down, and on the site now stands Roberts House an office block that houses the Inland Revenue!

My place of work in Altrincham

22. Work

My sleep had been rudely disturbed by the new alarm clock Mum had bought me, and bleary eyed I focused on the hands. Yes it was, seven o'clock. *"Peter, are you up yet? You're not going to be late on your first morning, or any other for that matter, so come on, up you get. NOW"* Reality dawned. The first day of the rest of my life had arrived. I couldn't make up my mind as to whether I was looking forward to starting work or not; at this time of the morning all I knew was that life had not given me any alternative.

After parking my bike in one of the racks, and with my parcel of sandwiches in my hand, I took a deep breath and ventured in through the small door within the large sliding factory door. Between the big printing machines I walked, nodding here and there to anyone who happened to look my way. Eventually I arrived at the brown sliding door that led through into the bookbinding department. I was feeling more nervous now, so bracing myself I said, *"Well Peter, here goes."* Sat amongst the ladies was, oh no, my girlfriend's mother, Mrs Downs, but she gave me a nice little smile and a nod.

I knocked on Mr Nightingale's office door and was shown into his sanctuary by a young lady only a few years older than I - Mr. Nightingale's secretary, Margaret Slack. After a brief chat about my responsibilities, and what I would be taught, Mr Nightingale took me to meet my work colleagues.

The first port of call was to meet the sheet folder. The flat sheets from the print room were folded on his special machine. He had a young lady assistant whose job was to feed the large sheets into the machine whilst he kept watch over the intricate machinery. What came out at the other end was a folded section of a book. The sections were taken to the collating table where they were put together in book order. Arthur, the machine minder, was the union man; I was told to see him at a later date so he could sign me up, as they called it, for the union. Looks like I've no choice in the matter, I thought!

The next operation was stitching the sections together - a row of girls on special machines. My heart missed a few beats I am sure - the most beautiful young lady I had ever seen, with black hair and red lips, was sat at one of them. I would never have the remotest chance with her, never in 10 years of Sundays.

My next port of call was the foreman, Vernon, and he and the boss gave me a little pep talk. Mr Nightingale handed me over to Vernon to complete my tour and give me my first assignment. He took me to meet the straight guillotine operator, Len Leonard, who cut all the board and paper to size. Vernon told me that I would not be allowed to operate any machinery until I was eighteen. Ian Sheldon was next; he worked the three-blade guillotine that trimmed the ends and front of the books, after the sections had been sewn.

After the spines had been glued and dried, someone belted them with a hammer to round off the spine. This was Freddie Flowers, who also pasted the covers on.

"Now then, your partner in crime, so to speak, should be lurking around here somewhere," said Vernon as he led the way through a gap in a partition wall. *"Aha! There*

you are, come and meet your new work colleague, if work is the operative word."

"Now then Peter, this is Kenneth Mottram; you'll be working with him from time to time. Carry on with your baling, Kenneth." "I'll take you to the gluing bench now to give you your first task," he said nodding at me.

Three men stood gluing the spines of a pile of books. Seeing the look of anticipation on my face Vernon said, *"No, not that.... that,"* and he pointed to a large wooden barrel. *"Yes, it's glue, it needs cutting up into chunks about 6 inches square with this knife, so they fit into those glue pots. OK get started."*

Months later - *'and for about the tenth time'* - I asked Freddie to lend me some sugar for my tea. Freddie chucked a bag over to me and I ladled three teaspoonfuls into my mug and stirred it; I was so thirsty I was spitting feathers. Ugh! Did I get a shock. To teach me not to forget my own sugar in future, Freddie had come prepared and put salt in the bag. There was nothing else I could do other than spit it back into my mug; how I managed not to be sick I don't know. I made sure I never forgot my sugar again.

Len Leonard was always pulling my leg, helped along by Alan Sheldon. Len had been in the army and had been stationed in Egypt. He told Kenneth and me many a tale of his trips into Cairo and of the sideshows he had visited; like the donkey show and the ladies who caught coins in a certain part of their anatomy that were rolled towards them down a table. I never knew whether to believe him or not.

Playing tricks and teasing apprentices I suppose was par for the course; you learnt to take it in your stride and laughed with them - or they would make your life a misery.

There were two ex-Polish soldiers working in the department, one had been a sergeant, and was a well built man. One day he came into work with all his hair shorn off -yes, as bald as a coot. He told us that it was a family tradition to stop baldness. Well all I can say is that it all grew back rather quickly, so maybe it did work. The other Pole had been a major, and apart from the fact that he talked posh, something in the way he conducted himself said that he had had a far different upbringing and life to his compatriot.

One morning, at break time, the ex-sergeant had everyone's complete attention as he related his experience of the previous night on his train journey home. A young Polish couple got in his compartment, and they talked non-stop about their love making the previous night, and in great detail. He just carried on reading his evening paper until he had to get off at Old Trafford, when he bade them good night - and many more nights like the one they had just enjoyed.

For our tea break we just sat on the bench that we were working at. One day I sat near to the guillotine. *"There goes your heart-throb,"* teased Len, as he pointed to Sheila O'Hara walking over to her machine. Talking of beautiful girls, in those days newspapers were beginning to get a bit daring and printed photos of girls in bathing suits. These were shown around amongst the men. But one day, as Len finished the sports page, an unprintable exclamation passed his lips - like a man possessed he dropped from his bench and rushed over to Freddie in great excitement. Waving his copy of the Daily Mirror under Freddie's nose he exclaimed. *"Just look at that, I couldn't believe my eyes"*. A mind blowing photo of a young lady in a bikini!

I was now the undisputed glue cutter-upper champion of the World. Kenneth took a back seat, so to speak - mind you he was three years older than me, and well into his apprenticeship. Vernon put me to work with the team of ladies who made the cases for the nearly finished books. The gluer was first in line, then me, to set the cloth over the cardboard and on to two folder-overers. These two young ladies folded the edges over, and last, but not least, the mangler put the covers through the mangle to make sure they were stuck down properly. A Mrs Doyle, who was getting on a bit, held this exulted position. I was getting more efficient by the day so the speed of the team increased - and poor Mrs Doyle was in tears on a few occasions because she couldn't keep up.

Kenneth and I got on well. A few months after I had been there, he said to me, *"Come into the waste room, I've something to show you, but it's a secret, promise."* We climbed up the big steps of bales, and round the back was a hole; wow, there was a room amongst the bales. *"Great isn't it, we can hide in here sometimes."* Yes we did - and we got sent home without pay for our trouble!

He was a member of a youth club in Altrincham where he played table tennis, and he invited me to join as well. Some time later I was in the team in the Cheshire league. The club was Fern Lee, a very large Victorian house on Dunham Road and close to where Lord Pilkington lived. His gardener was a member and he gave me a ticket to a garden party in aid of some charity. There were hundreds walking the gardens with a drink in their hand, and some were very posh. I arrived by bus and walked up the long drive, past many a Rolls Royce, Bentley and Daimler. Some had their chauffeur, sat there waiting for the call *"Home James"*.

During the summer of 1949 I went on the Works' outing to Blackpool. Oh boy, a lie in; we did not have to be at the factory till 9:00 am. The coach was ready to whisk us off for whatever adventure fate had in store.

Someone shouted *"First one to spot the Tower gets five bob from the management."* This was met with remarks like *"you'll be ruddy lucky"*, *"don't hold your breath"*, and *"if that happens, I'll double it."* After the jeering and laughter, the manager of the print room stood up and asked for some order, then announced, *"If the print room foreman was serious in his offer, then he would also put five bob in, doubling the offer to whoever spotted the Tower first!"*

That set the cat amongst the pigeons, howls of laughter and comments to the foreman like *"you'll have to pay up, pay up, pay up,"* calling his bluff. Someone was in for a nice little earner of ten shillings. As we neared our destination things quietened down - we were all busy looking out of the window - a lady who worked in the readers' room won the ten bob.

The coach park was at the rear of the Amusement Park and the driver advised everyone to be back *"by 5.00 - the coach will leave at ten past; anyone not on will be left behind."* All the men headed for the nearest pub, Kenneth included - well he had reminded everyone that he was now well over 18 so he was entitled to have a drink. I think the women headed for the shops. Me, I just stood there and wondered how so many people could vanish into thin air like that. I wandered round the fun fair, having a go on this and that. I looked at some of the big dippers and had a go on 'The Grand National', two strings of cars on adjacent tracks which raced each other up and down very steep gradients.

Two years into my apprenticeship I arrived home one evening - it must have been a Wednesday because Dad was home. I sensed that something was not quite right. We had finished our pudding and Mum came in from the scullery with a pot of tea, and as she poured, she said to me, *"We've something to tell you that is important"*, and then the bomb exploded, *"We're selling the house and we're buying a corner shop in Stockport."*

My world suddenly seemed shattered; I was enjoying my job, there was my new girlfriend, Barbara, and what about all my other friends, especially Harry. There was my amateur dramatics and all the other things. I didn't want the rest of my cup of tea; I went and sat in the front room, on my own.

Mr Nightingale and the union agreed to try to arrange a transfer for me, to a company nearer my new home, but until then I would have to travel in every day. After many months of very early starts, and a long journey, a small firm in Stockport agreed to take me. I was hoping that Dean's in Cheadle, who were like Sherratts, would take me on, but no luck. Hooley's promised to take me under their wing; they specialised in the making of stationery books, leather-bound ledgers and the like - the type of binding that I was taught at the night school by two brothers at Manchester College of Technology. They also taught gold and silver blocking and decoration of books with hand tools.

I visited all my pals and said my goodbyes over the last few days, and then the day of the move had arrived. It was getting on for half past nine when the removal van eventually pulled up outside our house; I was hoping they had forgotten, they were supposed to have been there before 9.00 according to Mum.

It was like history repeating itself, men from the van were invading our home and carrying it out; just the reverse of sixteen years ago, almost to the day. From my bedroom window I watched them close the large doors of the van. Slowly the monster inched its way down the avenue.

The house was an empty shell, every footstep seemed to echo the happy times we had spent within those walls. I saw the taxi arrive from my bedroom window. I looked at the gates and remembered the football I had played with the gang. I glanced up and down the avenue remembering all the times spent with my pals. Tears were in my eyes.

"Come on Peter love, it's time for us to go now." One more look round. As we walked down the drive together Dad put his arm round my shoulders and said, *"It'll be alright, son, you'll see."*

The good thing to come out of it was that I would meet the girl who would become my wife and the mother of our two lovely girls.